To Bill Gra...
With Best Wishes
Nelson Ash...
5-10-76

Education, Inequality, and National Policy

Education, Inequality, and National Policy

Edited by
Nelson F. Ashline
Illinois Office of Education

Thomas R. Pezzullo
University of Rhode Island

Charles I. Norris
University of Rhode Island

Lexington Books
D.C. Heath and Company
Lexington, Massachusetts
Toronto   London

Grateful acknowledgement is made for permission to reprint an excerpt from *Let Us Now Praise Famous Men* by James Agee and Walker Evans, published by Houghton Mifflin Company, Boston, Massachusetts, published in the British Commonwealth by Peter Owen, London; and for permission from the Center for Civil Rights, University of Notre Dame, and the Center for National Policy, Catholic University Law School to reprint Chapter 12 of this volume from the Symposium on School Desegregation and White Flight held on August 15, 1975 in Washington, D.C. Also, permission to reprint (last stanza) of "Burning in the Night" from *A Stone, A Leaf, A Door: Poems by Thomas Wolfe*, Selected and Arranged in Verse by John S. Barnes. Copyright 1945 by Maxwell Perkins as Executor (Charles Scribner's Sons). Originally in prose in *You Can't Go Home Again* by Thomas Wolfe. Copyright 1940 by Maxwell Perkins as Executor. By permission of Harper & Row, Inc., publishers.

Library of Congress Cataloging in Publication Data

Main entry under title:

Education, inequality, and national policy.

Based on an invitational conference held in Newport, R.I., in June, 1975.
1. Federal aid to education—United States—Congresses. 2. Educational equalization—United States—Congresses. I. Ashline, Nelson F. II. Pezzullo, Thomas R. III. Norris, Charles I.
LB2825.E26   379'.121'0973   75-21833
ISBN 0-669-00053-1

Published simultaneously in Canada.

Printed in the United States of America.

International Standard Book Number: 0-669-00053-1

Library of Congress Catalog Card Number: 75-21833

In every child who is born, under no matter what circumstances, and of no matter what parents, the potentiality of the human race is born again. . .

Let Us Now Praise Famous Men
James Agee and Walker Evans

Contents

viii

List of Tables

Foreword

As of 1975 federal aid to education approximates 10 percent of total expenditures at local and state levels combined. But the effect of these funds is to suggest national goals and priorities for all education. The largest single categorical aid program supported by federal funds is Title I of ESEA—Compensatory Education. It follows, therefore, that adding dollars for programs designed to compensate for educational deficiency related to poverty is the highest policy priority at the federal level. The argument for compensatory education, simply put, goes something like this:

- Poverty within groups of people in our society and how well they do in school appear to be connected.
- The economic improvement of individuals in America appears to be directly related to the amount of education they have.
- And concentrated effort, via the provision of money for increased or improved school services for poor, unsuccessful children, should help break the poverty cycle.

Also underlying the Title I ESEA policies is a fundamental commitment to the elusive goal of equality—the achievement of the good life for all—with the school being used as the primary vehicle in its pursuit.

The courts, in rulings pertaining to constitutionality, and the Congress, through the Civil Rights Act, have also viewed schools as primary providers of equal opportunity to the children they serve. One immediate consequence has been the requirement that traditional attendance patterns in many school districts be dramatically altered to provide for racial desegregation.

A thread of conviction about the pivotal role that schooling plays in the development of individuals in our society runs through many federal activities. Federal policy in education is, in part, implicitly based on the idea that schools *do* have the demonstrated power to reform society in the direction of more equality through their effect on young people. Yet, increasingly, during the late 1960s and early 1970s, arguments which challenged this view of education as the great equalizer became a subject of debate. Jenck's *Inequality*, based largely on a reanalysis of data collected in James Coleman's monumental study, raised serious doubts about the power of schools to provide the ingredients essential to reducing or eliminating poverty in our society. In his controversial articles on the heritability of intelligence Arthur Jensen even questioned whether we could defend the essentially environmentalist view of human development which was implicit in a view of equality that placed so much faith in the school milieu as a potential equalizer.

During that period, and to this day, those of us in the field of policy development and implementation have had a serious problem: all too often the debates raging around these issues have been heated and focused on emotional rather than rational arguments. Communication to us has been at best unclear, and at worst misleading. We have rediscovered the fact that education is not immune to the cudgels of the lunatic fringe and, further, that lunacy is not solely the property of the undereducated.

In discussions with Christopher Jencks during early 1973, it became increasingly apparent that at least one cause for the cacophony could be the heavy reliance on "open forum" discussions as a method of debate and analysis of these issues. An additional conclusion was that academics tend generally to communicate best to other academics. Their primary consumers are not necessarily either policy formulators or implementers.

At that point the idea of an alternative, invitational forum was conceived and the concept discussed with a number of people who were in the midst of the tempest. There was general agreement that a relatively tranquil climate for discussion was necessary and that, further, the basic focus should be on communicating to those who develop and implement national policy (e.g., congressional committees or state and federal administrators). With those two purposes in mind, an invitational conference was planned and conducted in Newport, Rhode Island, in June 1975. This book includes an edited record of that conference as well as additional papers which were developed by participants as a consequence of their conference experience.

In reading this record one should be aware that policy was not developed or set at Newport—the effect of that meeting will largely be a consequence of how widely its papers are disseminated and what their effect is on policymakers. The reader should also keep in mind that not all questions vis-à-vis a given position get asked. This is particularly true when the number of participants in a conference is limited by its organizers, as was the case at Newport.

Finally, one meeting is not enough to analyze exhaustively the major issues; the Newport conference was no exception in this regard. A year or two of cloistered debate would have been preferable to the four days available to us. But a short period of calmly reasoned argument was, in our opinion, a major step forward.

In no small measure our gratitude, and the graditude of the readers who may be enlightened by what they read, is due the George Gund Foundation of Cleveland, Ohio, which invested both its hope and its capital in this venture. We are also indebted to a great many people who generously gave their time and advice during the planning phase of the conference. To them, and to the staff who helped to conduct the event and complete this effort, a genuine and heartfelt thank-you.

Nelson F. Ashline

October 1975
Springfield, Illinois

Preface

The publication of this volume in our bicentennial year is most appropriate. The ideal of equality has been a key tenet in the promise of America from its earliest history, and the perception that education plays a crucial role in the fulfillment of that promise has long been recognized.

A reexamination of our thinking in regard to the role of education in achieving this country's egalitarian ideals is particularly timely in light of the controversy that has surrounded this topic in the past decade. The increasing number of studies by social scientists into the effects of heredity, family background, race and social class, integration and compensatory efforts in learning, and on social and economic mobility has deepened the debate. Some of our most cherished assumptions have been sorely challenged by these inquiries.

There is an urgent need for quiet discussion of the critical issues that confront public education in the 1970s. Both researchers and policymakers must be part of that discussion, for the social scientists have often failed to confront the policy implications of their research findings. This book and the conference which was its genesis are to be commended because they attempt to make that connection. It is written with the policymaker in mind. Its goal is to establish a historical and philosophical perspective on the education inequality link and to clarify the issues which impinge on it today. Beyond that, the book seeks to delineate the alternatives suggested by the various interpretations of recent social science findings and ultimately to assist us in achieving a more equitable society. This goal is worth our most strenuous efforts.

Frank Newman

November 1975
Kingston, Rhode Island

Introduction

The belief in education as the means of achieving social mobility and economic equality in this country has a long and respectable history. The public school has been seen as a primary vehicle for the fulfillment of our egalitarian ideals. It was assumed that, if given equal access to both education and an ever-expanding economy, everyone would be included in the ever-improving standard of living. This faith has been tested in the last decade. When we rediscovered poverty in this country in the early 1960s and declared war on it, it was not surprising that the school was designated as the primary arena for waging the battle. Other targets, including housing and employment, were also selected, and community action programs were inaugurated. However, these efforts were politically more sensitive, and more and more of the burden in the War on Poverty was shifted to the school. Former teacher Lyndon Johnson was quoted by an economist who sat at the planning table as saying

> This is going to be an education program. We are going to eliminate poverty with education, and I don't want anybody ever to mention income redistribution. This is not going to be a handout, this is going to be something where people are going to *learn* their way out of poverty. [*paraphrased*]

As a result, Congress passed the Elementary and Secondary Education Act (ESEA) in 1965. The bill authorized grants for elementary and secondary school programs for children of low-income families, school library resources, textbooks, and other instructional materials for schoolchildren. It also sought to strengthen state education agencies, educational research, and research training.

During this same period, the results of several major research efforts severely challenged the assumptions of ESEA and the underlying faith in school as the equalizer. Sociologist James Coleman's massive study *Equality of Educational Opportunity* (1966) was commissioned by Congress in 1964 to investigate the availability of equal educational opportunity in the U.S. Coleman found, as expected, that for the most part blacks and whites attended different schools. The schools, however, were much more alike than had been predicted in terms of measurable inputs such as teacher education, chemistry labs, number of volumes in the library, etc. Yet there were significant differences in the achievement levels of the two groups: the blacks began school with a one-year deficit in comparison to their white peers and ended with a three-year deficit by the 12th grade. By graduation, blacks were reading, on the average, at a 9th grade level and achieving at a

7th grade level in math. School differences, such as they were, had little impact on these achievement differences; school similarities made even less difference. Furthermore, the achievement differences were within schools, not between schools. Coleman concluded that family background and social context were much more significant variables than school facilities and services as far as academic achievement was concerned.

Arthur Jensen, educational psychologist and psychometrist, published an article "How Much Can We Boost IQ and Scholastic Achievement?" in the *Harvard Education Review* (1969). This article provided one possible explanation for the disparity in achievement between blacks and whites and added another dissenting opinion to the education equality link. Jensen's lengthy article reviewed all the previous studies on twins separated at birth. He found that regardless of environmental influence, intelligence remained fairly constant. This led him to advance the hypothesis that intelligence as measured by IQ tests was primarily inherited (80 percent heritability ratio). Because blacks tended to score lower than whites on IQ tests, Jensen surmised that the gene pool from which blacks in this country draw is inferior to that of whites, in regard to IQ. This was admittedly a tentative hypothesis. It was also heresy in the liberal academy with its environmental orthodoxy. And the reaction from academia was loud and emotional. The faith in the efficacy of compensatory efforts in education to achieve greater equality had been dealt another damaging blow. However, as can be seen in Chapter 7, Equality and Diversity in Education, Jensen has shifted his emphasis from group to individual differences as the appropriate focus for educational intervention.

The final major research effort, Christopher Jenck's *Inequality: A Reassessment of the Effect of Family and Schooling in America*, was published in 1972. Jencks and his colleagues at the Cambridge Policy Studies Institute reanalyzed both Coleman's and Jensen's data and other studies related to compensatory education, and attacked the education equality myth head-on. Jencks found that there was very little correlation between family background, schooling, cognitive skills measured by standardized tests, and later adult success. Brothers raised in the same environment differed in economic status about as much as any two randomly selected individuals in society. The factors which contribute to eonomic and social mobility are apparently idiosyncratic—"luck and personality" in Jencks's terms—and if this is the case, equalizing opportunity will not do much to reduce economic inequality in America.

Jencks went on to advocate a more direct, more explicit program of income equalization rather than the manipulation of "marginal institutions" such as the schools. It is his opinion that, unless we are willing to implement direct measures through taxes and legislation, poverty and inequality will persist at essentially the same current level. Those with more competence and luck would have to subsidize those with less. In order for this to be accomplished, the equity norms—i.e., the political and moral premises to which most of us subscribe—must change. Establishing political control over economic institutions, socialism, or welfare state capitalism is called for. Anything short of that, in Jencks's opinion, is doomed to fail in achieving greater economic equality.

Add to this the furor surrounding enforced bussing and integration and a less-than-robust economy, and one has another American institution under severe pressure. Certainly the policymakers have to be confused by the controversy and dissent surrounding the school. It would not be surprising to find them reluctant to authorize additional programs and expenditures given the lack of agreement among social scientists after ten years and $16 billion invested in policies and programs which in retrospect appear dubious at best.

It is telling that these issues and the resulting controversies have been the result of the social scientist scrutinizing the public school. The policymaker must be in some doubt as to the credibility of the various studies because all too often there is an equally convincing argument for an opposite conclusion that many times uses the same data base but ends with a different interpretation. This would lead one to believe that perhaps there is a pseudoprecision involved in measuring complex social, psychological, genetic, political, and economic factors influencing human characteristics that may not be quantifiable. It is also true that a piece of data, a fact, in itself does not carry an explanation or interpretation. Judgment or bias must inevitably enter into the evaluation of a given set of data and even more so into the formulation of policy based on that data. Chapter 5, Education, Life Chances, and the Courts: The Role of Social Science Evidence, by Henry Levin raises this issue cogently; and it is hoped that the inclusion of this chapter will help stimulate the debate on his thesis that Levin calls for.

Diversity is a theme which emerged at the conference and which is evident in several of the chapters of this book. Edmund Gordon can be credited with helping to shift the emphasis away from the apparently nebulous goal of equality toward a potentially more appropriate objective—that of justice in a diverse society. The whole emphasis on equality is fraught with contradictions, perhaps because of the dialectical tension between it and the promise of liberty that is also a key tenet in our democracy. By shifting the emphasis to justice and recognizing the uniqueness and diversity of human beings, we may be able to be more productive both in the area of educational technology and in the formulation of economic and social policy. In Chapters 7 and 8, both Jensen and Bereiter make a strong case for the individual as opposed to the group as the appropriate focus for educational intervention. Also, in the afterword to his lengthy definitional chapter on equality, Miller makes an important observation in regard to the limiting effect of a society with a single materialist standard of success. By narrowing the income ranges we open the possibility for other avenues of success and achievement and provide the opportunity for greater diversity and individualization within society.

In his concluding remarks as conference moderator, Torsten Husén said, "educational reform is not a substitute for true social and economic reform"—this insight should guide the reader throughout this book. Education may be a necessary condition for economic and social mobility, but it apparently is not a sufficient one. Current research has even begun to indicate a narrowing of the traditional income gap between high school and college graduates. This obviously does not suggest that education is of no value but rather than our expectations of it have been inappropriate. The chapters in this book are offered as an attempt to clarify the school's role in achieving this country's egalitarian ideals and to bring the multifaceted topic of equality into better focus. Perhaps if our expectations are more realistic, we will not be disappointed as often. More importantly, we can be more effective in achieving a more just and equitable society.

Charles I. Norris

December 1975
Kingston, Rhode Island

Conference Participants

Gordon Alexander. Special assistant to U.S. Senator Birch Bayh, staff assistant to U.S. Senate Subcommittee to Investigate Juvenile Delinquency.

Robert Andringa. Minority staff director, U.S. House of Representatives Education and Labor Committee.

T.H. Bell. United States Commissioner of Education.*

Carl Bereiter. Professor of Applied Psychology and Curriculum, Ontario Institute for Studies in Education.

Ronald Berman. Chairman, National Endowment for the Humanities.

Kenneth B. Clark. President of the Metropolitan Applied Research Center, Inc., and Professor of Psychology at City College, New York.*

Joseph C. Cronin. Illinois State Superintendent of Education.

John B. Davis, Jr. Superintendent of Schools, Minneapolis, Minnesota.*

Edgar Epps. Professor of Urban Education, University of Chicago.

Patricia Fleming. Former assistant to U.S. Congresswoman Shirley Chisholm. Current assistant to Representative Andrew Young, U.S. House of Representatives' Committee on Rules.

Herbert Gans. Professor of Sociology, Columbia University. Senior Research Associate at the Center for Policy Research, Inc.

Edmund W. Gordon. Chairman of the Department of Applied Human Development and Guidance, Teachers College, Columbia University. Director of ERIC/Information Retrieval Center on the Disadvantaged. Director of the Institute of Urban and Minority Education, Educational Testing Service and Teachers College, Columbia University.

Fred M. Hechinger. Editorial Board, *The New York Times*.*

Harold L. Hodgkinson. Director, National Institute of Education.*

Torsten Husén. Director of the Institute for the Study of International Problems in Education, University of Stockholm.

Christopher Jencks. Professor of Sociology at Harvard University. Research Associate at the Center for the Study of Public Policy.*

---

* Indicates those who accepted invitations to participate in the conference but were unable to attend. These names are included in the list of participants because they often played a significant role in planning the conference, including framing issues and suggesting additional participants. In many cases they sent representatives to the conference and have been a part of the continuing dialogue which has resulted since the event.

Arthur Jensen. Professor of Educational Psychology and Research Psychologist at the Institute of Human Learning at the University of California, Berkeley.

Sidney Johnson. Staff director, U.S. Senate Subcommittee on Children and Youth.

Henry M. Levin. Professor of Education, Stanford University.*

S.M. Miller. Chairperson, Department of Sociology, Boston University.

Frank Newman. President, University of Rhode Island.

Claiborne Pell. Chairman, U.S. Senate Subcommittee on Education. Honorary Chairman of the Gund Foundation conference on Education, Inequality, and National Policy.*

Reed Saunders. Deputy Assistant Commissioner for Planning, Budgeting, and Evaluation, U.S. Office of Education.

Sandra Scarr-Salapatek. Professor of Psychology, Institute of Child Development, University of Minnesota.

Robert Schwartz. Special assistant in education to Mayor Kevin White of Boston.

Marshall S. Smith. Visiting scholar and assistant director, National Institue of Education. Professor of Education, Harvard University Graduate School of Education.

Louis Stokes. Member of the U.S. House of Representatives.*

Lester C. Thurow. Professor of Economics and Management, Massachusetts Institute of Technology.

Stephen J. Wexler. Counsel, U.S. Senate Subcommittee on Education.

1

Public Education as the Great Equalizer

Fred M. Hechinger*

The new American role of education to strengthen the foundations of republican government had its origin in the revolutionary vision of Thomas Jefferson. Few concepts could have been more upsetting to the established order than Jefferson's idea of a "natural" aristocracy of talent—the very opposite of the existing aristocracy of inherited privilege. It was, if Jefferson's dream of the new American society were to come true, nothing less than the end of the old order.

This is not to suggest that Jefferson believed in, or wanted to bring about, absolute equality. What he was writing about when, at the age of 35, he drafted a "Bill for the More General Diffusion of Knowledge in the State of Virginia," was the need to clear the way for talented children and youths to continue their education and thus to rise to top positions of responsibility and power in society, without regard to their families' economic and social status. It was a plan that would have ensured elementary learning for all children, district schools for the further instruction of the brightest among that mass, and guaranteed admission to higher education for the cream of the crop.

It was an idea whose time had clearly not yet come, and when his blueprint was defeated in 1817, Jefferson acknowledged in sad disappointment that the members of the legislature "do not generally possess information enough to perceive the important truths, that knowledge is power, that knowledge is safety, that knowledge is happiness."

If Jefferson had any doubt about the future role of education—and this ought to be kept in mind for any assessment of America's education problems in the second half of the twentieth century—it was whether the school could muster the strength to counteract what he foresaw as the problems of an urban society. In 1787 this revolutionary, whose roots were firmly implanted in the society of the landed gentry, wrote to James Madison:

I think our governments will remain virtuous for many centuries; as long as they are chiefly agricultural; and this will be as long as there shall be vacant lands in any part of America. When they get piled upon one another in large cities, as in Europe, they will become corrupt as in Europe. Above all things I hope the education of the common people will be attended to: convinced that on their good sense we may rely with the most security for the preservation of a due degree of liberty.

---

* Editorial Board, *New York Times*.

1

But the urbanization of America was still far in the future. For the moment, Jefferson's vision of the power of education to build bridges between the different levels of society was gaining powerful allies. In 1821, Daniel Webster said:

For the purpose of public instruction, we hold every man subject to taxation in proportion to his property, and we look not to the question whether he himself have or have not children to be benefited by the education for which he pays; we regard it as a wise and liberal system of police, by which property, and life, and the peace of society are secured. . . . We do not, indeed, expect all men to be philosophers or statesmen; but we confidently trust . . . that by diffusion of general knowledge, and good and virtuous sentiments, the political fabric may be secure as well against open violence and overthrow as against the slow but sure undermining of licentiousness.

The concept of education as the ladder on which able children from humble homes might rise to wealth and influence was not readily accepted in Jefferson's time, and it continued to be violently opposed by those who saw it as a threat to the existing power structure and to the quality of American life and institutions. A proposal to levy a tax in order to finance public education was violently attacked by Philadelphia's journal, *The National Gazette*, in 1830. To do so, the newspaper warned, would make moderately successful families feel that "they had toiled for the benefit of other families than their own."

"We have no confidence in any compulsory equalizations," said the editorial. "It had well been observed that they pull down what is above, but never raise what is below. . . . A scheme of universal equal education, attempted in reality, would be an unexampled bed of Procrustes for the understandings of our youth. . . ."

But as the process of building a nation and creating the "new American" became the uppermost concern of many politicians and social philosophers, conservative efforts to maintain elitist restrictions were challenged by a growing commitment to egalitarian plans for a classless society.

Horace Mann was the high priest of a growing faith in education that fell little short of a new religion. He believed as deeply as Jefferson in the power of knowledge as the engine of republican government and a democratic society. Although he admired America's diversity, he was also fearful of the ultimate divisiveness of pluralism. In his view, only a new institution, capable of embracing so diverse a population, could create a sense of community and ensure enough unity to safeguard the new nation's foundation. Such a common purpose could be achieved only through the common school.

Before Mann, the term "common school" had always had the connotation of service to the poor—those who had been shunted aside and excluded from such elite institutions as the academies. Even those earlier reformers who had begun to plead for more humane treatment of children had been concerned largely about the fate of the offspring of affluent or middle-class families; the children of the poor were either ignored or termed, and treated as, "vicious." Not even so forward-looking and humane a philosopher as Locke had found it within himself to include poor children among the scope of his liberal proposals, exposing them instead to the workhouse and whippings.

Mann's view of America's future could brook no such dichotomy. On the contrary, he saw the school as the single most powerful tool with which to erase the social and economic distinctions. "Now, surely, nothing but Universal Education can counterwork this tendency to the domination of capital and the servility of labor," Mann wrote. And he continued:

If one class possesses all the wealth and education, while the residue of society is ignorant and poor, it matters not by what name the relation between them may be called; the latter, in fact, and in truth, will be the servile dependents and subjects of the former. But if education be equally diffused, it will draw property after it, by the strongest of all attractions; for such a thing never did happen, as that an intelligent and practical body of men should be permanently poor. Property and labor, in different classes, are essentially antagonistic; but property and labor, in the same class, are essentially fraternal. . . . Education, then, beyond all other devices of human origin, is the great equalizer of the conditions of men—the balance-wheel of the social machinery.

Mann believed that, even if greed and power were to continue to work to the disadvantage of the poor, education would give to ordinary citizens the means to "resist the selfishness of other men." Indeed, in Mann's approach there was a hint of the strategy of a "war against poverty" that would become so prominent a feature in American reform politics more than a century later. Education, Mann said, "does better than disarm the poor of their hostility toward the rich. The wanton destruction of the property of others,—the burning of hay-ricks and corn-ricks, the demolition of machinery because it supersedes hand-labor, the sprinkling of vitriol on rich dresses,—is only agrarianism run mad. Education prevents both the revenge and the madness."

While Mann considered it essential to the process of nation building that the schools inculcate in all children an understanding of government and politics, he was realistic enough to sense the danger—he called it "catastrophe"—of a political domination of the educational process. He was less realistic, however, in foreseeing the difficulty of separating the one (instruction about politics) from the other (the politicizing of instruction). The proper course, he counseled, would be to teach to all "those articles in the creed of republicanism, which are accepted by all, believed in by all, and which form the common basis of our political faith."

Not unlike Jefferson and Franklin, Horace Mann was still convinced that the unifying process of the common school would create sufficient political consensus to make it possible to teach a generally accepted "creed" of republicanism while avoiding divisive and partisan politics. Hindsight shows this to have been an idealist's perhaps inevitable miscalculation.

One third philosophical approach—added to the Jeffersonian concept of an aristocracy of talent and Mann's faith in the equalizing capacity of the common school—must be placed on the table. The exact opposite of Mann's effort to insulate the schools against power politics, this view was given its most concise expression in 1932 by George Counts, one of the spokesmen of post-Dewey progressivism. Counts "dared" a national convention of teachers to use the schools as the instrument to "build a new social order." (Dewey himself responded with a warning that political realities made it impossible for schools to determine the course of political, intellectual, and moral change in the society at large.)

It is nevertheless against these three philosophical underpinnings—the school as the ladder that lets the able climb to the top, the school as the great socioeconomic equalizer, the school as the instrument of political change—that the relative success or failure of public education to accomplish its mission and its mandate must be judged.

No assessment of public education's record as an equalizing force is possible without a brief examination of the schools' actual approach to such a goal in the years between Horace Mann and the contemporary era from the mid-1950s to today.

From the beginning of the period under examination, it was clear that the educational and political leadership continued frequently (although not necessarily always) to be satisfied with the education of those who willingly adjusted to the way of life of the majority and the parallel majority view of education.

The key to successful education, and its reward of socioeconomic equalization, was assimilation. Immigrant children were expected to reject their native culture and cut their ties with the language and the *weltanschauung* of their families. Children's names were Americanized by teachers, often without the parents' knowledge, let alone consent. Leonard Covello, who later rose to a respected position as an educator, recalled his father's shock upon learning that his son's teacher had ordered the "i" to be dropped from the original Coviello, in addition to the Americanization of "Leonardo." "We soon got the idea that 'Italian' meant something pretty inferior, and a barrier was erected between children of Italian origin and their parents," Covello recalled.

In 1851, *The Massachusetts Teacher* offered this comment on the effects of immigration, particularly from Ireland:

The constantly increasing influx of foreigners during the last ten years has been, and continues to be, a cause of serious alarm to the most intelligent of our own people. What will be the ultimate effect of this vast and unexampled immigration is a problem which has engaged the most anxious thought of our best and wisest men. Will it, like the muddy Missouri, as it pours its waters into the clear Mississippi and contaminates the whole united mass, spread ignorance and vice, crime and disease, through our native population? Or can we, by any process, not only preserve ourselves from the threatened demoralization, but improve and purify and make valuable this new element which is thus forced upon us and which we cannot shut out if we would?

Adele M. Shaw, in *The World's Work* of 1913, quoted a teacher asking a pupil: "You dirty little Russian Jew, what are you doing?"

It would nevertheless be misleading to omit from this account the fact that untold thousands of immigrant children did find the schools to be that tool of successful self-advancement and subsequent equalization that Mann had envisioned. Particularly those who had come from families which, though poor, enjoyed a long tradition of learning and had maintained that tradition even amid the most hostile and threatening surroundings—such as political persecution in Russia and Germany—not only managed to adjust to the schools' demands, but did so gratefully and even joyfully.

For example, Mary Antin, in her book *The Promised Land*, recalled her life in an American school in the 1890s:

There was no free school [in Russia] for girls. . . . At the high school, which was under government control, Jewish children were admitted in limited numbers . . . a nine-year-old Jewish child had to answer questions that a thirteen-year-old Gentile was hardly expected to understand . . . and there was no appeal. . . . No, the Czar did not want us in the schools. Education in America was free. That subject my father had written about repeatedly, as compromising his chief hope for us children, the essence of American opportunity, the treasure that no thief could touch, not even misfortune and poverty. It was the one thing that he was able to promise us when he sent for us; surer, safer than bread or shelter. . . . No application was made, no questions asked, no examinations, rulings, exclusions; no machinations, no fees.

She spoke for countless others for whom the schools were indeed the escape hatch from poverty. And yet, too many were allowed to fall by the wayside. Mann's hope that merely opening the schools' doors would clear the way to equality was shown to be optimistic. After a national investigation, the Federal Bureau of Education reported in 1914 that "chaos existed throughout the nation's schools. . . . There was no real national policy for helping immigrants."

Even the absence of such a policy, however, was better than the existing policy of discrimination and exclusions that confronted the children of black Americans. For a substantial part of American history, the black child was not just discriminated against, but invisible. Black education was an issue left to Supreme Court decisions; it was not part of any systematic review of American education.

In the South, where so much of the pattern for black education had been established, the lot of black children was submerged in the educational deprivation suffered by severely neglected poor white youngsters. In a society that could characterize its poor as "white trash," the cruelty of neglect toward the even poorer blacks becomes comprehensible, though not excusable. Such cruelty was reinforced by the poor whites' fear that they would sink even lower if blacks were allowed to rise on the scale of status and opportunity.

In *Plessy v. Ferguson* the Supreme Court in 1896 codified educational inequality by upholding the theory of "separate but equal" schooling, the code word for segregation and inequality. In general, the ruling echoed the views expressed earlier in *Roberts v. City of Boston* when the majority had turned down Charles Sumner's plea for equal rights in school attendance, holding that "legislation is powerless to eradicate racial instincts." The historic tragedy of the *Plessy* decision was that it rejected Justice John Marshall Harlan's prescient warning: "In the view of the Constitution, in the eye of the law, there is in this country no superior, dominant ruling class of citizens. There is no caste here. Our Constitution is color-blind." Acceptance of that fundamental truth was postponed for almost 60 years with awesome consequences to the nation and the cause of equality.

It was not until the 1954 *Brown* decision by the unanimous Warren Court—"We conclude that in the field of public education the doctrine of 'separate but equal' has no place. Separate educational facilities are inherently unequal."—that the officially imposed and sanctioned theory of black inequality was rejected.

Finally, no examination of the dichotomy that assured educational equality for some children, but denied it to others, would be complete without reference to the long history of child labor. Without reviewing the dismal conditions under which children labored in the mines and in the sweatshops, it must be recalled that as late as June 3, 1918, the Supreme Court, by a vote of 5 to 4, held in *Hammer v. Dagenhart* that the Keating-Owens Act prohibiting the worst abuses of child labor was unconstitutional. The act, the majority ruled, had given to Congress "power as to a purely local matter to which the Federal authority does not extend" and which would threaten henceforth "all freedom of commerce."

In a historic dissent, Justice Oliver Wendell Holmes, reminding his brethren of the congressional authority to enforce Prohibition, underscored the unequal treatment to which children are often exposed. "If there is any matter," Holmes wrote, "upon which civilized countries have agreed—far more unanimously than they have with regard to intoxicants and some other matters over which this country is now emotionally aroused—it is the evil of premature and excessive child labor."

It was not until the 1930s, when the Depression and a permanently changed labor market had made child labor unprofitable and unwanted, that this policy of inherent inequality was finally outlawed, although its evil persists even today in the case of the children of migrant farm workers.

Despite the schools' evident shortcomings, mainly as a result of the dichotomy between the opportunities of the mainstream and the deprivations of the poor, the positive side of the record is impressive. Today, for example, more than 75 percent of the pertinent age group finish secondary school in the United States, and almost half of these high school graduates go on to higher education—a record not yet matched by any other nation. Even more important, statistics corroborated by the Institute for the International Evaluation of Educational Achievement (IEA) show that the academic elite among American high school seniors (the top 9 percent that might well be viewed as the modern equivalent of Jefferson's aristocracy of talent) contained a far larger percentage of children from lower-class (unskilled or semiskilled workers') homes than the same sample in any of the other 21 nations surveyed. Specifically, the American newly risen group constituted 14 percent of the entire group, compared with only slightly more than 1 percent in West Germany, to cite only one typical example.

It is against such a historical and statistical background that the contemporary debate over the question of equality and over the schools as an instrument of equalization should be measured.

The issue moved to the center of the national stage when President Johnson assigned to the schools the major burden of closing the gap between the children of poverty and the children of the American mainstream. Through such devices as Project Head Start and compensatory education to be provided via the Elementary and Secondary Education Act of 1965, the schools were to become the heavy artillery in the War on Poverty and eliminate the deficit created by a long history of inequality and neglect. In particular the black children's learning achievements were to be raised through a combination of integration and compensatory education.

New questions, however, were raised almost as soon as this new push toward equalization got under way. James Coleman, then professor of sociology at Johns Hopkins University, in his report on *Equality of Educational Opportunity* (1966), maintained that in terms of teachers, facilities, curricula, and other yardsticks studied, the differences noted between black and white schools were negligible. Coleman concluded that, while the schools' efforts made some difference, family and socioeconomic background were far more important indicators of, and influences on, children's achievements. However, Coleman also found that black pupils who were enrolled in schools with a white middle-class majority appeared to be strongly influenced by the latter's motivation and achievement, while such an approach to integration did not appear to interfere with the white pupils' success.

Although these findings were subject to a variety of different interpretations, their immediate impact was to highlight the schools' relative impotence as a vehicle for dramatic change and equalization. Less attention was paid to the fact that the Coleman findings also suggested the importance of effective integration—the equalizing advantages to be gained by lower-class black children placed into high-achieving classrooms whose majority was middle-class white. (If heeded, these findings might have averted the Boston integration debacle that resulted from efforts to integrate blacks into lower-class white schools—under conditions which caused the insecure whites to react with the same hostility that had created such antiblack feelings among poor whites in the post-Civil War South.)

Up to this point, however, the debate remained largely confined to questions of strategies. Coleman had not challenged the basic assumption that, under certain circumstances and given the appropriate tools, the schools could successfully perform at least a limited equalizing mission. True, Coleman's findings underscored the need for a more effective partnership between school, home, and society, but that was hardly a point to be seriously challenged by educators. On the contrary, the profession was anxious to extricate itself from the prevailing view that the schools could do the job, if only left alone by laymen—a view which was, in large measure, the result of the profession's exaggerated claims during the era of the professionalization and bureaucratization of public education in the first part of the century. Given the magnitude of society's problems (see, for example, James B. Conant's *Slums and Suburbs*), it was hardly reasonable to expect the schools to do the job of closing the inequality gap in splendid isolation from the other sectors and agencies of contemporary life. Indeed, it could be argued that the schools might do well to concentrate on erasing the very inequalities which they had helped to perpetuate—through acquiescence to the long-standing dichotomy between poor and rich, black and white, male and female, etc.

One of the inequities the schools had helped to create had arisen from the misuse of an educational device, known as measurement or testing. Edward L. Thorndike, at Teachers College, Columbia University, had written in 1903 that "the science of education, when it develops, will, like other sciences, rest upon direct observations of and experiments on the influence of educational institutions and methods made and reported with quantitative precision." Educational measurement became an increasing preoccupation, and the use of intelligence tests to classify children in school gained wide acceptance.

Somewhat ironically, the popularization of intelligence tests was has-tened by their use for the classification of Army recruits in World War I. The results were a disaster, largely because the tests assigned to the military were poor adaptations of tests designed for children. The data eventually pegged the average mental age of adult Americans at 14. Half the American population and almost 90 percent of blacks emerged from this process labeled feebleminded. Moreover, immigrants from Southern and Eastern Europe were "shown" to be inferior to those from the northern countries, and a number of psychologists appended their studies with warnings that a genetically inferior influx from certain regions would de-press the nation's intelligence level.

Later, the schools still applied similarly misleading "scientific" yardsticks to nonwhite minority pupils, once again misusing testing devices for the purpose of permanently categorizing—and often tracking—children instead of making the tests instruments for the detection and pedagogical response to individual strengths and weaknesses. (A growing body of opinion, led by John Hersey in an early study of the misuse of IQ tests, held that group testing may be too inaccurate a yardstick to be taken seriously, calling instead for the use of individual tests, except for purposes of the most flexible, preliminary sorting.)

Shortly after initial reassessments of pupils' achievements in the light of Coleman's findings, the testing issue once again became a matter of heated controversy in the context of the debate over educational equality. This time the debate was to take an even more acrimonious turn when several social scientists advanced the thesis, based on what they said was new statistical research data, that heredity might be more important than environment in determining a child's IQ. The new theory's leading propo-nent was Arthur Jensen, professor of educational psychology at Berkeley, who presented his findings in a 123-page article in the Winter, 1969 issue of the *Harvard Educational Review*.

Jensen, on the basis of a study of largely European and North American middle-class populations around the turn of the century, concluded that "the heritability of the IQ . . . comes to about 80 percent. . . ." In other words, he suggested that the low scores among certain groups—racial, ethnic, and socioeconomic—may be caused by genetic inheritance to a larger degree than had been assumed, with the environmental factors contributing to the result in a relatively lesser measure. (Alfred Binet had written half a century earlier: ". . . our personal investigations . . . have demonstrated that children of the poorer class are shorter, weigh less, have smaller heads and slighter muscular force, than a child of the upper class; they less often reach the high school; they are more often behind in their studies.")

The instant response to Jensen, and to related statements by Dr. Richard Herrnstein, a Harvard psychologist, was one of political outrage rather than scientific dialogue. Attacks launched against Jensen and others approached the dimensions of censorship and persecution. But even many of those who were shocked by such attempts at repression raised questions about the validity of Jensen's claims or, at least, about the popular interpretation of his often tentative conclusions.

The statistical approach to determine the relative influence on the IQ by either heredity or environment remained subject to scientific, as well as political, disagreement. To what extent, for example, could the two factors contributing to measured intelligence be meaningfully distinguished? If a group had been subjected to poverty and intellectual deprivation for generations, would not the deficiency in psychological as well as intellectual nutrition, which are clearly environmental, also come to appear to be hereditary—at least until such a time as drastic and long-term reversals of such handicaps could, in turn, register their impact on successive generations? Jensen himself wrote, in answer to charges of racism leveled against him: "I believe that the cause of the observed differences in IQ and scholastic performance among different ethnic groups is scientifically still an open question, an important question, and a researchable question."

(The concept of the IQ as a fixed and predetermined indicator of an individual's potential had repeatedly been challenged in the past. In 1960, for example, Albert Upton, a professor of English at Whittier College, California, announced that, after eight months of "exercises" involving the comprehension of words and analysis of ideas, the IQ of a class of first-year students had been raised by an average of 10.5 points, with the largest individual gain being a phenomenal 32 points.)

While the Jensen debate had been confined largely to the campuses, another controversy over the issue of inequality transcended the world of academia and affected the national and political reappraisal of public education's past and future roles. Christopher Jencks, an educational sociologist at Harvard, in 1972 published a widely noted book, *Inequality: A Reassessment of the Effect of Family and Schooling in America*. Jencks maintained that, based on a reevaluation of previous data, particularly Coleman's, the public schools had failed to achieve the social goals set for them by their founders and claimed for them by their supporters. Specifically, Jencks held, the schools had failed to close the economic inequality gap, a goal that he concluded could only be accomplished politically through the redistribution of income by way of socialism.

While the schools did not, in Jencks's view, really matter as instruments of socioeconomic reform, he did not ask for their abolition. Let them continue, he said in effect, to do the best they can for the children, and do it in the most pleasant environment to which children are entitled. But, he implied, it would be misleading to promise that great social reforms would emerge—none of the equalizing miracles that Horace Mann had predicted as the consequence of rich and poor rubbing elbows in the same classroom.

In many ways, the Jencks doctrine tends to be politically less dangerous for the schools than the earlier appeal by some progressives, such as Counts, to sue the schools for the creation of a new social order. If they are shown to be impotent as a social reform force, the schools might at least be spared the wrath of conservatives who would accuse them of doing something that Jencks insists quite accurately, in the light of past history, they would be incapable of accomplishing even if they wanted to—spark a social or political revolution. Jencks's efforts to usher in socialism would, after all, be fought on nonschool grounds.

For similar reasons, too, Jencks's views are potentially less dangerous educationally and politically than the efforts of those educational revisionists (Ivan Illich, *Deschooling Society*; Colin Greer, *The Great School Legend*) who advocate the dismantling of the public schools largely as a means of dismantling the institutional structure of American government itself.

In replying to the Jencks thesis, Daniel Patrick Moynihan (*On Equality of Educational Opportunity* by Moynihan and Frederick Mosteller), using the same Coleman data base, argues that the schools have, in fact, been party to major social improvements, particularly the elimination of social class as the determinant of educational advantage. What makes a compromise between Jencks and Moynihan difficult is the fact that the latter counsels moderation and gradualism in efforts to move toward greater equality—or less serious inequality—while Jencks is convinced that gradualism not only has already failed but is not likely to close the gap even in the long run.

Criticism of the public schools' failure to reach sufficient numbers of the urban poor is obviously justified. In fact, the public schools have, throughout their history, often failed many of the children of the poor, unless the parents themselves made extraordinary efforts to demand effective schooling and to inspire a love for learning in their children. Many youngsters fell by the wayside. What makes such ''dropping out'' infinitely more serious in the postindustrial society is that jobs for the uneducated have dwindled. Whatever low-level jobs remain provide so little reward and incentive that failure in school paves the way for alienation and despair.

Although the revisionists have been sensitive to that alienation and despair, the question remains whether their solutions—downgrading or abolishing the schools and breaking with the concept of compulsory education—will help or hurt children, particularly the disadvantaged. Will greater freedom of choice—whether or where to go to school—though intended to increase everybody's options, once again give the advantage to the affluent, who would send their children to school with or without compulsion and who, given a voucher to spend where they wish, would be the first in line at the best schools?

In a historical framework, the question may be not whether the schools have failed because they were unable to eliminate inequality (although such a failure would clearly disappoint Mann), but rather what measure of success they have achieved in helping substantial numbers of children to rise on the material and social scales of affluence, influence, and status in relation to what Mann called their "natural capacities." And it seems difficult to assess the degree of their success on that score without comparing it to education-induced conditions in other industrial countries. Whether a nation opts for the gradual or drastic redistribution of incomes, regardless of educational achievement or natural capacities, is not properly an issue either to be decided by the schools, or to be taken into consideration in judging the success of the educational system.

The danger inherent in the collective voices of those who claim that the schools have failed, or that they do not really matter, or that they will never be able to solve, or contribute to the solution of, the problems of poverty is that they may add to the previously largely conservative outcry in favor of reducing school budgets and relieving the taxpayers' burden. The confluence of such views could also diminish the sense of urgency in present efforts to close the inequality gap in school expenditures between communities with high and low taxable property bases.

A final comment is in order. While Horace Mann would undoubtedly be shocked by the failure to erase the gap between poverty and affluence to which Jencks has addressed himself, Jefferson might hail the concrete gains clearly traceable to the schools in efforts to allow a natural aristocracy of talent to avail itself of educational opportunities up to the highest level of scholarship. Yet, it should also be recalled that Jefferson had serious doubts about whether his prescriptions for an equitable and successful republic would survive in an urban environment. Jefferson had a nagging fear that the untutored "mob" of cities steeped in corruption might undermine the great democratic experiment.

Virtually all the contemporary unanswered questions are related to Jefferson's original doubts. These questions seem to ask not whether public education in America has failed, but whether and how it can be made to succeed in modern, predominantly urban America.

References:

Gordon, C. Lee, ed. *Crusade Against Ignorance: Thomas Jefferson on Education*; Teachers College Press, Columbia University, New York, 1961.

Mann, Horace, *Twelfth Annual Report of the Secretary of the Board of*

Education, West Newton, Mass. November 24, 1848. Dutton, Wentworth State Printers, Boston, 1849.

Webster, Daniel, *The Works of Daniel Webster*, Little Brown, Boston, 1854. Volume 1 Pg. 41-42.

2 Types of Equality: Sorting, Rewarding, Performing*

S.M. Miller†

Introduction

The failure of the growth of gross national product to eliminate poverty has resulted in discontent in many advanced industrial nations. Inequalities have not been reduced, despite the great absolute advance in the condition of the working class; an underclass or marginal working class living under distressing conditions has been discovered once again. A profound issue is becoming recognized: in many countries national income is no more equally distributed today than it was twenty years ago, despite the importance of taxation and governmental transfer programs.[1] In some socialist countries, the tension between economic incentives for productivity and a more egalitarian distribution of income is acutely sensed. The specter of "the equal sharing of low incomes" supports nonsocialist reforms which offer the possibility of "the unequal sharing of greater income" which might result from the widespread use of production incentives. Absolute and relative differences are the staple of current discussions of stratification and equality.

Despite the long discussions in the sociological field of social stratification, the issues of equality have been inadequately conceptualized. True, equality of opportunity is differentiated from equality of conditions or results; the difference between the concept of an open-class society and a classless society is clearer than before. But conceptualizations have not gone much further.[2] In the 1950s economic growth was at the forefront and was expected to be the resolver of the issue of poverty; prevailing conceptualizations were perhaps adequate, for equality was not an active social and political concern. Today, however, we need a much more delineated understanding of the goals of equality.

The attacks on inequality and on the goal of equality of opportunity have come from a variety of directions. In the U.S., at least, a confusion has developed about the various objectives of those espousing "more equality" or equality of conditions or results. This chapter strives to delineate the goals which are embodied in the objective of equality.

*I am indebted to Jean Baker Miller and Ronnie Steinberg Ratner for a critical reading of an earlier draft.

† Boston University.

15

Four types of equality are delineated. Type 1 is the well-known standard of equality of opportunity. The other three, which are of more central importance, are about equality of conditions or results. Type 2 is representative equality, which deals with who gets the preferred positions in society. Type 3 is the most frequently discussed form of equality—income equality—or my preferred term, "resource equality." Type 4 is task equality, which connects the rewards or resources tied to positions to the redistribution of tasks or performances.

Each type is discussed in turn. The general procedure followed is first to distinguish each type from the others; then some of the issues involved in pursuing the type are analyzed. Philosophical and political support for and opposition to each type are then briefly discussed.

As we can see from this typology, it is no longer useful to say that equality of opportunity is about "opening doors" to talent, while equality of conditions is concerned with "providing floors" so that differences in society are narrowed. The quality-of-conditions goals—the central issue of this chapter—can be characterized by relating to: *who* gets *what* positions, which is a question of sorting; what rewards or *resources* do they get in these positions; and what activities, performances, or *tasks* do they engage in?

Type 1: Equality of Opportunity

Equality of opportunity means that family background, religion, race, or sex should be neither an advantage nor a disadvantage in obtaining the desirable occupations in society. Ability, not privilege, should count, and all individuals should have the same chance of moving into the desirable occupations (upward social mobility). Where one starts in the social structure—the socioeconomic level of one's parents—should not affect where one ends—the occupation attained.

The goal of equality of opportunity has been very attractive. It has a surface appeal of removing privilege and discrimination, rewarding merit, and achieving efficiency because the meritoriously accomplished perform the important tasks with high motivation and effectiveness, meeting the "functional imperatives" of a society. It is also appealing because it seems only mildly disturbing. It does not seek to change a society fundamentally except to remove false (i.e., productively inappropriate) barriers.

The equal opportunity goal leads to an emphasis on schooling as the appropriate public policy. Increasing the access of those of low socioeconomic origins to secondary and higher education is regarded as the main way of achieving equal opportunity, for educational level is thought to affect people's future occupational level and income. The desired goal is a "meritocracy" where ability (and perhaps drive) alone determines position. And schools do the sorting of ability.

One attraction of the meritocratic ideal is that it emphasizes education, not economic structure, correcting abuses of discrimination by emphasizing individual merit, not by changing the situation of large groups of people. The goal of "a career open to talent" is exhibited in who and how many are deemed to fit the meritocratic ideal. The equal opportunity ideal is attractive because it does not seem to require large changes in society; rather, unseemly discrimination, prejudice, and snobbery are to be reduced. Increasing the numbers who are rising to the top will raise societal efficiency by widening the pool of talents available for high positions at the same time social harmony is promoted by reducing the disquiet resulting from unreasonable and categorical discriminations.

Many nations pride themselves on the advances that they have made toward increasing mobility opportunities. Secondary school and university places have been greatly expanded. Widespread urbanization has offered access to higher education and occupations to a much greater proportion of families than before. Privilege has been reduced, and merit has become more important in attaining positions.

Nevertheless, in many nations educational opportunity and social mobility are acute political issues, for many with merit and potential merit who are born to low-income families clearly do not have as good a chance to rise as do individuals raised in families that have already reached relatively high standing. While in a number of nations the advantages of being born into high socioeconomic families have been reduced, they are still substantial in terms of entry to higher education.

It is important to realize that *relative* chances are the important issue in equality of opportunity. If youths of low-income families move in greater proportions than before to graduate from high school (as is the case in this country) while youth of middle-income families move to graduate from college, the educational gap between the two groups of youths may not have narrowed.

Even if educational differences between socioeconomic levels were narrowed, there is no assurance that the relative educational gains of the low socioeconomic groups would pay off in terms of occupation and income. We do not live in a meritocracy where merit determines educational, occupational, and income level. As Jencks has reported, the links between education and occupation and between occupation and income are weak. People of the same educational level have an enormous range of incomes, as do people of even the same occupation.[3]

Swedish data indicate that socioeconomic background affects what happens to one after schooling. Those of the same level of schooling but with different socioeconomic levels have different occupations and incomes. Holding educational level constant, those of high socioeconomic background do much better.[4] Class counts. Education is not the great equalizer.

Despite the spread of education and the presumed reduction of privilege in access to positions, studies of social mobility in the United States suggest the tentative conclusion that no decline has occurred between 1962 and 1972 in the relative advantage sons of nonmanual workers have over the sons of manual workers in attaining nonmanual positions.

If we do not live in a meritocracy, where merit alone determines educational, occupational, and income levels, is this an attainable goal? Can meritocracy be achieved? Many American conservatives and liberals believe that a higher degree of meritocracy can be attained than is now the case, but a sizable number of people, especially those who feel discriminated against, are much less optimistic. They believe that it is not possible to provide an equal footing, an equal start, for those who have come from many different places in society. It is exceedingly difficult to achieve equal opportunities without prior equal conditions.[5]

Those from better-off families can more easily prepare themselves for higher positions. Cultural differences are important:

To be born in different positions within society molds the ability to handle access to institutions and the development of levels of aspiration and achievement motivation. In this sense, then, equality of opportunity can never be fully present in a society with great social divides within it.[6]

Nor does equality of opportunity prevent the stigmatizing of those at the bottom—indeed a "more perfect meritocracy" might strengthen stigmatization: "failure" to climb would be attributed only to personal inadequacies. Nor does "equal opportunity" diminish the overemphasis on "material success" and materialism. Nor would it likely promote fraternity if successfully running the "rat race" is the essence of the more open society.

The expansion of opportunity is regarded as the way of incorporating discontented, disadvantaged groups into society. Expanding changes of ascent are not particularly costly nor disturbing to the usual modes of operation of a society; the snobbery of the already settled smooths the irritations produced by the push of the newly arrived. In recent years this reassuring scenario of incorporation of some of the talented disadvantaged with minimum discomfort to those in desirable positions has been rent. Unrest, disturbance, and violence have resulted from the equal-opportunity-in-education approach. Mass enrollments in universities engender strains there; unrest, as in France, may spread to other sectors of society. Academic elites feel threatened by the expansion of universities and the new demands made upon them. The schooled who are underemployed and unemployed may become a disturbing, rebellious group. The struggle to increase opportunity cannot be won only in the university, and the university is strained by its role in the opportunity process.

Beyond Equal Opportunity

Dissatisfactions, on both the feasibility and the normative levels, with the goal of equality of opportunity have led to stress on the goal of equality of conditions or results. Here, the emphasis is not only on fairly arraying people at the beginning of the race so they all have an equal chance of winning, but also on seeing that at the end of the race these differences in education, occupation, and income are not very great.

Type 2: Representative Equality

This form of equality of conditions has a direct continuity with the equal opportunity perspective of Type 1, as it focuses on the sorting process— who gets what position. It is concerned with the occupational outcomes for particular categories of individuals; it also specifies activities which should ensure that a category is adequately represented in desirable positions in a particular society. In the United States, there has been particular concern about the low percentage of women and blacks in the higher levels of university faculties and at the managerial level of large corporations; there also has been agitation about the low proportion of blacks in the construction field.

Representative equality can be another form of equality of opportunity if the demand is only to ensure that groups discriminated against on the basis of ascriptive characteristics of race, ethnicity, or sex have a chance equal to that of the overadvantaged groups to attain higher positions. Indeed, a good deal of the struggle for equality of opportunity in this country has been to reduce the barriers against blacks. The newness of the contemporary demand for representative equality is that it insists upon results—looking at what has happened at the end of the process of selection, and not only at the degree of apparent openness in the steps of the selection process. Consequently, the representative equality demand today is for greater equality of results.

This demand is disturbing since it involves much greater pressure for change than most equality of opportunity measures. Unlike equal opportunity, representative equality does not stress increasing the educational level of the discriminated. Rather, it directly stresses breaking the barriers of discrimination in institutions. It seeks to use governmental power to pressure institutions to change their behavior. Results are to be seen in the short run, not after a generation has had increased schooling. Since representative equality is about employment, not only schooling, it more directly confronts economic livelihoods, institutional practices, and the positions of the privileged. It is a much more disturbing objective than equality of opportunity.

The methods employed to pursue representative equality are also upsetting to many. Targets, quotas, and preferences have been used as ways of moving institutions to increase the representation of the underrepresented groups. The struggle for greater equality of opportunity has frequently been against quotas and preferences. These devices result in discriminated groups receiving only a token number of positions while individuals from these groups are not treated solely in terms of their own merits. Now, these discriminating practices of the past are turned around, and targets for the representation of particular groups are supported as a major way of ending discrimination.

A variety of terms has been used in the U.S. and in the United Kingdom to refer to such practices: affirmative action, compensatory opportunity, positive discrimination.[7] What underlies them all is the concern not only to end discrimination but also to overcome the results of long periods of discrimination. The argument is that many qualified persons are discriminated against on the basis of race and/or sex, and many highly qualified persons from these groups are available for high-level positions. To move to anywhere near appropriate proportions requires direct, concerted, pressured action. Slow, gradual change will not overcome the past.

This position disturbs because the other side of discrimination, or accumulated disadvantage, is the less frequently mentioned situations of privilege and advantage. Therefore, some of the privileged inevitably must lose out if disadvantage is to end. How much losing out depends on the criteria used to define representative equality. If farm-worker and working-class youths are 60 percent of the university-age cohort but furnish only 10 percent of university students, then many middle-class youths who would have been admitted to universities would lose out if the goal is a strictly proportionate representation of farm-worker youth. Or, if blacks or women are to be represented on the higher levels of university faculties somewhat akin to their proportion in the general population or among graduate students, many white males would have reduced likelihood of becoming full professors. Exactly what percentage is considered as constituting representative equality or engendering the cessation of discrimination or overcoming the accumulated effects of disadvantage is obviously an important issue.

Daniel Bell[8] has pointed out that if various ascriptive groups (e.g., women, blacks, other ethnic groups) asked for exactly proportional representation on university faculties, their demands would soon add up to more than 100 percent. Usually the target is not precise proportions but definite movement in the directions of greater proportionality.

It is my general impression that those who espouse greater representativeness do not see it as an enduring principle. That is, they see it as necessary to end discrimination and to overcome the effects of discrimination on both the discriminated and the privileged. Once there is roughly comparable opportunity for all groups, then it will rarely be necessary to continue the requirement of proportionality or representativeness among the occupants of desirable positions.

Representative equality seems thus a short-term goal, even if it may in fact persist as a social policy for a long time as one and then another discriminated or disadvantaged group demands action to rectify what it believes have been abuses against itself. What constitutes discrimination or disadvantage is therefore a crucial issue. Is the fact of a low proportion of a particular group in certain positions evidence of discrimination? It might not always be a sign of disadvantage that a society or particular group may wish to overcome.

The philosophical basis of the desire for representative equality is that it is instrumental to a larger goal of reducing discrimination or disadvantage, eliminating privilege and advantage. It is also espoused on the basis of assumed rights that individuals have under the implicit social contract—rights not only for freedom from discrimination but rights to have equal *likelihood* of getting a position. In equality of opportunity, the concern is with the fairness of the chase for favored positions in the selection process. In representative equality, eliminating discrimination in the race may not be adequate; the objective is to get greater proportionality in outcomes. Proportionate or appropriate results rather than ''equal opportunity'' is at issue. Or, it is argued by some, equal opportunity will be pursued effectively as a goal only where there is governmental pressure to show appropriate results.

Who is for representative equality? Obviously, *economic gainers* in the discriminated populations, who will get higher-level positions, more authority, higher pay, more interesting jobs, support it. Since the groups involved can be large, there are *political gainers* who seek to win support by supporting representative equality. For example, the Nixon administration had been surprisingly strong in pressuring universities to hire more female faculty members. *Psychological gainers* are those from nondiscriminated groups who believe that a less privileged society is more satisfying and less politically disturbed. Finally, there are those *social doubters* who doubt that meritocracy prevails and believe that other systems of sorting and selecting individuals may be more reflective of merit than the pseudomeritocratic processes which currently prevail. A variant of this position rests on the premise that jobs are resources and should be allocated on a basis that provides benefits to those at the bottom. Merit is irrelevant; the relevant question is only who is to benefit.

The philosophical opposition to representative equality is based on the equity concern, that it is unfair to introduce representative equality: ability, hard work, and/or experience should not be supplanted by other considerations in hiring, promotion, and layoff. Traditional and/or meritocratic processes should not be transformed in midstream. Those who work hard or long for a company or university should be rewarded, not penalized because of ascriptive characteristics over which they have no control.

Representative equality is an agonizing political issue today. With layoffs and unemployment, seniority competes with representative equality as a principle of employment policy. Layoffs endanger the employment of women and blacks who have only recently been hired. If those with long employment in a factory will be laid off only after those with shorter experience, then women and blacks will lose out. If white males are laid off despite their longer service, a strong principle of nonarbitrary layoffs will be impaired. A nasty struggle is brewing between seniority and affirmative action.

Representative equality is characterized by some as "reverse discrimination" in that favor is given to some on the basis of attributes which have nothing to do with the position that they are to fill. Discrimination, it is argued, can be overcome in the long run without producing new forms of discrimination to favor the formerly disprivileged. Meritocratic selection processes with full efforts to achieve equality of opportunity are seen as desirable and achievable. The operation of the principle of representative equality is seen as incurring the resentment of the displaced, creating unrealizable expectations, and lowering the productivity of the institutions which are being challenged to include the disadvantaged. The reply is that in the short run, at least, there can be no denial that even open competition without discrimination would not produce great changes; representative equality is an attempt to shorten the time it takes to change both institutionalized and individual discrimination and the psychological and social burdens of past discrimination.

Among those opposed to representative equality are the *economic losers* who would not get positions that they might have obtained if representative equality had not been practiced. The operation of an institution like the multinational corporation might not be threatened directly by an injunction to have a more representative hierarchy, but the white male managers might become anxious if women or blacks had increased chances of getting the preferred positions. Opposition also comes from *status or psychological losers* who feel that their positions are made less attractive because lower-status or less-qualified individuals are in similar positions.

The *economic worriers* are those who fear that efficiency or effectiveness will be lowered because meritocratic procedures are not as strictly enforced as before. The *social worriers* fear backlash, that pinpointing the particular groups who will gain in special ways in the effort to obtain representative equality will focus attention on them and that the aggrieved losers will make things difficult for the formerly discriminated.

Many oppose representative equality because they feel that meritocratic standards are the best hope of keeping a society from being ruled by privilege. They see particular criteria again intruding in the effort to achieve a meritocratic, universalistic social order. As Daniel Bell has argued, the need is for a "well-tempered meritocracy" rather than representative equality.

The principle of meritocracy thus duels with the principle of ending disadvantage. Those who clash on the goal of representative equality differ on how much significance they attach to current discrimination, what yardstick should be applied to measure progress (which includes the time period in which change is desired), and what prices are appropriate to pay for overcoming discrimination.

The sociological issue centers on how profoundly and how rapidly discrimination and disadvantage can be overcome. My belief is that considerable pressure and sanctions are necessary and that short-run strategies of representative equality are necessary if there is to be sizable change in the situation and outlook of the discriminated.

Despite the strong opposition that representative equality can incur, it is a specialized form of the search for equality. It does not seek to change the return to position but who gets the position. Thus, representative equality is compatible with very large differences in benefits available to occupants of various positions. It is not economic or resource equality. It tries to achieve a different sorting of particular categories of the population; it does not aim at achieving a narrowing of the differences among positions. It sorts people, not positions.

As Jean Baker Miller points out, however, it may be the most important form of equality—and therefore the most contentious. For one, it deals with those ascriptive characterizations—race and sex—which are more enduring agents of discrimination than those of class alone. Advantages accrued because of maleness and whiteness may be particularly hard to give up. Further, as the occupational structure becomes more differentiated, then race and sex discriminations may affect much greater numbers than those disadvantaged by their class origins. Finally, attempting to achieve representative equality means more frequently that there are clear-cut and immediate losers—if a woman or black gets that opening, then a male white does not. The other forms of equality do not demonstrate such quick, evident, and disturbing changes.

Type 3: Resource Equality

We turn now to the most common objective of equality-of-conditions efforts—the reduction of the economic differences among (occupational) positions. It was until recently the form of equality most commonly discussed when equality of conditions was studied.

"Income equality," a fairly common term, does not capture the issue of wealth or assets and fringe benefits, an increasingly important element of wage-salary income. Consequently, a broader term is useful. Possibilities are "resource equality," which suggests the command over resources, to use Titmuss's term, as the key issue, and "reward equality," which indicates that individuals are being repaid for their effort and skill. Another possibility, which is interesting for its startle quality, is "meritocratic equality," for it stresses that the reduction of economic inequalities is not incompatible with the maintenance of meritocratic selection procedures. The obvious term "economic equality" is too frequently regarded as referring only to income. I will be using "resource equality," for it suggests the finiteness and comprehensiveness of what is to be distributed.

In its post-1960 reemergence, a concern with resource equality followed the recognition of poverty in presumably affluent, capitalist countries. The belief that economic growth not only made people better off but also distributed more evenly the expanding command over resources withered with the recognition of the existence of a submerged population living below the standards of society. After initial resistance, it has been increasingly recognized, in the U.S. and the United Kingdom, at least that the issue is not that of bringing people up to some poverty line, even if adjusted for changes in the average standard of living. The issue is rather that of comparative or relative position, of degrees of inequalities rather than sheer insufficiency as implied in the poverty-line approach.[9] The reappraisal of the concern with poverty as basically a concern with equality has been uneven. Paradoxically, in the United States as the Johnson administration sought to reduce poverty, liberal and progressive intellectual analysis moved beyond the poverty concern to the more profound and pervasive issue of inequality.

The concern with narrowing resource differences among occupations (and thereby among individuals and households) is the typical interest when sociologists discuss equality and stratification. The Davis-Moore analysis[10] of the functional bases of stratification is about resource equality, not representative equality of conditions. The Davis-Moore analysis contends that differential rewards are necessary in order to obtain and maintain the best talent for high positions in society. While representative equality is criticized as interfering with the meritocratic principle because it is interpreted by some as introducing nonmeritocratic criteria in the selection process, resource equality is indicated by the functional analyst because it upsets the efficiency-inducing distribution of rewards.

It is criticized on the basis of who decides what are the most needed positions, how talent is best developed and screened, what range of difference in rewards provides needed incentive, and the possibilities of nonmonetary incentives. The basic perspective of resource equality is that, with due regard for circumstances such as family size, individuals should have roughly similar resources over their lifetime regardless of the position or occupation they fill.[a]

Rewards or resources of income and prestige are only one set of issues in the context of equality of results. The clash between adherents of the functional theory of stratification and meritocrats, on one side, and those espousing equality of conditions or results, on the other, can be on the issues of selection, reward, or, as we shall soon see, task.

It is important to recognize that efforts to reduce the range within the reward structure do *not* involve change in the basis of access to position. They are concerned only with the return to position. Nor are they concerned with who gets the high position. Thus, those who espouse resource egalitarianism—the overwhelming majority, at least until recently, of those seeking greater equality of conditions—are not aiming at changing who is in what position, as in representative egalitarianism, and are not demanding changes in the basis of access to position. Thus, a fully meritocratic outlook based on a highly selective procedure can be compatible with the desire to reduce differences in incomes. That is why calling it meritocratic egalitarianism is not a contradiction in terms. Indeed, it is my belief that an increasing number of people in various societies are interested in reducing the income differences among occupations while maintaining or expanding the presumably meritocratic bases of selection into the positions. Thus, as Rawls contends, resource equality and equality of opportunity are not incompatible.

The question of the extent of resource equality is obviously of great importance. Some exponents of equality have limited goals in mind; they are interested in achieving what Martin Rein and I have called "lessened inequalities." They seek "to constrain inequalities, to have 'tolerable or

[a] Obviously it makes an important difference whether individual or family is the unit for which we strive to achieve equality. For the purpose of the present analysis, it does not seem crucial to pursue this important difference. Ray Pahl has argued that the important issue is not a near-sameness in income but that individuals who are low in one dimension of equality (e.g., income) should not be low in others (e.g., occupational prestige or job satisfaction). The nonconvergence of dimensions is his objective. Oskar Lange suggested a somewhat similar scheme in that everyone should receive the same income; then those who wanted to have interesting jobs would pay a tax for that pleasure. What seems to be involved is that the total utilities or resources should not be very different, although the permutations may differ. In Pahl's suggestion, the objective is to prevent the emergence of an underclass, a pariah group, in society.

acceptable inequalities' rather than to eliminate them altogether.''[11] A greater degree of resource equality is sought by the "normative egalitarians," for they "hold equality as the orienting goal, although in practice [they do not] seek a complete leveling." Gans's analysis is oriented toward normative equality.[12] Those we have termed "practising egalitarians" espouse the bold goal that everyone should have the same resources except for adjustments for family size and the like. "But these modifications are not to reward unequal talent but to accommodate difference in individual circumstances. Therefore, the band of income variation would be very narrow indeed.''[13] What we have then in the classification of lessened inequalities—normative egalitarianism and practising egalitarianism—are degrees of resource equality.

The standard methods of achieving lessened inequality are taxation and transfer which deepen the importance and progressivity of the tax systems and spend a disproportionate amount of government funds on the disadvantaged. These welfare-state-type policies have failed to achieve more equality in the last twenty years of postwar capitalism, because progressivity is not the usual tax practice and transfers are not great enough or sufficiently concentrated on the nonaged disadvantaged to make a big difference. Obviously, much more will have to be done along both these lines if great equality is to be produced. The strong use of taxation or an incomes policy might prevent, as in wartime, the gaining of work-related income above a certain level and the inheritance of wealth.

The tax-transfer approaches are essentially redistributive. A more basic concern with affecting the *original* distribution of resources is slowly emerging. This preventive strategy requires affecting basic economic policy and structure rather than trying to offset their antiegalitarian or nonegalitarian effects.[14] The sociological significance of this is that the issues of distribution and stratification are raising basic questions about the sweeping changes needed to produce desired outcomes. Even more fundamental and disturbing than the bitter disputes about taxes and transfers would be efforts to affect what is produced within a society. Thus, the differences between lessened inequalities and normative egalitarianism are not only a matter of how much change can be effected in what time period but how profound these changes might be. The lessened-inequalities approach may center on rectifying the abuses of the tax system; normative egalitarianism may focus more on the transfer system and affecting the original distribution of income; and practising egalitarianism may seek to produce pockets of communitarianism within a society that is largely unequal.

The philosophical or value or ideological basis for the resource form of egalitarianism is either in utilitarianism or in social contract beliefs. The utilitarian approach argues that the greatest good will be produced for the greatest number by a redistributional approach that reduces resource differences. While utilitarianism has fallen into disuse among sociologists, Christopher Jencks espouses it in his recent demand for socialism.[15] The thesis that utilities will be augmented through equality rests on the assumption that those who lose out are fewer in number than those who will gain. (We can assume that the treacherous issue of individual differences in utility is not as important as the question of sheer size.) At one time, that assumption was unquestionable; the worst-off class was clearly the largest class in society. In many societies today it is not obvious that a redistribution toward the bottom would not harm sizable numbers. To a large extent, the issue is who is defined as "at the bottom?" that is, who should benefit from redistribution? If, for example, all those over median income lose some income to all those below the median in order to gain greater equality, it is not inescapable that overall utilities would increase. Or, if, in order to benefit sizably the bottom fifth of income recipients, it becomes necessary to redistribute from the upper two-fifths, then the effects on aggregate utility may not always support a redistributive policy.

Indeed, this issue of who is to benefit from a redistribution is exceedingly complex. For many, efforts to improve the conditions of those "at the bottom" benefit the least worst off of those "at the bottom" and little help or may worsen the situation of the very worst off.[16] Frequently, as is now the case in the United States, a "respectable disadvantaged"—the organized worker of mass production industry—is split off from the worst off—those in irregular low-wage situations with heavy needs for transfer payments. The respectable disadvantaged, for example, are provided extension of unemployment benefits and the like, while the worst off lose rights to transfer as welfare rolls are slashed. The result is to deepen the antagonism of the respectable disadvantaged toward the worst off so that thorough-going redistribution is unlikely.

A different and sounder basis for supporting resource egalitarianism is in the implicit social contract within many societies. This view differs from that promulgated by John Rawls,[17] which speculates on what individuals would opt for if they were confronted by a veil of ignorance about their prospects. On this basis, he constructs a new social contract. But in many nations there is an already-existing, implicit social contract which recognizes certain ranges of income differences as appropriate and others as unacceptable. The belief is that there is or should be a rational, appropriate basis for inequalities. The legitimacy of differences is based on the implicit or explicit social contract of what is right or necessary. What many who demand greater equality are questioning is the rational or reasonable basis for current inequalities. There is a loss of confidence in the rationality of income differences. Despite the certainty with which many economists embraced human-capital theory, evidence increasingly questions the importance of the relationship between education and income. As cited earlier, Jencks[18] shows that in the U.S. education explains only a minor part of the variations in income, and in Sweden data suggest that family origins are still important in affecting income even when education is held constant.[19] Since education has been offered as the important determinant of income differences, the rational basis for income claims is eroded.

The second underpinning of the belief in the rational basis of the prevailing social contract is the belief that income is related to economic contribution. The wide gap in 1973 between an automobile worker with a wage of $12,000 and the president of General Motors Corporation with a salary of more than $800,000 is difficult to defend on the basis of the contribution of the executive. Furthermore, the recognition is spreading that many wealthy individuals escape the heaviest burden of taxation and that in many nations those just above the poverty line may pay as high a percentage of their income in taxes as the wealthiest persons in the nation despite the avowed commitment to rates of taxation which increase with income. This disenchantment with the tax system as an equalizer and equity-producer undermines the acceptance of income differences as fitting and appropriate. This questioning of the acceptability of income differences is deepened as more believe that governmental practices could produce different distributions of disposable income.

Resource equality can also be viewed as instrumental to the larger goal of reducing conflict, strain, and violence in a society. Crime and delinquency, for example, may be seen as class and caste issues which will not recede with expansion or reformation of the police-judicial-prison system; their reduction depends on a change in the fortunes and reception of the deprived populations. Similarly, political violence is a response to inequality. Thus, without greater equality, the chances of obtaining a less crime-harrassed and more cohesive society are very small. Obviously, the acceptability of the instrumental outlook depends on how effective greater equality would be in reducing such strains and dissatisfactions in society.

Who is for greater income equality? Those who favor resource equality are those *economic gainers* who will directly benefit from redistribution; the *political gainers* who seek an alliance to further other objectives by joining with the deprived groups that will gain from it; the *social gainers* who believe that their society will be easier to live in if greater personal equality prevails; and the *psychological gainers* who sense greater personal satisfaction in a more just society. The political, social, and psychological gainers are largely made up of noneconomic gainers.

If the number defined as disadvantaged is large, then the size of the economic gainers increases. But in order to provide gains to a large group, the number of those adversely affected is likely to increase. The result is not only an increase in the number of economic losers but a possible deepening in their reactions to their losses.

Those opposed to greater resource equality no longer do so on the basis that inequality is a good thing in itself. Rather, their philosophical or value argument is that there is a *rationality* in the reward structure, that reward is roughly proportionate to contribution or to effort. This is the basic perspective of the important school of human-capital economists. A second value emphasis is on the upsetting of tradition, that wage differentials represent historically justified differences, and that changes in these differentials are unfair—too narrow, for example, the difference between an unskilled and skilled worker is a violation of *equity*. Equity or fairness based on past practice is seen as violated by equalization.[20] The implicit social contract about wage differentials is upset by a drive toward greater equality.

A third perspective is that of the costs of equality—that equality is expensive, would reduce efficiency, and would cost everyone. Reducing income differences, the argument runs, will reduce *incentive* and therefore lessen productivity and innovation with the resulting threat of a smaller economic pie to distribute. All would suffer in absolute terms in order to improve some relatively. This perspective follows the Davis-Moore functional argument that inequality is necessary for motivation. Finally, there are those who see governmental regulation as a threat not only to economic but to political liberty as well—the less government, the greater freedom. In this view, inequality is not necessarily regarded as instrumental to or an obstacle to liberty; rather, efforts to decrease inequality are regarded as reducing liberty. The stress here is on the political costs of equality in terms of libertarian models.

The opposition to greater resource equality comes from those who are *economic losers*, those who would stand to lose income because it is shifted to others for the sake of greater equality. They have an economic stake in the prevailing system of inequalities. *Status losers* might also suffer reductions in income, but at least equally important would be their feeling of resentment that the less deserving have a high position in society.[21] The "notch group"—those just above the population that will benefit from redistribution and greater equality—are believed to be those most beset by resentment, although I am not sure that this is always so.[22] The *economic worriers* may not be economic losers; but they *are* concerned that economic production may contract as a result of the loss of economic incentives, so that many would lose. The *social worriers* fear that the traditional social fabric would be rent by greater equality and that endemic conflict would ensue.

It is more difficult than it is with representative equality to pinpoint the political gainers from resource equality. Where it is easily possible, as in the U.S., to concentrate on a public assistance or welfare population (largely believed to be black), a backlash resentment may develop from which there could be *political gainers*.

It is, of course, misleading to discuss issues of resistance to equality only in terms of individual attitudes, values, and dissatisfactions. Crucial economic and military institutions are involved. In Chile, truck owners/drivers, small in number, precipitated the crisis which led to the downfall of Allende by the military. Large corporations are obviously opposed to greater equality and may mobilize in opposition to it.

The political difficulty of resource equality is that it is important, at least in many nations like the U.S., to have many people feel that they will benefit from redistribution. The most politically efficacious case is where it is possible to take enough income from a small number of very rich to give to a large number of the disadvantaged without worsening the position of those in between. The 1972 McGovern presidential concern in the U.S. failed to convince many people that this is what was sought. Can such a situation prevail? Without a definition of income broader than that now utilized by the U.S. Internal Revenue Service, it is unlikely that the very rich possess sufficient resources to support by themselves sizable and widespread distribution. Indeed, some calculations that I have made of a shift of income to the bottom two-fifths reveals it is not possible to make important gains by taxing more of the income of high-income recipients.[23]

Political support and resistance partly depend on what is meant by "equality" as a norm. What is the appropriate range of income in a normatively egalitarian society? The goal of "lessened inequalities," a wide though a much narrower range in the distribution of resources than now prevails in most nations, may permit movement toward equality without incurring much resistance. Even corporation executives and wealthy stockholders might feel that mild income reform would be good for the social and political stability of the society. On the other hand, lessened inequality is only "some" equality, although it is definitely "greater equality." "Normative egalitarianism," with its narrower ranges of differences, may produce much greater resistance. Similarly, rapid moves toward greater equality may build up more resistance toward equality than would slower steps. But the slower path may be continually subverted by manipulation of advantage to maintain inequalities or by the accumulation of resistance to it. One can see why some advocate a big change taken at once with a willingness to face the consequent resistance rather than a slow and ineffective forgoing of great equality. But even those who espouse the "big step" have to recognize that inequalities are hardy and fast-growing. They do not easily erode; they reappear in one form or another with great facility.

Can greater equality be achieved without a change from capitalism and concentrated business power? Is resource equality incompatible with concentrated business power? One can envisage situations where lessened inequality is achieved but where large corporations continue to be large and important. Their managers receive less absolute and relative income, but there is persistent effort to undermine this achievement by augmenting the fringe benefits of executives. Even if this effort were frustrated, managers would continue to have the noneconomic satisfactions of doing important and satisfying work, occupying high-status positions, influencing developments. This might well be a case where noneconomic incentives work. The corporation as an institution would not be threatened by reducing the economic advantages of its managers.

If the view of John Kenneth Galbraith and others is accurate—that corporations are run by managers who seek to preserve and expand the institution rather than maximize profit—then this scenario is reasonable. Even more thorough-going equality might be compatible with corporation functioning. Conceivably, the large corporation, without an economic necessity to maximize or distribute profits (stockholders in practice are essentially treated as secondary bondholders who lend money to the corporation), could function under conditions of greater equality; indeed, based on experience with other reforms, like the Factory Acts in the United Kingdom and Franklin D. Roosevelt's New Deal in the U.S., it might even prosper from the reforms. But what about the stockholders who might lose their wealth or the return on their wealth if equality were thorough-going? If dominant stockholding interests felt threatened, they might strive to activate military and business groups into resistance. Then the political, if not the economic, character of capitalism is inconsistent with much greater equality.

A normative egalitarianism which does not strike at the economic sources of power may always be in jeopardy as it strives to make equality more profound. The economic power of business must be offset by the political power—electoral and confrontational—of great numbers who favor equality. It will have to be viewed as a desirable individual and social goal. That is why the philosophical or value basis of equality is not a post hoc rationalization of positions taken on various economic grounds, but rather an important ingredient of the political struggle.

The likelihood is that small businesses as well as large and medium-size corporations would strongly oppose the move toward far-reaching equality. Small businesses are perhaps the most likely to be adversely affected; this sweeping statement is based on the experience that it is those closest to the disadvantaged who bear most of the burden of social change. The larger and more important economic blocs usually can escape many of the acts of change or can more easily absorb them.

Resource equality is not incompatible with a concern for representative equality, although the two are not usually linked. Even if income differences were sharply narrowed, it might be important to many that various groups of people no longer be disadvantaged in getting particularly important or desirable jobs. Equalizing rewards for jobs does not necessarily eliminate the questions of who gets certain jobs because positions still would continue to differ on other dimensions than income.

Disturbing though resource equality may be to many, it does not touch the bases of selection for position nor the distribution of tasks among individuals. It affects the rewards to position but not access to position or nonmoney aspects of position. Jobs may still be very hierarchical in power and status, even if income differences have become narrowed. The next type of equality objective—task equality—seeks to remedy these inattentions.

Type 4: Task Equality

Resource equality in itself does not directly redistribute power, status, or work satisfaction. It might have such effects over time, for diminishing the importance of such discriminators as wealth and income may disrupt other patterns of domination and hierarchy. But graded positions do not easily die out; even antiquated bases of status and authority can have powerful afterlives, as Weber sought to demonstrate.

Resource equality is inadequate in another way. It redistributes income but not tasks, while representative equality redistributes positions but not resources or tasks. As long as individuals have positions which give them great power over others at the workplace, resulting in great variations in prestige, the move toward resource equality may be unstable. It is subject to the subtle and not-so-subtle pressures of the holders of the more important or powerful positions to subvert resource equality by demanding direct bribes of greater income and privilege or by covertly providing themselves with new or manipulated benefits.

At another level, not as broad but perhaps as significant, the issue is that of job satisfaction. Currently there is a maldistribution of the potentials of job satisfactions; some jobs offer many more possibilities of performing interesting tasks than do others.[24] The usual practice is that jobs which are high on power and status and income usually are high on intrinsic job satisfaction, i.e., involve a variety of tasks which are more interesting than occupations which are low on power, status, and income. Reducing income differences among occupations may not only maintain power and status differences but may also leave untouched differences in job enjoyment. Just as some prestige jobs accumulate the positives, other jobs are stuck with the negatives—"dirty" work, debilitating routine, narrow tasks. Task equality seeks to reduce resource differences at the same time that it aims at redistributing the tasks which now make up occupations, so that individuals do not have mainly satisfying or mainly unsatisfying tasks to perform. It is misleading to believe that attitudes alone are central in response to jobs: some jobs are inherently limited in what they offer in terms of work satisfaction.[b]

At the philosophical-value level, task equality is regarded as instrumental to the more basic aspiration for brotherhood, fraternity, or humanhood (to use a word less cloaked in male perspectives). Individuals should not be doing only the drudge jobs even if resource equality prevails and they have incomes that are similar to those who do the exciting jobs in a society. Since the situation is that good jobs have little of what bad jobs have and vice versa, those in the bad jobs have much less chance of developing their capabilities, aspirations, and consciousness. A sense of universal human destiny which engenders cooperation and humane values is not likely where there is competition for scarce jobs offering satisfaction. Divisions in society are not only about the class splits in income but also about the styles of life and status distinctions associated with the kinds of tasks one is engaged in. A habit of action, to reverse Veblen, is a habit of thought. Work is not the person, but it is not extraneous to her or him.

Ray Pahl has suggested the narrower goal of social improvement as a substitute for equality. Rather than seeking to reduce the economic differences among individuals, he suggests rather that these differences not be allowed to concentrate negatively at the bottom or positively at the top. Hard, difficult jobs should not get low pay and status; interesting jobs should not have the reverse treatment. It is the clumping together of all goods or all bads that is the danger. The *non*crystallization of the dimensions of stratification is the Pahlian objective. Task equality seeks that goal within the context of resource equality, unlike the Pahlian acceptance of variations in resources.

The task equality approach takes the Tawney concern with fraternity[25] and the Young concern with overcoming materialism[26] and argues that resource equality will not be enough to achieve these goals, essential as they are. Tasks must be redistributed.

Can tasks be redistributed without great loss in the economic output of a nation? Those who espouse task redistribution are, in effect, challenging the degree to which rationality prevails in the distribution of occupational tasks, just as some who seek resource distribution challenge the rationality (and national economic benefits) of the prevailing distribution of income and wealth.

In the U.S. a growing body of data demonstrates the following:

---

[b] The fact that some people seem to enjoy limited, routine jobs or at least prefer them to more demanding jobs does not mean that everyone in routine jobs prefers them or would prefer them if attractive alternatives were available. Satisfactions are related to expectations: low aspirations do not mean that consciousness might not be altered in different circumstances. Nonetheless, task equality efforts would have to make arrangements for those who prefer routine, noninvolving, and nondemanding tasks.

(1) many educational requirements for jobs are inappropriate; (2) those of higher education frequently do more poorly on a job than those with lesser education; (3) the belief of heads of enterprise that there are effective grounds for selecting employees is based on the flimsiest of evidence; and (4) the clustering of tasks into occupations is a result of accumulated and often outmoded practice and tradition which make it desirable that tasks be reassembled and redivided into different occupations. These findings overlap with the desire of the resource egalitarian who declares, "who says occupation does not say income?" The task egalitarian, on the other hand, asks "who says task does not say occupation?" How tasks are combined into occupations is not necessarily ordained by technology.[27] A variety of ways of combining tasks may be possible. An example is the move of some automobile factories, notably Swedish, away from the long assembly-line, simple-routine-task mode of producing automobiles in which each individual performs one or two very atomized tasks to a system where a small group of workers form a team which performs all the tasks involved in automobile assembly.

One general aim is to construct jobs which combine a variety of tasks at different levels of skill and satisfaction. An alternative approach is to rotate tasks among individuals so that all share in the difficult, less-satisfying, or low-status positions. This can be done, as in the Israeli kibbutz, where an individual holding a premier post can also be daily involved in the washing of the supper dishes or where premier posts are held for relatively short periods and rotated. Another policy is that for periods of one's working life (including the student period as part of work life), one does the difficult, dirty, or needed tasks of society as students might do farm work during harvest periods in Cuba and China. Or, as in the U.S., many of the most difficult, low-paid jobs are held by youths, many of whom (but unfortunately not all) can confidently expect not to have to do them for much more than a summer or for some years as part-time workers while they complete their education. Less-satisfying work can be concentrated in a few years at the beginning or end of one's lifetime or may be part of the annual work cycle. A great variery of arrangements is conceivable. The theme is that all share in the performances of the "goods" and "bads" of work.

In the U.S. some interesting innovations in the occupational structure are developing. "New careers" have been constructed to open up highly professionalized, highly schooled occupations to people of low education. Some tasks of the professional, lower-level tasks, in the main, have been given to the new careerist, sometimes called the subprofessional or paraprofessional; some new tasks that had not been provided by the professional service have been added to the service and are offered by the subprofessional. In some cases, job ladders and new educational routes are developed so that the subprofessional after several years can move into a traditional or an alternative route to a professional position.

The concern with task equality puts the question of social mobility in a different context than that in which it is usually regarded. If there were greater resource equality, social mobility might still be important in giving people the opportunity to have a variety of interesting tasks over their lifetimes. Social mobility in the context of resource equality would then be less competitive and compulsive, less caught up in economic and status struggles. Rather, it would be an instrument to promote the self-realization of individuals, as people sought to engage in tasks which were interesting and satisfying to them at that time. Obviously, the structure of education would change, as is already foreshadowed in the concept of recurrent or permanent education.[28]

The fundamental assumptions are that most occupations can be changed and most people can develop beyond limited tasks. Indeed, I believe that an underlying assumption and an aspiration of task egalitarians are that a committed society can develop individuals and that education and personnel offices should not serve as sorters and excluders of individuals but should operate as aids to the development of all individuals. Coupled with this is the transformational aim to redistribute work satisfaction for all. In the case of task egalitarianism, it may be possible to avoid a zero-sum gain in which some must lose for others to gain. The redistribution and restructuring of tasks may lead to a much greater total of job satisfaction.

I have written at length about task equality and its possibilities, for it is frequently dismissed as romantic and utopian, and yet it captures many today, especially among the young. Task equality has a cyclical attraction—it languishes and then reappears as a compelling vision. It is difficult to conceive of its actual operation. Nonetheless, it shows the profundity of the goals of equality and raises the image of the possibilities of the individual and society that go beyond the economists' calculations of tax and transfer tables.

It is also educational for intellectuals to consider it seriously, for it more directly confronts those who might rather easily accept resource equality but find task restructuring and redistribution intellectually and emotionally disturbing. It is important to keep social scientists from believing that all others have ideologies and vested interests, but that they have successfully managed to escape into an unencumbered world of carefully tested ideas.

Without some movement toward task equality, a great degree of resource equality may be unachievable. That is one of the reasons that Herbert Gans does not insist on a thorough-going resource equality, for he sees the division of labor as more difficult to change than I do. On the other hand, achieving task equality may not be possible without a great degree of resource equality, for in the absence of the latter, low-paid employees would be assuming the obligations of the higher-paid without their recompense, which violates the principles of equal pay for equal work. Some measure of task equality may be achievable in the absence of resource equality, but I doubt if a great deal.[c]

The other side of the issue is perhaps more significant: can significant steps toward resource equality be maintained if large differences in tasks persist? If wide gradations in task and status coexist with lessened inequalities, will there not be great pressure to make the reward structure mirror the task-status structure? I think that this is likely, and therefore I see task equality as instrumental to the achievement and maintenance of resource equality as well as serving as an important objective in and of itself.

The task approach is attractive because it pushes the concern with equality beyond the economic. Gans is right to stress that income and wealth, rather than occupation, should be the concern of sociologists in the study of stratification. But we should not correct the mistaken emphases of sociologists by exclusively focusing on these two economic categories. Issues of status and satisfactions, of power and hierarchy, are significant, and we should be learning how to think about them in the context of economic issues.

Power and Philosophy

Power has not been discussed in this chapter as one of the important dimensions of inequality. Obviously, it is important to go beyond the income-wealth and occupational dimensions of inequality, for without a redistribution of power in a society, it will be impossible to achieve and sustain greater equalities. Power is the most difficult dimension of inequality to discuss, for here it is not only a question of redistribution of the power that is already generated, but, more clearly than in other dimensions, the question of the very nature of the dimension is involved. The possibilities of change in that dimension are basic. Political power can be more evenly distributed in a society that is still oppressive or repressive. A truly democratic society still has the question of what are individual rights against the majority will.

I have not attempted here to grapple with the intricate issues of equality and political power, citizen participation and bureaucratic and expert roles,

---

[c] Some status differences in treatment and in amenities may be reduced without great changes in resource equality. Indeed, in some teaching and research offices, that may be happening between faculty and secretarial staff.

and the like. The discussion of power has been relegated to its place within the scheme of occupational inequalities. Obviously, it should not be left in this restrictive place.

The issue of power extends much beyond that of a dimension of inequality. The question is, Can power be developed to make the changes that greater equality requires? On this difficult question I would make only one point that seems neglected by many who talk about power. The frequent tendency is to see it in the purely political term of who controls the state and not in the broad perspective of political economy in which political and economic forces interact, what Meynaud calls "the bias of the system."[29] The state may be in control of forces seeking greater equality, and yet they may be ineffective in their equality accomplishments because there are economic processes which offset the effort to utilize state power to produce greater equality. If, for example, the economy is in a sudden severe contraction, it is difficult to have sizable redistribution of a decreasing economic pie. When sociologists have discussed economics recently, the discussion has been largely about economic power. But it is important to recognize that the concentration of economic power is not the same as control over economic processes, that demand and supply are important, that incentives are not only capitalist inventions, and that money is more than a veil.

Efforts to achieve greater equality should drive sociologists to a concern with understanding economic processes as well as structures. It should also drive them to another neglected connection of sociology, the philosophical basis of beliefs, values, political platforms. Positivism in sociology and linguistic analysis in philosophy have pushed the examination of values into a narrow box. In sociology, we describe who holds what values; in philosophy, the analysis of values or morals is largely restricted, except for those who believe in natural rights, to questions of the form of belief, degrees of consistency and coherence. The discussion of why equality and what type of equality demands that all of us address the question of the moral basis of society—an old, difficult question. The quest for equality is a quest for wholeness, for developing the unique qualities and common humanity of all. Philosophy and economics cannot continue to be residual bins of sociology, convenient resting places for difficult questions.

Some friends have described my examination of philosophical questions about equality as a fruitless enterprise: people will decide whether they wish to achieve greater equality on the basis of their economic status or position; philosophical or moral beliefs have little to do with the issue; and power, not philosophy, will determine the fate of drives to greater equality. These are strong arguments but not complete ones, for, as Jencks argues, some of the advantaged will need to support equality if it is to get majority support. And the support of the advantaged will have to be won on other than narrow grounds of economic self-interest. Further, political power grows where a slogan, a platform, or a revolutionary demand has a moral urgency behind it.

Which Equality? Whose Equality?

Representative equality seeks to affect who gets what positions. Resource equality aims at narrowing the differences in resources among positions. Task equality tries to affect the nature of positions as well as the resources attached to them. The three issues of equality, then, are: Who gets what positions? What are the rewards for being in these positions? What does one do in these positions? In representative equality, the issue is the group; in resource equality, the reward; in task equality, the activity or performance.

Is one always more important than the others? I doubt it. When there is powerful discrimination or a long history of discrimination against ethnic groups, as occurs to a large or small extent in all nations, and where there is powerful discrimination against women, which is probably the case in all nations, then representative equality cannot be bypassed as a less important goal. But there is a difficulty here, for if we simultaneously reduce resource inequalities, we may be downgrading positions as they become available to the formerly discriminated. The important thing would be to make sure that the most favored positions are not isolated from the equalizing process and are not restricted to the most favored groups as in the past.

Since resource equality is a long-term struggle, the progress that might be made in attaining representative equality should not be neglected because it does not produce resource equality. The same holds for the relationship between resource equality and task equality. Which type of equality should receive the major attention in a society cannot be decided abstractly, for it is a political, tactical issue, not only a philosophical, moral question. Even those who disdain liberal reform in favor of structural reform must also be concerned about how to engender the conditions which make structural reform possible. Issues and possibilities do not unfold smoothly. The onion of equality is not peeled off evenly.

Equality in its contemporary concern has emerged out of the disturbing and discouraging rediscovery of poverty. In the attention to the broader and more profound issues of equality, we should not neglect the worst-off groups in society. Which of the unequal should be given the most attention is always a core problem, just as what kind of inequalities we seek to end and which equalities we want to foster are central questions. We can be concerned with the bottom tenth, the bottom fifth, or the bottom half. Very different concerns, issues, and possibilities ensue from the choice of the relevant population.

My friends at Aide à Toute Détresse in France and elsewhere have counseled me and others that the concern with equality poses the grave danger that another "creaming" process[30] will occur where the least unequal of the unequal may benefit considerably while the most unequal will advance very little. Shifting conceptualizations bring different populations into focus and concern. The term "poverty," for all its inadequacies, did help to focus attention on the worst off, though of course poverty has its degrees, and antipoverty programs, their creaming propensities. The first task is always to relieve the plight of those at the bottom: the second task is to avoid stereotyping them if they do not immediately respond to our ministrations.

If political feasibility dictates an anticreaming policy, then it should be clear that that is what is going on and that it is ended as soon as possible. In delineating types of egalitarian objectives, we should never forget that we are dealing with human suffering and not abstractly considered societal malfunctioning. The choice and blending of goals are not just analytical processes, for they reflect and make our social realities. They delineate whose suffering is to be relieved and in what ways.

Economics has reclaimed the title of "the dismal science" after a postwar skirmish with optimism that led economists to believe that Keynesianism and managed economics could triumph over stagnation, inflation, and inequality. For a period, as Martin Rein has said, sociology had claim to the "dismal science" title, showing that nothing could be accomplished. With the advent of the equality theme, sociology has perhaps moved to a new position and may help us find the way to societal advances rather than chronicling impossibilities and inescapable and limiting imperatives.

The discussion of equality is moving from the assumptions of a social order believed to be ordained by technology and the consequent division of labor to a belief that the social order can be changed and molded. The new beliefs assert that issues of the quality of everyday life, not just the malfunctioning of the economy, may lead to changing the economic order and social stratifications. At the same time, many recognize that changing the economic order does not ensure that desired changes in the social order will follow.

Thus, the disturbing assumption of the current discussion of equality is that stratification is purposively made, as a result of priorities, of choices of decisions; it is not only a consequence of the inevitable unfolding of economic order and technology. This assumption is in conflict with the notion of functional prerequisites and obviously had to be tested. The issue, of course, is not whether any kind of change can be made but which changes and to what degree are they likely to be successful? The "what degree" is important to note, because some functionalists and Marxists, at least in the U.S., frequently assume a 100 percent efficiency and complete interdependence within a society. Obviously, the extent of change rather than a dichotomous view of present/not present, achievable/unachievable should be the question to which we address ourselves.

Even if we cannot answer the difficult issues of equality, a new agenda has emerged. It has moved the discussion of stratification to a search for equality. It has turned a presumably descriptive question into a normative one—from "how is a society stratified?" to "how *should* it be ordered and connected?" It has turned from the inevitabilities of social order, the presumed prerequisites of societal functioning, to the possibilities of change. Possibilities and inevitabilities are both positivist issues, although the former has not usually been regarded in that light.

What do we want? How can we get equality with minimal impositions on individuals?[31] Those are good questions to encounter. Many, both young and old, accept today the challenge of these questions. That search should be healthy for social science—and for societies.[d]

Equality and Diversity: An Afterword

Equality is usually indicated as threatening diversity. The more frequent truth is the other way around: Inequality threatens diversity and encourages uniformity of values, styles, approaches.

Where inequality prevails and success is enthroned, individuals are pressured to follow the mold and strive for "success." People treat themselves as "things" to be used to achieve material gains. The material gains of consumption and occupational success become the real objectives, not the development of the individual in special, unique ways. Those who do not "make it," those who are not successful, are failures to themselves and to others. The pressure, consequently, to follow the route to possible success is tremendous. The penalties are great for those who do not follow the route or do not achieve. Indeed, the only way, it seems, of avoiding the stigma of failure is to completely opt out of the well-worn pattern, to retreat to a rural way of life.

Those who stay within "the system," the overwhelming bulk of the population, have little chance of avoiding the stigma and strain of what is defined as failure unless they can build a strong, small community for themselves (and perhaps can demonstrate that they could be successful if

[d] An important, grave issue is ignored in this reference to "societies." The relation between achieving greater equality within a rich nation and attaining greater equality between rich and poor nations is unclear. Increasingly, advocates of greater equality will have to deal with it.

they wanted to). The result is that the range of styles and attitudes for the great bulk of Americans is exceedingly narrow. It will remain so as long as success or failure are so important and so limitedly defined by material and mobility achievements.

Opening up Americans to wider ranges for themselves requires greater equality. If income differences are much smaller, if individuals work out their satisfactions along a variety of dimensions rather a few economic, materialist ones, if conspicuous consumption and relative economic deprivation become less important—then, the individual is in a freer situation. Diversity in styles and attitudes, more individualization, is possible.

Materialism and narrow concepts of success are the enemies of diversity and individualization. Equality does not ensure that diversity will follow, but without equality, diversity will be severely limited.

The equality revolution is a sea change not only in economic conditions but in what we expect of others and what we encourage them to do. It is a change in values, a change that could dispel the pall of limited variation that so frightens many of our young.

Notes

1. S.M. Miller and Martin Rein, "The Possibility of Income Redistribution," *Social Policy*, May-June 1975.

2. For an important effort to systematize the discussion of equality and its remedies, see Herbert J. Gans, *More Equality*, New York: Pantheon Books, 1973.

3. Christopher Jencks, *Inequality*, New York: Basic Books, 1972.

4. T. Husén, "Ability, Opportunity and Career, A 26-Year Follow-up," *Educational Research*, 10 (3): June 1968.

5. See S.M. Miller and Martin Rein, "Poverty, Inequality and Policy," in Howard Becker, ed., *Social Problems*, New York: John Wiley & Sons, 1966.

6. Ibid.

7. For an extended discussion of the issues in the U.S. context, see S.M. Miller, "The Case for Positive Discrimination," *Social Policy*, 4 (3): November-December 1973, pp. 65-71. Not only ascriptive groups such as women and blacks may be involved. In some socialist nations, the concern for the over-representation of middle-class youth and the under-representation of working-class and farm youth in universities has led at various times to barriers to entrance to the former, preference given to the latter, or the institution of a requirement that all students engage in non-white-collar labor before admission or graduation.

8. Daniel Bell, "Meritocracy and Equality," *The Public Interest*, Fall 1972, pp. 29-68.

9. For a delineation of the three approaches of poverty line, comparative position, and inequality, see S.M. Miller and Pamela Roby, *The Future of Inequality*, New York: Basic Books, 1972. In the U.S., the poverty line has been adjusted for changes in the cost of living but not for changes in the average standards of society. Thus the poverty line is a much lower percentage of median income in 1974 than it was in 1960. This is one way of producing a statistical decline in the percentage of the population who are "poor."

10. Kingsley Davis and Wilbert Moore, "Some Principles of Stratification," *American Sociological Review*, 10: April 1945, pp. 242-49.

11. S.M. Miller and Martin Rein, "The Possibility of Income Redistribution," *Social Policy*, May-June 1975.

12. Herbert Gans, "An Egalitarian Approach to the Study of Social Stratification," Plenary Session 4, Eighth World Congress of Sociology, Toronto, 1974.

13. Ibid.

14. S.M. Miller, "Pour une Politique des Revenus," *Analyse et Prévision*, 1974.

15. Jencks, *Inequality*, New York: Basic Books, 1972.

16. S.M. Miller, Pamela Roby, and Alwine de Vos van Steenwijk, "Creaming the Poor," *Trans-Action*, June 1970.

17. John Rawls, *A Theory of Justice*, Cambridge, Mass.: Harvard University Press, 1971. Also W.G. Runciman, *Relative Deprivation and Social Justice*, Berkeley: University of California Press, 1966.

18. Jencks, *Inequality*, New York: Basic Books, 1972.

19. T. Husén, "Ability, Opportunity and Career," *Educational Research*, 10 (3): June 1968.

20. This position is analyzed in Martin Rein and Peter Marris, "Equality, Inflation and Wage Control," *Challenge*, March-April 1975, pp. 42-50.

21. See Adam Walinsky, "Keeping the Poor in Their Place," in Louis Ferman et al., eds., *Poverty in America*, Ann Arbor: University of Michigan Press, 1965.

22. Richard Hamilton, *Class and Politics in the United States*, New York: John Wiley & Sons, 1972.

23. S.M. Miller and Martin Rein, "The Possibility of Income Redistribution," *Social Policy*, May-June 1975.

24. Some evidence suggests no great differences among occupations in workers' expressed feelings about job satisfactions (Jencks, *Inequality*,

New York: Basic Books, 1972). This contradictory attitudinal evidence is based on individuals' appraisals of their current possibilities, not on what satisfactions they might have if job tasks were reassigned.

25. R.H. Tawney, *Equality*, New York: Barnes, 4th ed., 1964.

26. Michael Young, "Is Socialism a Dream?" Rita Hinden Memorial Lecture, December 1972.

27. Melman has argued that economic demands rather than technological imperatives govern the use of technology. Seymour Melman, "The Impact of Economics on Technology," *Journal of Economic Issues*, 9: March 1975, pp. 59-72.

28. Selma Mushkin, ed., *Recurrent Education*, Washington, D.C.: National Institute of Education, 1974.

29. Meynaud, quoted in Ralph Miliband, *The State in Capitalist Society*. New York: Basic Books, 1969. See also S.M. Miller, "Planning," *Social Policy,* September-October 1975.

30. Miller, Roby, and de Vos van Steenwijk, "Creaming the Poor," *Trans-Action*, June 1970.

31. Rawls states as his "first principle" of "justice for institutions": "Each person is to have an equal right to the most extensive total system of equal basic liberties compatible with a similar system of Liberty for all." Rawls, *A Theory of Justice*, Cambridge, Mass.: Harvard University Press, 1971, p. 302.

3

The Equality-Meritocracy Dilemma in Education

*Torsten Husén**

Introductory Observations

As shall be spelled out later, "equality" refers in this chapter not only to equality of opportunity at the starting point of the career race (the liberal conception of equality) but also to equality of life chances (the more radical conception which puts more emphasis on the results than formal equality of opportunity). "Meritocracy" refers to a system of strict selection on the basis of socially highly valued criteria of merit. In the educational system this criterion tends to be academic performance.

There are three major problems we are faced with when we talk about equality versus meritocracy or accessibility versus meritocracy. The first is, What should we mean by equality? The confusion about its meaning is often massive. The second problem area, which is indeed very intricate, has to do with the basic facts from which certain generalizations have been drawn by social scientists that have dealt with the problem area over the last few decades. I could limit myself in this context to refer to names like Coleman (1966), Jensen (1969), and Jencks et al. (1972). The third problem area relates to how the "facts" are converted into policy. I don't pretend to deal with these three problem areas systematically; I shall do it in a somewhat floundering way in this presentation. The main emphasis will be put on educational equality and the meritocratic dilemma that we are faced with in the modern society when trying to "democratize" higher education.

Before embarking upon an attempt to deal with these problem areas, let me make the following three observations.

Number one is that the equality-meritocracy dilemma has taken on another face in recent years due to the enrollment explosion. In the mid-1940s, I began to deal with the problem of equality of educational opportunity on behalf of the Swedish government. I conducted the first survey of the "pool of ability" which in the policy debate at that time referred to young people of working-class origin who didn't have the opportunity to get into higher education. At that time, the problem was conceived to be very simple. It was just a matter of seeing to it that material hurdles,

* University of Stockholm.

45

economic and geographical barriers, were removed so that those of working-class origin who were intellectually capable were given financial opportunity to get into academic secondary education, which was in Europe the main avenue into higher education. It was just a matter of framing a policy and devising techniques by which the talent from the depths of the society could be discovered and properly taken care of.

Since the end of the 1940s the enrollment explosion has been much more vehement in Europe than in the United States, where at that time already a fairly substantial proportion of the relevant-age cohort was in full-time higher education. An extra boost was given by the GI bill at a time when most West European countries had 2 to 5 percent of the relevant age group in higher education. Some twenty-five years ago, surveys began to be conducted in which the social background of university students was related to the participation rates. The picture obtained was disturbing. In the first survey that we conducted in Sweden, by 1945 we found that some 60 percent of the university students came from what was referred to as "socioeconomic group 1," which in the United States is referred to some-what euphemistically as upper-middle class. That group represented about 6 to 7 percent of the adult population in Sweden. Only 6 to 7 percent of the university students came from "socioeconomic group 2," which mainly consisted of manual workers and at that time made up some 50 to 55 percent of the adult population.

The picture was somewhat similar all over Europe. At the beginning of the 1960s (when I say Europe at the present moment, I mean Western Europe), surveys were conducted in, for instance, France, Germany, and the Netherlands. I have reviewed these studies for OECD (Husén, 1972), (Organization for Economic Co-operation and Development) and the picture was, by and large, the same as the one to which I just referred. Friedrich Edding and Roderich von Carnap (1962), for instance, studied the participation rates in the Federal Republic of Germany. At the beginning of the 1960s, Ralph Dahrendorf published a series of articles which then came out as a booklet on students of working-class background at German universities. The figures that Dahrendorf collated were very disturbing. They showed that, by the beginning of the 1960s when roughly 50 percent of the German work force consisted of manual workers, draftsmen, skilled manual workers, unskilled laborers, and farm laborers, only 5 percent of the university students came from homes of manual workers. Among these 5 percent about three-fourths had parents who were highly skilled or specialized workers. Thus, the majority of this tiny little group came from homes where the parents represented a more skilled type of work force. The bottom stratum of the status hierarchy that consisted of about 25 percent of the work force was represented by only 1 percent of the university students, whereas the top stratum of the status hierarchy, consisting of 1 percent, was represented by about 25 percent of the students at the universities (Dahrendorf, 1965). I shall not go into any further detail about surveys that were conducted in the 1950s in various places on both sides of the Atlantic, which, by the way, were conducted even more in the United States than in Western Europe.

Second, an observation about the socialist countries. Until about 1960 we knew very little about how access to higher education in the socialist countries was related to the social background of the students. One had a classless society—but a society where the work force was divided up in intelligentsia, workers, and peasants. A survey conducted in the Soviet Union was referred to by Premier Kruschev in the fall of 1958 when he introduced the new Education Act to the Supreme Soviet. He was then saying that something on the order of 75 to 80 percent of the students at the institutions of higher education in the Moscow area came from the intelligentsia and the functionaries, whereas only some 20 to 25 percent came from homes where the parents were manual workers or peasants. By the beginning of the 1960s, several surveys on aspirations for higher education and the home background of the students began to be made public in the U.S.S.R. (Yanowitch and Dodge, 1968). Some very interesting patterns of student aspirations, in terms of the relationship between participation in higher education and social background, began to emerge.

In the first place, the aspirations for top-quality higher education in institutions, such as the University of Moscow, were extremely strong. There was a striking discrepancy between the aspirations of the students and the available places at the high-quality universities. Second, surveys conducted showed what Western social scientists would call a strong social bias in terms of student's social background. The Soviet Union seems to me to be an interesting case in elucidating what happens when a country rapidly becomes industrialized and then needs to train professionals in large numbers. By about 1965, 80 percent of the Soviet professionals were first-generation professionals, i.e., were first-generation upper-middle or upper-class. Their parents were either peasants or manual workers. They were a rather status-conscious group. I dare say, after having looked at the problem at some length, they are more in favor of meritocracy than the corresponding social strata in Western Europe or in the United States.

Third, it has until recently been commonly believed that inequality of life chances, say in occupational status and earnings, could be heavily reduced by increasing equality in educational opportunities. The belief in the formal educational system as the "great equalizer" has, however, been shaken by the findings, and even more so by the interpretations of the findings, of Jencks et al. (1972). The debate elicited by this study, as well as the so-called Coleman (1966) report some years earlier, has, both conceptually and methodologically, brought the research on equality to a higher level of sophistication.

The preoccupation with equality of educational opportunity among "progressives" or "liberals" since the time of the French Revolution is accounted for by the fact that equal educational opportunity has not been seen as a goal per se but as the most important step toward equalization of life chances. Horace Mann, in the United States by the middle of the nineteenth century, hoped that education would serve as the "great equalizer." The attempt to launch massive compensatory programs for disadvantaged children at the beginning of the 1960s stemmed from the same conviction. But the faith in what education might achieve has been challenged in recent years, both by those who believe in inherited differences as the main determiners of life chances and by those who ascribe decisive influences to the manipulation of environmental conditions. Jensen (1969, 1973) bluntly attributes what he regards as the failure of Project Head Start to inherited differences in educability. Jencks et al. (1972) play down genetically conditioned differences but take an almost nihilistic view with reference to what can be done by manipulating the educational factors. They purport to show that differences in life chances, defined by income and/or occupational status, are only weakly related to formal scholastic attainments. They see the role of the school mainly as that of a sorting and certification agency. Greater equality in adult life can be achieved only by public policy that directly affects income distribution and job opportunities. Neo-marxist-oriented critics go a step further in maintaining that the role of the formal educational system in the capitalist society is mainly to prepare a docile and disciplined labor force that will suit the hierarchically structured society (Bowles, 1972; Bowles and Gintis, 1972-1973).

If the critique launched against the futility of formal schooling is right, i.e., that education does not contribute to equalize life chances, then the matter of equalizing educational opportunities would not be regarded as an issue. Nor would it be worthy of any further research endeavors which instead would have to be focused on factors outside the educational realm conducive to individual or group differences in life chances. But we should keep in mind that the key criterion employed by Jencks et al. (1972), when they talk about inequality, is income, with all its limitations, as a measure of real level of pecuniary success, not to speak of "success" in general.

The formal educational system is not primarily devised to maximize the income power of the individuals processed through it. It is there in its own right. In the modern, increasingly complex society, it serves the function of enhancing the individual's "coping power," his capability to take advantage of what is offered, including public services.

The Inheritance of Intelligence

The concept of the heritability of intelligence has played a dominant part in the U.S. debate over equality of educational opportunity. Jensen's ominous article "How Much Can We Boost IQ and Scholastic Achievement?" in the *Harvard Educational Review* (1969) stirred up the debate, and Jencks's book *Inequality* (1972) added more fuel to it. The concept of heritability is beset with so many shortcomings that it is practically useless. In the first place, it is a so-called population characteristic. It does not refer to a particular individual but is an average. Second, it refers to a particular social situation. If you create exactly equal opportunities, then heritability becomes very important (close to 100 percent), whereas if you have a society where the environmental conditions vary quite a lot, you have a very low heritability. This gives at least some hints about the shortcomings. Third, nobody has been able to establish any link whatsoever between genetic assets on the one hand and concrete behavior on the other. For example, we do not know anything about the specific genetic mechanisms that determine intellectual behavior.

The Changing Conception of Educational Equality

The Conservative Conception

According to the conservative conception of educational equality, God has bestowed different amounts of talent upon each human being, and it is up to the individual to make the best possible use of that capacity. A hyperconservative variant of this philosophy maintains that, by and large, God has given us all the aptitudes that corresponded to the caste or social class in which we are born. The more or less tacit assumption, then, is that we have not only to make optimal use of our capacities but be content with them, because we have been given what we deserve.

The Liberal Conception

"Equality" has for some time been one of the key words in the policy debate on educational problems at both the national and the international level. "Equality of educational opportunity" (*Chancengleichheit, égalité des chances*) has not, however, been regarded as a goal in itself, but as a means in achieving the long-range goal of bringing about equality of opportunity in social and economic careers. As we shall see later, the classical liberal concept of equality is that all individuals should be given the same opportunity to start their careers, not necessarily that greater equality should ultimately be brought about in terms of social and/or economic status.

The roots of what has been referred to as the "classical liberal" conception of "equality of educational opportunity" are to be found back in the eighteenth century. The famous Preamble of the American Declaration of Independence was first drafted by Thomas Jefferson in 1776 and read, in *his* original wording:

We hold these truths to be sacred and undeniable; that all men are created equal and independent; that from that equal creation they derive rights inherent and inalienable, among which are the preservation of life, and liberty and the pursuit of happiness . . .

The interpretation of the Preamble has to be made within the context of the political philosophies of Locke, Rousseau (who in 1755 had published his treatise on the origin of inequality among men), and Helvetius.

Jefferson used the phrase "natural aristocracy" to characterize those who, irrespective of birth, possessed outstanding innate talents. Society should see to it that no barriers existed for the promotion of those belonging to the natural aristocracy who deserved a social status matching their natural talents.

The natural aristocracy is allowed to emerge in a society which dissolves the privileges that form the basis for an "artificial aristocracy," which in sociological terminology would be labeled an "ascriptive aristocracy."

The classical liberal concept of equality of opportunity embodied in what is often referred to as the "American dream" is epitomized in the following quotation from a poem by Thomas Wolfe:

So, then, to every man his chance—
To every man, regardless of his birth,
His shining, golden opportunity—
To every man the right to live,
To work, to be himself,
And to become
Whatever thing his manhood and his vision
Can combine to make him—
This, seeker,
Is the promise of America.

The Weimar Constitution of 1919 talked about the reorganization of society according to (inherited) individual capacity. This new social order should supersede the one with allocation according to socially inherited privileges. The school had as one of its major tasks to "promote the talents" (*Begabtenfoerderung*). The newly established science of psychology was expected to provide methods whereby the individual ability could properly be assessed. The Constitution stated that educational career should be determined by "innate aptitute" (*Anlage*) and "inclination" and not by social background. The criteria for scholastic promotion should be "ability" and "will" (Petrat, 1969). By introducing a system of financial aid, an intensive social mobility could be promoted. The interplay of free competition and equal opportunity would see to it that the above would get access to careers that they deserved (*freie Bahn den Tüchtigen*).

The first large-scale attempt to elucidate empirically the extent to which equality has or has not been achieved in a particular national educational system is presented in the Coleman report (Coleman et al., 1966). This extensive survey was initiated by the Civil Rights Act of 1964. In accordance with it, the U.S. Commissioner of Education was requested to conduct a survey "concerning the lack of availability of equal educational opportunities for individuals by reason of race, color, religion, or national origin in public educational institutions at all levels in the United States" (Coleman, et al., 1966, p. 3). The survey set out mainly to elucidate how far the schools offer equal educational opportunities in terms of other criteria (other than segregation) which are regarded as good indicators of educational quality. Some of these criteria were quite tangible, such as libraries, textbooks, laboratories, and the like. Others—such as curriculum offerings, grouping practices, and methods of instruction—were less so. Some, finally, were rather elusive, such as teacher competence and teacher attitudes.

In commenting upon some of the implications of his big survey, Coleman (1966) raises the question of whether equality means that one wants to have equal schools (i.e., equal treatment) or equal students. He points out that his survey had mainly focused on what comes out of education in terms of student achievement in areas such as reading and arithmetic—skills that are important for success not only in further schooling but also on the labor market. This, of course, does not permit any absolute judgment about the real levels of equality or inequality of the schools the students are attending, because more of the individual differences in achievement are accounted for by their home and peer environments than by the school. However, what matters to the student "is not how 'equal' his school is, but rather whether he is equipped at the end of school to compete on an equal basis with others, whatever his social origins"(Coleman, 1966, pp. 71f). Schools "are successful only insofar as they reduce the dependence of a child's opportunities upon his social origins. . . . Thus, equality of educational opportunity implies, not merely 'equal' schools, but equally effective schools, whose influences will overcome the differences in starting point of children from different social groups'' (Coleman, 1966 p. 72). This implies differential pedagogical treatment.

In preindustrial society, with its extended family and patriarchal kinship system and the family as the unit of production and as the center of social welfare responsibility and education, the concept of educational equality had, as Coleman (1968) has pointed out, no relevance at all. Geographical, occupational, and social mobility were minimal.

The industrial revolution changed the role of the family. It ceased to be a self-perpetuating economic unit or a training ground. Children became occupationally mobile outside the families. Training became a community responsibility, and institutions were provided where young people could learn skills that made them marketable outside the family.

Both liberals and socialists in Europe for a long time thought of equality of opportunity as being equality of *exposure* to a given program. It was up to the children and their families to take advantage of the exposure offered. If the children failed, they had only themselves to blame. Thus, the important thing, from the point of view of policymaking, was to construct the system in such a way that all children, irrespective of social background, would be offered formal equality in terms of equal and free access to education.

But the liberal conception tacitly took the child's future for granted. The problem of assigning students to different programs in a comprehensive system is to find programs that will ''suit the individual needs'' of each child. But the real problem is, as Coleman (1968) points out, that what is taken for granted is *the* problem. No guidance program, even if it is based on the most elaborate system of testing, can predict what will ''suit'' a student in terms of his or her educational and/or occupational career.

Somewhat schematically, this classical liberal philosophy could be described like this. Each individual is born with a certain, relatively constant capacity or intelligence. The educational system should be so designed as to remove *external* barriers of an economic and/or geographical nature that prevent able students from the lower classes from taking advantage of their inborn intelligence which entitles them to due social promotion. One reformer, Count Torsten Rudenschiöld, in his book on ''Thoughts Concerning Social Mobility'' (*Tanker om stånds-circulationen*, 1854) developed a blueprint for a school system that would promote a maximum of social mobility in seeing to it not only that able young people from lower classes were duly promoted, but that upper-class youngsters with limited capacities should be given humble schooling and channeled into humble occupations as well! Everybody, via education, should be given the social status to which she or he is entitled by innate talents.

Major educational reforms in Europe during this century have at least partly been guided by this philosophy. By extending education to more advanced levels, by making the compulsory part of it less differentiated, and by making it available to children from all walks of life, one can remove the handicaps that are inherent in being born poor and living far from a school.

The 1944 Education Act in England, which made secondary school education universal and available to all, not only to those who could afford it, was regarded by many as a "democratic breakthrough." But about ten years later when a survey was carried out to elucidate its effects on the social structure of the enrollment for the academic secondary school, it was found (Floud et al., 1956) that at least in certain regions the proportion of working-class children admitted to grammar schools was *lower* than before the "breakthrough." When the economic barriers were removed and all the places were thrown open for competition within the framework of the 11-plus examinations system, children from the middle- and lower-middle class homes were in a better position to compete than those from less privileged backgrounds and thus achieved an increased representation. Previously, a certain quota of places had been available to those from poor backgrounds. Floud and her coworkers were the first investigators to demonstrate clearly that selectivity does not go together with equality of participation. A certain amount of social bias always goes into a selective education system (Husén, 1971).

The Radical Rethinking of Educational Equality

In analyzing the educational system in industrialized and technological societies, the French sociologist Bourdieu (1964) contends that there are indications that the educational system tends to assume the function of reproduction, i.e., to preserve or even reinforce the existing structure of society, instead of being an agent of social mobility for inherited ability and the motivation to use it. Other researchers, such as Jencks et al. (1972) and Bowles (1972), have followed suit.

Recent surveys of existing research on participation rates and school achievements as related to social class (for instance, background studies to the 1970 OECD Conference on Policies for Educational Growth, OECD, 1971) provide fairly consistent evidence that extended provisions for education, and thereby increased formal accessibility to free secondary and higher education for all children of a given age, have not considerably changed the social structure of the enrollment to any great extent. Students who take advantage of the increased opportunities are already in a favored or semifavored position.

What has been demonstrated by drawing upon empirical data could just as well be brought out by scrutinizing the logic behind the liberal philosophy. According to this philosophy, admission and promotion in the educational system should be guided by individual capacity or aptitude, not by socioeconomic background. The concrete criteria of "capacity" are grades (marks), scores on objective tests, and examination results. All these criteria are to a varying extent correlated with social background.

Thus, access to and promotion within the educational system in accordance with objectively assessed capacity by no means exclude the influence of socioeconomic factors which, according to the liberal philosophy, are discarded by employing criteria of academic merit. As long as admission to a certain type of education is generous in terms of the proportion admitted from those who apply and the attrition rate during a given stage is low, and as long as education is available to all free of charge, socioeconomic background plays a less prominent role. But as soon as a competitive selection takes place, either on admission or in terms of grade-repeating and dropout during the course, then the correlation between background and indicators of performance increases considerably. A case in point is the selection for the faculties of medicine in Sweden which, as with all lines of study with *numerus clausus*, is carried out on the basis of marks obtained in the gymnasium. With the possible exception of the intake to the training program for psychologists, there is no other program that is so highly selective. Also, there is no other faculty with such a grossly unbalanced representation of the social strata.

Peter Schrag (1970) has pointed out that the establishment of the common school has been part of the "American dream," that the schools and universities held the promise of providing equality of educational opportunity, and that they were expected to guarantee an open society unaffected by social and economic inequities. In the middle of the last century Horace Mann foresaw that a school for children from all walks of life would be "a great equalizer of the conditions of men, the balance wheel of the social machinery. . . . It does better than disarm the poor of their hostility toward the rich: It prevents being poor. . . ." Apart from being an equalizer, the educational system was seen as a prime instrument for the individual born in humble circumstances to move up the social ladder. Everybody should be given equal opportunity to achieve and to be promoted, provided he or she had the talent and the energy to go ahead.

Schrag (1970, p. 70) observes that until about a decade ago "equality of educational opportunity" was interpreted in terms of social Darwinism: "Everyone in the jungle (or in society, or in school) was to be treated equally: one standard, one set of books, one fiscal formula for children everywhere, regardless of race, creed, or color. Success went to the resourceful, the ambitious, the bright, the strong. Those who failed were stupid or shiftless, but whatever the reason, failure was the responsibility of the individual (or perhaps of his parents, poor fellow), but certainly not that of the school or the society.''

It has not been realized until recently that these two objectives, as they are commonly conceived, are not in fact compatible. The school cannot at the same time serve as an equalizer and as an instrument that establishes, reinforces, and legitimizes distinctions.

As long as we are applying one uniform, relatively linear standard (bright, average, slow learner, or whatever labels we want to use), some students are, *by definition*, destined to fail.

In an article in which he deals with the philosophical implications of an open-admission policy to college, Karabel (1973) realizes the dilemma between selectivity on the one hand and equality on the other. He states the problem in the following provocative way (Karabel, 1973, p. 40):

The ideology of academic standards brilliantly reconciles two conflicting American values: equality and equality of opportunity. Through the system of public education, everyone is exposed to academic standards, yet only those who succeed in meeting them advance in our competitive system. Everyone enters the educational contest, and the rules are usually applied without conscious bias. But since the affluent tend to be the most successful, the net result of the game is to perpetuate intergenerational inequality. Thus academic standards help make acceptable something which runs against the American grain; the inheritance of status.

The rethinking about individual differences that has been going on in recent years has important practical implications. According to the ''social Darwinism'' view, equality had to do only with what goes *into* the system—its input resources. The question is now being asked of whether one should not also consider what comes *out* of the system and thereby waive the equality at the input side by providing extra resources for those who are regarded as socially and/or culturally deprived.

The glaring contrast between the official rhetoric about equality of opportunity and the existing differences in life chances has, in recent years, led to the emergence of a philosophy of equality of *results*.

Removal of economic and social barriers which, according to the liberal philosophy, would open the gates to more advanced education for all whose natural aptitudes qualify them, patently does not suffice. Inequalities in a highly selective and/or competitive system do in fact remain, or even tend to increase. The difference between comprehensive systems with a single-track basic school covering the compulsory school age and those with a dual-track structure, where selection in one way or another actually takes place or is prepared earlier, is that in the comprehensive system the inequalities tend to move up to the preuniversity or university level. This is the case, for instance, in Japan (OECD, 1971).

The basic distinction between equality of opportunity and equality of results has been elaborated by John Rawls in his book *A Theory of Justice* (1971), where he develops what Charles Frankel (1973) refers to as a "new" egalitarianism. The "old" one, which in the liberal vein was concerned with equality or access or equality of opportunity, advocated a policy of correction. It is referred to as "corrective" egalitarianism. Society had to rectify formal inequalities by providing help to the disadvantaged to overcome the hindrances or barriers which prevented them, for instance, from taking advantage of the opportunities of schooling.

But the fact that a person is born with certain genes into a family with certain material and cultural assets is, as Rawls puts it, "arbitrary from a moral point of view." The fact that some are born with a brilliant mind, and others with a slow-moving one, is to be ascribed to the "natural lottery." Thus, the moral problem is to "redeem" the individual who, due to this "lottery," has been born with less favorable genes or to less favorable circumstances. Society should see to it that the burdens and benefits are distributed according to each individual's abilities. This, briefly, is the message of the "redemptive egalitarianism."

The redemptive philosophy has been challenged by Frankel (1973), Coleman (1973), and Bell (1973). Frankel's main objection to Rawls's theory of justice is that it "treats the individual as not an active participant in the determination of his fate." A model of life as a lottery is not very conducive to a sense of personal responsibility. Bell (1973) looks at the equality problem in very much the same way as Frankel. But he also views it within the framework of a society where rationality, technical competence, and educated skills become more and more important and where they, since they are more sought after, are also more highly priced.

Coleman (1973) in reviewing Jencks et al. (1972) poses the crucial question of whether—and to what extent—equality of opportunity is an appropriate goal. Each individual is born with a highly varying set of "private resources, genetic and environmental." If nothing is done on the part of society, this will result in quite unequal opportunities. Society can try to "infuse" resources selectively so as to achieve greater equality, but such a policy is faced with two problems. In order to compensate fully for the inequalities of private resources, "the publicly-provided resources for the privately disadvantaged must be sufficient to provide to all children the same opportunity as held by the child with the greatest private resources, genetic and environmental" (Coleman, 1973, pp. 134-35). Such extreme implementation is obviously not possible. The other problem is that an inverse policy of equality of opportunity with the aim of establishing equality of results would have disincentive effects upon parents, which could reduce the total amount of resources available and be detrimental to a system of redistribution. This, in the long run, could lead to less favorable effects for the disadvantaged. Coleman (1973, p. 135) concludes:

For both these reasons, first because it is impossible to achieve, and second because if achieved it would lower the general level of opportunity for children, the ideal of equal opportunity is a false ideal. A society cannot make an implementationable decision to create equal opportunity for all children within it. What it must do instead is to decide what level of public resources and what imbalance of public resources it should invest to reduce the level of inequality that arises from private resources.

In retrospect, from the point of view of individual satisfaction, Coleman doubts whether public investment in bringing about equality of results more than equality of opportunity is to be preferred. The ability to overcome obstacles may lead to at least as much satisfaction as the attainment of these goals per se.

Concluding Observations

As we have seen, until recently the overriding policy problem in "democratizing" advanced education, that is to say, formal education beyond mandatory schooling, was conceived of as a problem of paving the entrance routes into institutions of higher education. But one has begun to realize that equality of opportunity of access is different from equality of opportunity of success, either in school or in adult economic careers. The "corrective egalitarianism" emanating from the liberal thinking has been challenged by those who, on the basis of a Marxist philosophy, sometimes advocate a "redemptive egalitarianism."

The basic difference between the liberal and the radical conceptions is, as already indicated, how they view the role of the educational system. According to the liberal conception, the system's task is primarily to remove external barriers, allowing each child's original capacity to develop. Success and failure in school depend primarily upon the individual. Once the avenues have been opened up for free competition, the students' natural intellectual and moral resources are the decisive factors. If they fail, they have to cast the blame upon themselves, because they have been given the opportunity and not taken proper advantage of it. According to the radical conception, students' success, or failure, must be ascribed mainly to the school situation, particularly to the way instruction is organized. The basic problem, then, centers on the extent to which the educational institution has been able to provide the conditions conducive to satisfactory student development.

The implication in terms of policy that ensues from the rethinking of the concept of equal opportunity is that it is not very fruitful to put the responsibility for scholastic success or failure on the individual. One has to shift the burden of responsibility to the *system*—to the educational system or to society at large.

In the long run, then, it seems that the problem of achieving equality of

58

opportunity is one of "restoring multiple options" based on different values, but values that are not ranked along only *one* dimension. Schrag (1970, p. 93) puts the problem very succinctly: "By definition, no society with but one avenue of approved entry into the mainstream of dignity can be fully open. When that single instrument of entry is charged with selecting people out, and when there are no honorable alternatives for those who are selected out, we are promising to all men things that we cannot deliver." No wonder, then, that we are beginning to amass so much evidence for *uniform* provision within the educational system not being the solution to a more "equal" society. To paraphrase Orwell: those who at the outset are more equal than others will take more advantage. That is the lesson learned from equalization programs at all levels of education.

Finally, the more radical conception of educational equality is that, in order to achieve the long-range objective of more equality in occupational career and standard of living, remedial action must be taken in the wider context within which the schools are operating—that is, society at large. Educational reform cannot be a substitute for social reform.

References

Bell, Daniel (1973). *Coming of Post-Industrial Society: A Venture in Social Forecasting*. New York: Basic Books.

Bourdieu, Pierre (1964). *Les Héretiers: Les Etudiants et la Culture*. Paris: Editions de Minuit.

Bowles, Samuel (1972). "Schooling and Inequality from Generation to Generation." *Journal of Political Economy*, (2) 80 (3): May-June 1972, 219-251.

———, and Herbert Gintis (1972-1973). "IQ in the U.S. Class Structure." *Social Policy*, 3 (4-5): 65-96.

Coleman, James S. (1966). "Equal Schools or Equal Students?" *Public Interest*. (4): Summer 1966, 70-75.

———. (1968). "The Concept of Equality of Educational Opportunity." *Harvard Educational Review* 38 (1): Winter 1968, 7-37.

———. (1973). "Equality of Opportunity and Equality of Results." *Harvard Educational Review*, 43 (1): February 1973, 129-137.

Coleman, James S., et al. (1966). *Equality of Educational Opportunity*. Washington, D.C.: U.S. Department of Health, Education and Welfare, Office of Education.

Dahrendorf, Ralf (1965). *Arbeiterkinder an deutschen Universitäten*. In Recht and Staat, Heft 302-303. Tübingen: C.B. Mohr (Paul Sieback).

Edding, Friedrich, and Roderich von Carnap (1962). *Der relative Schul-besuch in den Laendern der Bundesrepublic 1952-1960*. Frankfurt A.M.: Hochschule fuer Internationale Paedagogische: Forschung.

Floud, Jean E., et al. (1956). *Social Class and Educational Opportunity*. London: Heinemann.

Frankel, Charles (1973). "The New Egalitarianism and the Old." *Commentary*, 56 (3): September 1973, 54-66.

Husén, Torsten (1971). "The Comprehensive-Versus-Selective School Issue." *International Review of Education*, 17 (1): 1971, 3-10. Hamburg: Unesco Institute for Education.

_____. (1972). *Social Background and Educational Career*. Paris: OECD.

Jencks, Christopher, et al. (1972). *Inequality: A Reassessment of the Effect of Family and Schooling in America*. New York: Basic Books.

Jensen, Arthur R. (1969). "How Much Can We Boost IQ and Scholastic Achievement?" *Harvard Educational Review*, 39 (1): Winter 1969, 1-123.

_____. (1973). *Educability and Group Differences*. London: Methuen.

Karabel, Jerome (1973). "Open Admissions: Toward Meritocracy or Democracy." *Change*, (3): May 1973, 38-43.

Mann, Horace, *Twelfth Annual Report of the Secretary of the Board of Education, West Newton, Mass. November 24, 1848*. Dutton, Westworth State Printers, Boston, 1849.

OECD. (1971). *Educational Policies for the 1970's*. General Report, Conference on Policies for Educational Growth, Paris, June 3rd-5th 1970. Paris: OECD.

Petrat, Gerhardt (1969). *Soziale Herkunft und Schullaufbahn*. Weinheim: Beltz und Deutsches Institut für Internationale pädagogische Forschung, Frankfurt/Main. 2d ed.

Rawls, John (1971). *A Theory of Justice*. Cambridge, Mass.: Harvard University Press.

Schrag, Peter (1970). "End of the Impossible Dream." *Saturday Review*, 19th September, 1970, 68-96.

Sjöstrand, Wilhelm (1973). *Freedom and Equality as Fundamental Educational Principles in Western Democracy: From John Locke to Edmund Burke*. Studia Scientiae Paedagogicae Upsaliensia No. 12. Stockholm: Almqvist and Wiksell.

Yanowitch, Murray, and Norton Dodge (1968). "Social Class and Education: Soviet Findings and Reactions." *Comparative Education Review*, 1968, 248-267.

4

The Role of Education in the Escape from Poverty

*Herbert J. Gans**

In the conventional American wisdom, education has long been viewed as a major device for upward occupational mobility, the notion being that what children learn at school will enable them to obtain a viable foothold in the world of work. As a result, education has also been conceived as a major agent in the escape from poverty, and many of the programs in the War on Poverty of the 1960s emphasized improvements in education for the poor.

By the poor, I mean here the approximately 20 percent of the population which now earns less than half the personal median income, (almost $13,000 in 1974). Part of this population consists of the aged, children, and female heads of households, who earn below the official poverty line (just over $5,000 in 1974), but it also includes many "normal" two-parent families with full-time but poorly paid breadwinners, the so-called working poor.

Like some other social scientists, I am dubious that education plays a significant role in the economic and occupational mobility of this population, and that schooling can therefore be a significant force in antipoverty policy or in the achievement of more equality in American society.[1] Although little is known even about the role education plays in the upward— and lack of downward—mobility in the middle class, it has clearly not been a major factor in the upward mobility of the poor. While some poor children have always been, and are now, able to escape from poverty as a result of their superior performance in school, most poor children follow one of these patterns: they do not attend schools in which a superior performance is a stepping-stone to occupational success; they are kept out of good jobs by the many noneducational status indices and credentials which poor people cannot obtain; or, most importantly, they graduate into a labor market in which jobs are increasingly scarce even for people with the right educational and social credentials. In addition, many poor children do not do particularly well in school to begin with, and it is ironic that even while many educators continue to believe that education can provide an escape from poverty, they also believe, and rightly, that the schools have not yet learned how to educate poor children.

Much of the discussion about education among the poor has sought to

---

* Columbia University.

put the blame on the schools, on poor children, or on their parents; but ultimately, little is to be gained by blaming anyone, for the fault rests with much larger and more powerful forces. In American society, as elsewhere, public education has functioned, if not necessarily intentionally, to support the existing stratification system, channeling many children into the strata of their parents and into those occupations most in demand in the current economy, and only a handful of children have been able to transcend the channeling process.[2]

As a result, poor children go to schools which are, on the whole, inferior in many ways to middle-class schools, where they are often taught by teachers who do not consider them capable of learning. Some teachers are simply hostile toward the poor; a much larger number, however, adhere to widely accepted stereotypes of the poor as being stupid and apathetic, and then it becomes a self-fulfilling prophecy. Nevertheless, despite the considerable evidence that poor young children are as intelligent, curious, and hungry for learning as their middle-class peers—many of whom are not half as interested in learning as educators like to believe—some poor children do behave in school as if they were stupid or apathetic. Aside from the fact that they sense, and react to, their teachers' stereotypes of them, they also enter the schools with several handicaps. Some come from such crisis-ridden homes that their parents have never even had the time or energy to teach them the kinds of play that are a crucial part of early learning, and many more lack the prior "booklearning" that curriculum-makers and teachers take for granted. More important, upon entering the schools, they encounter an academic middle-class culture and a set of bureaucratic rules which not only diverge sharply from the culture and rules they have learned as necessary for survival and mobility in their neighborhood, but which often seem to have little direct relevance to learning per se. Equally significant, as poor children get older, they become aware of the fact that the culture and rules of the school are also irrelevant to their future. As they discover that even with a diploma they may not find a decent job and the chance to escape poverty, they become alienated from the school and from learning, "enrolling" instead in the so-called school of hard knocks, in which they learn more of the culture necessary to their survival as poor people.

To put it another way, poor children realize that the school functions in part as a preparatory institution and anticipatory recruiting station for what economists call the *primary labor market* of well-paid, permanent, secure, and relatively interesting jobs; that neither their teachers nor the rest of middle-class society considers them eligible for this labor market; and that their future is in the *secondary labor market*, of underpaid, temporary, unstable, and dead-end jobs—preparation and recruitment for which takes place on the streets of the urban slum.[3] One illustration of poor children's awareness of their future is the consistent finding that school performance, particularly among boys, declines as they become old enough to realize what is in store for them, so that by the time poor children enter their teens, many drop—or are pushed—out of school, in spirit if not in body, and some resort to protesting what they consider to be imprisonment in a hostile institution, either by seemingly senseless verbal or physical violence or by more explicit political protest.

To be sure, some teachers are able to overcome this pattern, either by personal charisma or by their ability to translate the curriculum into meaningful teaching; and some poor children are able to absorb the culture of the school and obey its rules because they have been imbued with the drive for individual mobility and believe that they can escape from poverty through education; but such teachers and children are, in the end, only exceptions that prove the rule. Unusually gifted teachers and exceptional children are rare in all populations, poor or affluent, and it would be illusory to expect that they will ever be produced in large enough quantities to overcome the drawbacks of existing institutional arrangements.

Escaping Poverty—the Historical Experience

Instead of expecting the school to function as a major causal factor in the escape from poverty, I believe it is more useful to ask what institutions and agencies, educational and other, have been and are most helpful in enabling the poor to enter the more affluent sectors of society. This question can be addressed in several ways, but I shall here use a historical approach: to discover how previous generations of poor people escaped from poverty, and to use this experience in constructing an alternative escape model. American history is, of course, a treasure trove for this purpose, for most of the people who came to America arrived as poor people and were able, somehow, to achieve a measure of affluence.

If one looks, for example, at the European immigrants who arrived in America in the last half of the nineteenth century and the first quarter of the twentieth century, it is clear (1) that they came as very poor people; (2) that insofar as their children went to school at all, they went to schools that were worse in all respects than today's schools for the poor; and (3) that they nevertheless were able eventually to escape poverty. I am referring here especially to what I call the "peasant immigrants," the people who came from the rural areas of Southern, Eastern, and Southeastern Europe—for example, the southern Italians, Sicilians, Poles, other Slavs, Hungarians, and Greeks, among others—most of them unskilled and most of them with little or no education. Their experience is relevant particularly because they were similar in many ways to today's poor, who were only a generation or so ago rural migrants from the South, Appalachia, and Puerto Rico. At the same time, they must be distinguished from what I call *urban* immigrants, with some artisan or other urban occupational experience, with more education, and, in some cases, with a little capital in their pockets. During the nineteenth century, America became home for urban immigrants from many countries, including those who sent mainly peasant immigrants, but the most frequently mentioned, and thus most visible, urban immigrants have been the Jews, particularly those emigrating from Eastern Europe.

The case of the Jews deserves somewhat more detailed discussion because many educators believe that they relied mainly on education to escape poverty, ostensibly because Jewish culture places especially high value on education. Recent historical research suggests, however, that immigrant Jewish children and the children of the first Jewish immigrants did not stay in school very long, so that very few could have used education to achieve upward mobility.[4] In addition, the Talmudic education valued by the Jewish immigrants—actually only by the religious minority among them—was antisecular and discouraged learning for the sake of occupational mobility, so that it could not have been used for escaping poverty.

No one yet knows how many Jewish immigrants valued secular education, or whether they valued it more than other urban immigrants, but most of the Jewish newcomers were so poor that they had to send their children to work as quickly as the other immigrants—although there is some evidence to suggest that the second, or first native-born, generation of Jews attended school in larger numbers and performed more successfully than other second-generation groups, at least among the peasant immigrants. Unfortunately, the many educators and other policymakers, then and now, who pointed to the Jews to support their claims for relying on education as a means of escaping poverty vastly overestimated the educational performance of the Jewish immigrants; they failed to consider that other urban immigrants (for example, southern Italians and Sicilians) may also have escaped more quickly from poverty than the peasant immigrants, whether or not they went to school; and they ignored the difference between urban and peasant immigrants.

One historical fact is well established, however: the peasant immigrants did not escape poverty via the schools. They came from countries in which education had been either inaccessible or irrelevant to them, and many of them made strenuous efforts to keep their children out of school in America, partly because these schools treated them with hostility and believed that they were unteachable, but also because parents wanted the children to work and contribute to the family income, and the jobs which were available to them did not require education.[5]

Instead of the schools, the peasant immigrants relied on the labor market; wherever feasible, as many family members as possible went to work at whatever jobs were available, and though many were never able to progress beyond positions in the secondary labor markets of their time, and many died prematurely from exhaustion, illness, and other consequences of being poor, some were able, by mere persistence, to achieve a modest family income, if not in the first, then in the second generation. They were able to escape from poverty not only by their own efforts, and because generations of previous poverty had prepared them for surviving at a fantastically low standard of living, but also because their sole resource—unskilled labor—was in demand at that time. The immigrants came, after all, at a time when America was undergoing particularly rapid industrialization and urbanization, so that except during the frequent periods of depression, there were jobs in building factories, transportation systems, and cities. In addition, the immigrants arrived at a time of incipient unionization, and the unions played a large role in the achievement of job security, and thus in the escape from the secondary labor market. Indeed, in those days unions were in many ways organizations of the poor, which they are not today.

Finally, I suspect that those immigrants who were able to stay—or move quickly—out of low-paying factory jobs and engaged instead in petty entrepreneurial activities, even peddling, were able to make their way out of poverty more rapidly than those who had to rely on factory work. The rapid expansion of consumer goods, industries, and retailing during the late nineteenth century often allowed peddlers to become shopkeepers fairly quickly; and although many of those who opened shops soon went bankrupt, others were able to move themselves or their children into the middle class. Needless to say, the urban immigrants were usually in a better position to exchange the factory for the entrepreneurial enterprise than the peasant immigrants, if only because they had had some entrepreneurial experience in Europe.

Over the long run, of course, both urban and peasant immigrants were able to leave poverty behind, but even so, the peasant immigrants escaped from poverty much more slowly than is generally believed; many were still poor or in the secondary labor market in the second generation, and only in the third and fourth generations have the majority established themselves in well-paying and secure blue-collar and white-collar jobs.[6]

Significantly, the slow escape from poverty took place without major changes in the attitude toward education. As long as enough semiskilled blue-collar and service jobs were available, and since employers were not yet concerned with credentials unrelated to performance, the descendants of the immigrants did not give up the peasants' belief in the limited relevance of education. Equally important, they could not yet afford to do so; they still needed the children's contribution to the family income, and thus encouraged them to leave school as quickly as possible. Of course, by then child labor laws were sufficiently enforced so that the children often stayed in school until the legal leaving age, but whether they learned anything relevant to their later occupational activities is still a moot question.

Only in recent years have these attitudes changed. As blue-collar wages began to go up, parents no longer needed their children's paychecks. Also, as parents realized that automation and the decline in manufacturing would eventually lead to a reduction in decent blue-collar jobs, and that white-collar jobs could not be obtained without the proper credentials, they began to insist that their children graduate from high school, and that boys, at least, consider going to college.[7] Such changes in attitude have escalated in the last decade; since then the descendants of the peasant immigrants, now often fourth generation, have begun to stream into the publicly funded colleges and community colleges.

These observations suggest a hypothesis about the role of education in upward mobility which is just the reverse of the conventional wisdom. Education, at least for the poor, is not a causal agent in the achievement of mobility, but one of its effects, and education is not thought to be relevant to mobility until after parents have achieved a threshold of economic security in the primary labor market.[8] Only then are parents able and willing to encourage their children to go to school, and to be able to live in neighborhoods with schools worth attending; and only then do children decide that education may indeed be useful to them. Whether the interest in and the willingness to use education require prior middle-class status, and whether the change of attitude applies to education in general or only to higher education, which is more directly relevant to occupational mobility, remains to be seen. In any case, the history of the European immigrants suggests that economic success leads to educational success, not the other way around.

Some Policy Implications

This analysis is based on limited historical and mobility data, but if it is accurate, it suggests that education should play a smaller and, as will be shown below, a different role in antipoverty policy than it did, for example, in the War on Poverty. Although there are dangers in trying to repeat history, the most effective way to eliminate poverty is through employment, with income grants in lieu of employment for those who cannot work or cannot find work, until poor people have enough economic security to be able to use education to achieve further mobility, either for themselves or for their children.

Since jobs, particularly for the unskilled, are now scarcer than they were during the time that the immigrants escaped poverty, it will be necessary to resort to deliberate job-creation. The jobs to be created should mesh with the needs of the private and especially the public economy, but they must also mesh with the long-range need of the poor: to become part of the primary labor market. In other words, such jobs must provide enough income, security, and opportunity for advancement to enable their holders to feel that they are participants in the economy and the society, so that their children will be able to advance further through education.

The historical record suggests that parental establishment in the primary labor market was a prerequisite and a takeoff point for using education to achieve further mobility, but whether history must repeat itself, or whether a different takeoff point can be found is as yet an unanswered question. No one now knows where the takeoff point is at which people feel that they are participants in the economy and society, so that their children will feel it is useful to go to school. Thus, research would have to be undertaken to determine whether that takeoff point requires parental establishment in the primary labor market, or whether it could be reached even if parents are still in the secondary labor market. Or for that matter, does it only require a specific level of family income, either through work or income grants, or a degree of income security, or some combination of work and income prerequisites?

The exact requirements for the takeoff point are particularly important in view of the fact that without major transformation of the contemporary economy, it is unlikely that many of today's poor, particularly women, can be employed. Hopefully, the takeoff point may not even require jobs, but simply a degree of economic security, in which case it may be achieveable through a system of income grants providing a decent living to poor people unable to work or find work.

The history of the immigrants also suggests that it may take two to three generations before poor people are ready to reach the point at which they are able to make effective use of education. However, whether this is a justifiable hypothesis remains to be seen; it is possible that under other labor market conditions, the European immigrants could have moved out of poverty more quickly. Also, today's poor people do not, for the most part, suffer from the language barriers the immigrants faced, and in addition, their aspirations and expectations are higher, so that they would bitterly resent any policy planning that asks them to wait for yet another two to three generations. In addition, it is always possible that educational breakthroughs will be made which will enable poor children to use the schools to escape poverty, although such breakthroughs would be irrelevant if the economy is not able to employ them up to the level of their education.

Conversely, many of today's poor carry one stigma not carried by the

European immigrants; they suffer from racial discrimination, which hurts them both in the schools and in the labor market. Of course, many European immigrants were initially also discriminated against—for having a dark skin and ''swarthy'' features—but they were redefined as whites the moment they had escaped from poverty, a possibility out of the reach of today's poor blacks.

Finally, and most important, even if history suggests that economic success must precede educational success, and that the process may take two or more generations, it may also be possible to speed up the process by focusing policy efforts directly on poor children, and specifically by reversing the traditional pattern of having schooling precede entry into the labor market.

Rather than keeping poor children in school even though they perform poorly there, it may be more desirable to allow them to go to work instead, in adolescence, and in some cases even earlier, with the idea that they can return later to school. Certainly many poor youngsters today, as in the past, would like nothing better than to leave school for a job, and there is no reason to believe that they cannot perform in at least most semiskilled jobs, particularly if they are supplied with job training once they are hired.

Revoking the child labor laws may appear to be a regressive proposal, but while history offers considerable evidence of exploitation of children before these laws came into effect, it is also true that young people were able to perform creditably in the labor market and offer income support to their families, particularly at times when adults could not find jobs. Even so, I would not advocate a return to a nineteenth-century practice, and any policy to put adolescents to work would have to be accompanied by stringent safeguards to prevent exploitation, both of them and of other workers, i.e., adults whom they might replace. Consequently, the youngsters should be given specially created jobs, which (1) fit their youthful needs, (2) call for job training, (3) provide opportunities for developing a career, and (4) do not allow employers to fire older, better-paid workers instead. Indeed, I am arguing not that poor young people should be put to work, but that they should be enabled to begin careers at an earlier age.

In addition, their jobs should have two built-in educational components. First, the young workers should be enabled and encouraged to continue their education while working, and even to be aided financially to do so, assuming that there are schools available where they could learn. Second and more important, the young workers should be able to return to school on a full-time basis when they are older, and when they may be more interested in schooling than they are at present. Many young people today who have gone to work at an early age are often sorry later that they did not stay in school, and although their judgment is based on hindsight, it does reflect a greater appreciation of the utility of education (or credentials) with increasing age. The return to school could take the form of a leave of absence from work, which many corporations already give their executive trainees, or of the equivalent of the GI Bill, which war veterans receive to train themselves for better jobs.

If scholarships were available for such young people so that they could return to school in their twenties and even in their thirties, with enough funds in the scholarship to enable them to support their families while they are in school, the educational investment would produce a higher payoff for them and for society than the present investment required for keeping poor adolescents in school into late childhood. Consequently, a work program for young people should be combined with a later educational program, with the federal government setting aside enough funds at the time adolescents go to work to allow them to return to finish their education—through college—at a later date.

Allowing poor adolescents who are truant from school—or who have dropped out emotionally—to go to work might also have a salutory effect on the schools themselves. Teachers would no longer have to cope with unhappy and unruly youngsters and could devote themselves more fully to students with academic interests. In addition, the threat of losing students to the world of work, which would lead to a reduction in teaching jobs and school budgets, might encourage the schools to make education relevant to poor young people in an attempt to keep them from going to work. Perhaps the schools might even begin to draw some educational lessons from the mass media and the peer group, both of which have long been able to educate children more effectively than teachers and textbooks. Conversely, the schools might become more involved in preliminary forms of job training, in order to give some anticipatory job socialization to youngsters who want to drop out to go to work. Finally, if the schools are likely to lose at least some of their students when the job market beckons, they could recoup the declining enrollments by matriculating young children at an earlier age, before kindergarten. Head Start, private-school nursery programs, and some day-care programs have shown that prekindergarten children are particularly eager to learn, and the poor ones among them are then still too young to know that their schooling may not help them occupationally when they are older.

In effect, I am suggesting that whether or not the aim is the elimination of poverty, the schools should not be used to postpone entry into the labor market, as they are at present. Their contact with poor young people ought to be timed for those periods at which people are most ready to learn, i.e., when they are very young, and later, when they have had sufficient job experience to realize that they need more education.

Some Caveats

As already noted, the proposals for changes in antipoverty policy and the schools rest on a sparse data base, about both the occupational mobility of the European immigrants and the takeoff point at which education becomes an effective device for mobility. Moreover, neither the poor nor the labor markets nor the schools of the 1970s are exactly like those of the late nineteenth and early twentieth centuries. For example, today's poor appear to have much higher expectations about the utility of education than did the poor of the past, and poor parents now put considerably more pressure on their children to stay in school and to perform effectively. Indeed, many studies have shown that poor black parents have high educational aspirations for their children, and higher ones than poor white parents, which encourages some observers to argue that the former therefore resemble the European urban immigrants more than the peasant ones. Although it is undoubtedly true that poor people today have higher educational aspirations for their children than did the European immigrants, parental aspirations do not necessarily predict children's performance. Actually, many poor Jewish children at the turn of the century did badly in school despite parental pressure, if only because they realized, as do today's poor, that for them occupational mobility can only rarely be achieved through educational success.

Finally, my proposals have several difficulties and defects, of which at least three are worth mentioning. First, they imply differential educational treatment for the poor and the rest of society, for while poor youngsters would leave school to go to work, affluent ones would stay in school and prepare for college, thus widening the gap between the poor and the nonpoor. Such inequality of treatment is not desirable, although in this case it only formalizes what already exists informally, and enabling poor children to work at decent jobs seems preferable to having them sit in school without learning. Nevertheless, formally unequal treatment of poor adolescents can only be justified if it is complemented by a later chance for education, if the adolescents who drop out to go to work are allowed to return to school later and to go on to college. Even so, I would suggest that if the goal is the escape from poverty, equality of *results* or outcomes is more important than the time-honored educational belief—if not practice—in equality of *treatment*. If unequal treatment can bring about more equality of results, it is preferable to equal treatment that helps to perpetuate poverty.

Second, the argument I have made here can be used, when taken out of context, to justify pushing additional poor children out of schools, whether jobs are available or not. Pushing children out of school is an unjustifiable policy even when jobs are available for them, however, and I want to emphasize strongly that when jobs are not available, as at present, keeping poor children in school is far preferable to forcing them out on the streets without work. Even when the schools are unable or unwilling to teach poor youngsters, they at least do not encourage poor children to become criminals.

Third, the entire scheme presented in this chapter rests, on the one hand, on a highly pessimistic assessment of the school, and on the other hand, on a highly optimistic assessment of the labor market and of the possibilities of job creation in particular. In effect, I am suggesting that the decisionmakers in American society, be they leaders or voters, are not likely to be able or willing to educate poor children to the level at which they can become part of the primary labor market, but that they are willing or able to create jobs for them. Given the disappointing record of job-creation and income-grant programs for the poor, my implication that it is easier to intervene in the economy to incorporate the poor and the young poor in the labor market than it is to change the educational system may be totally inaccurate.

There is no doubt that the proposals made here suffer from misplaced optimism; and in actual fact, I am as pessimistic about the possibility that the poor can obtain decent jobs or income grants as that they can obtain a decent education. The powerlessness of the poor and their economic superfluousness, at least in the current economy, strongly suggest that nothing significant will be done for them, either in the schools or in the economy. Worse still, in many parts of the American economy, machines continue to replace workers, and government policies (for example, in the granting of investment credits and depreciation writeoffs) only exacerbate this tendency. Consequently, if present trends continue, the number of unemployed is likely to increase, and unemployment may become a fact of life for people who are not now classified among the poor. These trends can only be reversed by a drastic change in national economic policy, which measures growth not by increases in the GNP, but by increases in employment, and by the replacement of capital-intensive production with labor-intensive production.

Ultimately, the proposals I have made here can only be implemented in a full-employment, labor-intensive economy, and at present the chances of bringing about the necessary political change to achieve such an economy are less than miniscule. As a result, my proposals are, for the moment, utopian. Nevertheless, even if they cannot be implemented, these proposals seem justified on another ground: that they will at least dispel the illusion, which has been created both for the poor and for the rest of society, that if and when the right combination of philosophy and technique is found, education can offer an escape from poverty. If that illusion, however, which Colin Greer has called the "Great School Legend," can be dispelled, it may be possible to achieve some progress by considering entirely new approaches, in which education takes an effective role within a larger and broader antipoverty policy. Such approaches are beyond the scope of this chapter, but they require not only the movement toward a full-employment, labor-intensive economy, but also some redistribution of wealth and income, as well as the greater equalization of tasks which S.M. Miller has suggested.[9] Poverty cannot be eliminated without a more egalitarian economy and polity, and only when such equalization has been achieved will it be feasible to bring about the educational equality which educators have sought for so long.

Notes

1. See, for example, I. Berg, *Education and Jobs: The Great Training Robbery,* Praeger, 1970; C. Jencks et. al., *Inequality,* Basic Books, 1972; and B. Harrison, *Education, Training and the Urban Ghetto,* Johns Hopkins University Press, 1972.

2. For a summary statement, see C. Greer, *The Great School Legend,* Basic Books, 1970; see also S. Bowles, "Getting Nowhere: Programmed Class Stagnation," *Society,* June 1972, pp. 42-49.

3. A good recent analysis of the two labor markets is in P. Doeringer and M. Piore, "Unemployment and the 'Dual Labor Market,'" *The Public Interest,* No. 38, Winter 1975, pp. 67-79. For a poignant sociological analysis of life in the secondary labor market, see E. Liebow, *Tally's Corner,* Little, Brown, 1967.

4. Fragmentary empirical evidence that most Jewish immigrants did not escape poverty through education can be found in two recent Columbia University dissertations: T. Kessner, "The Golden Door: Immigrant Mobility in New York City, 1880-1915," Department of History, May 1975; and S. Gorelick, "Social Control, Social Mobility and the Eastern European Jews: An Analysis of Public Education in New York City, 1880-1924," Department of Sociology, October 1975.

5. See, for example, S. Thernstrom, *Poverty and Progress,* Harvard University Press, 1964.

6. S. Thernstrom, *The Other Bostonians,* Harvard University Press, 1973.

7. See R. Schrank and S. Stein, "Yearning, Learning and Status," in S. Levitan, ed., *Blue Collar Workers,* McGraw-Hill, 1971, pp. 318-341; and H. Gans, *Urban Villagers,* Free Press, 1962, Chapter 10.

8. Greer, *The Great School Legend,* Basic Books, 1970, p. 85.

9. In Chapter 2 of this volume. See also H. Gans, *More Equality,* Vintage, 1975.

5

Education, Life Chances, and The Courts: The Role of Social Science Evidence

*Henry M. Levin**

Introduction

Public policy attempts to improve the "life chances" of youngsters from low income and minority backgrounds have focused primarily on the schools. "Life chances" is defined as a child's future ability as an adult to participate fully in the social, economic, and political life of society. More narrowly, "life chances" may be considered in terms of such outcomes as ultimate earnings, occupational status, and political efficacy. The crucial role of the school in preparing students for these eventualities has been tacitly assumed. It is no surprise, therefore, that in their quest for greater equality among persons of different races and social class origins, both policy makers and the courts have devoted extensive efforts in an attempt to alter the organization and financing of education.[1]

There are three principal areas of reform to which policy makers and the courts have directed themselves in the last two decades: school desegregation, the provision of additional resources for the education of children from low income families, and reform of state educational finance systems by reducing the reliance upon local property wealth as the determinant of local school expenditures.[2] Each of these reform measures comports with notions of basic fairness and, indeed, could be defended on these grounds alone. But this view of reforms—that they are essential in a "just" society—has been overshadowed by the claim that social science research has shown that the particular educational strategies offered to the courts enhance the life chances of children. Educational reform litigation increasingly relies on social science evidence, as seen in the challenges to school segregation, to the present methods of financing education, and to student classification policies.[3]

This article explores the appropriateness of using social science evi-

*Professor, School of Education and Department of Economics, Stanford University.

Reprinted, with permission, from a symposium on The Courts, Social Science, and School Desegregation appearing in *Law and Contemporary Problems* (Vol. 39, No. 1, Winter 1975), published by the Duke University School of Law, Durham, North Carolina. Copyright 1975, by Duke University.

dence as a basis for formulating public policy and for deciding law suits in these particular areas. In the course of this exploration, four questions have to be addressed: (1) To what degree can social science methodology determine the impact of schooling on such life chance outcomes as income and occupational attainment, separating out other factors influencing life chances such as family background and IQ? (2) To the extent that social science research presents conflicting theories of these relationships, why do some theories receive considerable attention in the policy arena while others do not? (3) What impact does social science evidence have on the evolution of law and public policy with respect to education? (4) Finally, what contribution can the social sciences make to the issues raised in litigation?

Effects of Education on Life Chances

How might the social scientist attempt to trace the effects of a particular educational strategy on the life chances of an individual or group of persons? The difficulties inherent in this task can be illustrated by considering the fundamental characteristics of the problem. At the outset, there is a complex multitude of psychological, social, genetic, political, economic, and educational influences that can determine occupational attainments and earnings. The actual effect of education and of a particular educational environment is particularly difficult to trace because the outcomes that we wish to review are very much removed in both time and context from the schooling process. Typically, research in this area is intended to relate the income and occupation of an individual or a group of persons to the schooling which they received many years before and under circumstances very different from their present situations. Also, the educational experiences of an individual are so closely tied to his social class origin and family experiences that it is virtually impossible to isolate the distinct influences of each on life chances.

In addressing this issue, social scientists have two basic approaches at their disposal.[4] The first is the purely experimental approach. In theory, an experiment would select persons who were similar in every respect and assign them to a different quantity and quality of education, and then monitor them over their life-times in order to determine how the differences in educational experiences are translated into differences in life-time experience. Such an experiment would probably require a minimum of thirty years and would have to ensure that the individuals in both the experimental and control groups were treated identically in their pre-adult years, with the exception of schooling. In other words, such factors as genetic background, family environment, community factors, medical care, nutrition, friendships, and so on, would have to be identical in order to draw an accurate inference about the effects of differences in schooling.

For obvious reasons, however, such an exercise is impossible. Not only do we lack the luxury of several decades or a life-time to carry out research for impending policy decisions, but the conditions that we would have to place on the human subjects in order to conduct the experiment could very well raise questions about a violation of their constitutional rights.[5] Even were such an experiment feasible, we would not be able to generalize beyond the actual educational strategies that were utilized and the specific persons or groups of persons that were involved in the experiment. Since there are infinite combinations of both, even a relatively large scale experiment would reveal information about only a limited range of alternatives and population groups. Moreover, in a society such as ours, the relationship of education to one's life chances is likely to change from generation to generation, meaning that the results obtained from a particular experiment might not be applicable to conditions some forty years later when the experiment was finally completed.

Thus, the most powerful investigative tool that science has to offer for an understanding of the relationship between education and life chances is politically and practically infeasible. At best, experimentation can be used to test minor hypotheses that may be related to some later outcome.[6] For example, it may be possible to set up an experiment to determine the effect of teachers' attitudes on student achievement or educational aspirations, assigning students randomly to two different types of teachers, and holding other factors constant for the period of the experiment. Outcomes would be measured by standardized test scores and such elements of educational aspiration as incentive for further schooling. Even with this more limited type of experiment, it is a formidable endeavor to fulfill the *ceteris paribus* conditions. And even more problematical is the relationship of the experimental outcomes to life success. One would have to make the assumption that student test scores and attitudes are related initially to educational attainment, and ultimately to income and occupational attainment. While the logic of such a relationship may be compelling, any conclusion in this respect is beyond what could be substantiated by results from the experiment just outlined.

An alternative social science strategy that is used when direct experimental research is not feasible is the quasi-experimental approach.[7] This latter strategy represents an attempt to parallel the experimental conditions by using statistical procedures to "correct" for those factors that cannot be controlled experimentally. Sometimes the quasi-experimental approach is termed a "natural" experiment because data are collected from an actual life situation rather than an experimental one. For instance, a researcher who is interested in the effects of schools on life chances might collect historical data for a sample of adult males or females. These data would include the present earnings and occupation of the individuals, information on their parents' class origins, characteristics of the schools that they attended, information on their friends, their work experience, and so on. A statistical model would then be constructed in an attempt to determine the relationship between the educational variables and the occupational and income attainments of the sample being studied.

Quasi-experimental studies attempt statistically to relate all relevant factors that might explain a particular phenomenon. The success of such an approach is dependent upon the ability to identify and measure these factors and to relate them in the statistical analysis in a manner reflecting the true phenomenon. As mentioned previously, however, there are an unlimited number of potential influences on adult outcomes and there are a variety of plausible ways that each can be measured and related to other variables in the analysis. In an area where choices must be made among the myriad of possible variables, measures, and relationships, the complexity and arduous nature of this type of statistical analysis necessarily limits the researcher to a narrow set of alternative formulations. The actual choice of factors to be included in a study, the measures of those that are ultimately selected, and the structure used to relate them is in part determined by the personal predilections of the researcher.[8]

In summary, there are enormous difficulties in determining how a host of genetic, psychological, social, cultural, political, economic, education-al, and chance factors determine a person's ultimate life attainments. These difficulties and the complex nature of the problem suggest the inability of social science research to derive answers that can be utilized with any reasonable degree of reliability. Indeed, it is little wonder that opinions on the subject differ as much among social scientists as they do among laymen. Because of the inherent inadequacy of our present tools, there is no social science consensus on the appropriate educational strategies for improving the life chances of children from low-income and minority backgrounds.[9]

Hypotheses about Schooling and Adult Attainments

The fact that social science has not provided a definitive or even a tenta-tively acceptable analysis of the relation between schooling and adult attainments does not mean that there exist no hypotheses on the subject. To the contrary, there are at least four such theories relating schooling to eventual adult occupation and income. Each of them presumes a relatively different educational approach toward improving the life chances of disad-vantaged students.

Skills or Cognitive Achievement

Much of the literature on schooling and adult income is dominated by the notion that education produces verbal and mathematical skills as well as other knowledge that translate into higher productivity in the market place and consequently higher earnings. Under this hypothesis, the more cognitive knowledge that children acquire in school, the greater will be their life attainments. Accordingly, the effect of schooling or income is determined by the effect that schooling has on skills and knowledge. Those schools that contributed toward greater gains on achievement tests ostensibly would have the greatest impact on improving the future adult attainments of their pupils. Hence, the appropriate educational strategies would be those that are consistent with increasing the test scores of children from low income backgrounds. The most notable of these approaches is the provision of additional educational resources as exemplified by programs of compensatory education in the elementary and secondary schools [10] and such preschool programs as Project Head Start.[11] It has also been argued that greater social class and racial integration of schools will have this effect.[12]

Noncognitive Characteristics for Work Relations

In contrast to the cognitive achievement hypothesis outlined above, the second thesis views the school as inculcating students with the appropriate behaviors for occupying particular positions in the occupational or organizational hierarchy. Such characteristics as respect for rules, dependability, and internalization of the norms of the workplace have been found to be strong predictors of employee ratings by supervisors and of income levels.[13] The workplace is seen as a hierarchically differentiated organization in which different positions require varying worker characteristics.[14]

those at the base of the hierarchy requiring a heavy emphasis on obedience and rules and those at the top, where the discretionary scope is considerable, requiring a greater ability to make decisions on the basis of well-internalized norms. This pattern is closely replicated in the social relations of schooling. Note the wide range of choice over curriculum, life style, and allocation of time afforded to college students, compared with the obedience and respect for authority expected in high school.

According to the second hypothesis, while minimal skills are necessary for productivity, most of the discrepancy in occupational attainment and earnings is attributable to noncognitive work traits. Four of these work prerequisites—proper level of subordination, discipline, supremacy of cognitive over affective modes of response, and motivation according to external reward structures—have been identified.[15] Also identified are the ways in which the schools are structured to foster these traits. For example, subordination and proper orientation to authority along hierarchical lines are necessary in virtually all modern work enterprises. Thus, "[a]s the worker relinquishes control over his activities on the job, so the student is first forced to accept, and later comes personally to terms with his loss of autonomy and initiative to a teacher who acts as a superior authority, dispensing rewards and penalties."[16] Similarly, it is argued that other school practices are related to the requirements of the workplace; students from lower social class origins are being prepared to occupy lower status occupations and those from higher class backgrounds are being socialized to undertake professional and managerial roles.

This hypothesis suggests that the contribution of schooling should be evaluated in terms of its impact on creating productive worker characteristics. Unfortunately, the work hierarchy is so unequal in terms of job requirements, satisfaction, income, and prestige that providing everyone with the "most productive" traits is not likely to increase life chances for everyone. Rather, it would simply redistribute opportunities among the population with some individuals improving their standing and others losing ground in terms of productive adult roles. In contrast with the thesis that everyone's productivity is enhanced by the attainment of greater cognitive skills, it is difficult to argue that productivity for all individuals would rise with the inculcation of higher echelon occupational traits, so long as the number of such positions is rationed by the occupational pyramid. In short, the view that the schools affect the life chances of students by preparing them for particular levels of the work hierarchy suggests that schools perform their function when they differentiate and produce the highly unequal outcomes that correspond to adult roles.[17] The most that could be accomplished by the schools in such a world is that students from disadvantaged backgrounds would have the same chance to be prepared for particular roles as those from diadvantaged backgrounds, in contrast with the present system which relegates racial minorities and the children of the lower class to corresponding lower-class adult roles.

Screening and Certification

The third major hypothesis of how education affects earnings and occupational status views the school as an organization whose principal function is to sort and select students. According to this interpretation, the schools carry out a sophisticated process of assessing the cognitive and personal attributes of a student and then assigning him to a particular educational fate. Through testing, ability grouping and tracking, curriculum assignment, grading systems, and stratification by social class among neighborhoods, the schools act as an enormous filter.[18] Students who have the low-level skills and personality characteristics suitable for the lower end of the work hierarchy are placed in slow ability tracks or in inner-city schools that provide them with little incentive for further schooling. In contrast, students with high test scores and with personality attributes that correspond with the upper level of the job hierarchy are encouraged to pursue further education and will be rewarded with the high grades which represent the admission requirement for obtaining superior educational credentials.

The screening and certification hypothesis assumes that the occupational and income attainment process for an individual is determined largely by the amount of schooling he has received, his field of study, and the prestige of the institutions that he attended.[19] Thus, the sorting and selection of each student according to his initial and developing characteristics are identified in the job market by an educational credential which is used to establish his place in the occupational structure. Since such credentials are awarded on the basis of "productive" characteristics, employers need only to find out which "certificate" an individual possesses in order to judge his suitability for a particular position.[20] The hypothesis thus suggests that schools do not serve to educate students but instead to select them for their future fates according to characteristics derived from their genetic heritage and non-school environments. It has been further argued that the traits used for selection have little to do with real productivity differences and that persons with higher educational credentials are simply placed in jobs that are ostensibly more productive because of such factors as, for example, greater capital investment per worker.[21]

Presumably, then, the reason that children from lower income and minority backgrounds do more poorly in both schools and later careers is that they are filtered out rather early on the basis of low initial test scores and personality traits deemed inappropriate for further educational selection. Their low educational credentials mean that they will occupy low productivity jobs with little hope of access to the more productive and remunerative ones.[22] The educational policy implications of this hypothesis are not unlike those of the second hypothesis discussed earlier, which is concerned with the noncognitive characteristics or behavior appropriate at various levels. In both instances, the schools tend to reinforce the initial attributes of students; according to the third hypothesis, through selection and certification procedures, and according to the second hypothesis, through selection, differentiated preparation by category of student (especially social class), and certification. The major distinction between the two views of the educational process is that the sorting hypothesis assumes that the school has no educational effect on the student and that the observed differences merely reflect variation in natural endowments and out-of-school influences. The noncognitive socialization theory, on the other hand, assumes that schools do have an effect—that of further reinforcing these initial differences.

Only by eliminating all sorting and selection based on characteristics that coincide solely with race and social class will educational credentials be distributed in a more nearly random manner. Yet, since grades and examination scores are based substantially upon behavior and language styles which in turn are heavily determined by racial and social class backgrounds, drastically different criteria would have to be developed for determing a student's educational success.

Reduction of Social Class and Racial Frictions

The final hypothesis considers the attitudes of all students towards racial and social class differences. The premise is that the better all racial and social class groups understand each other, and the greater the number of intergroup contacts, friendships and interactions, the less racial and class conflicts there will be in adult life.[23] The role of the school in this regard is crucial, for racial, cultural, and social class diversity in the educational environment is considered to be a prerequisite to greater justice in the distribution of jobs and earnings among the population. It is assumed that such a policy would have a marked impact on reducing labor market discrimination against racial minorities and members of the lower classes.

The obvious educational strategies that are consistent with this hypothesis are those which lie at the heart of the school desegregation movement. These include greater social class and racial heterogeneity among students and the introduction of a more multi-culturally oriented curriculum. The former action would be accomplished through massive desegregation of schools, thereby increasing the diversity of student populations and of the resultant educational and social interactions. The latter approach, which emphasizes a greater balance among the cultural contributions of different social and racial groups, would be implemented through changes in instructional materials, teacher training, and teacher selection.

Empirical Support for the Hypotheses

According to the conventional image of science, mere application of research methodology to competing hypotheses will reveal which one best describes the world. Thus, through the use of sophisticated empirical research techniques we should be able to distinguish among those approaches worthy of elevation to the level of explanatory theory and those which should be banished as falsehood. But, as noted previously, the tools of social science are inadequate for this task. The social science evidence that does exist is incomplete, fragmented, and applicable to narrow populations only. It cannot, therefore, be conclusive.[24]

Although each hypothesis can be shown as consistent with some observable facts, the same facts often lend support to more than one of the hypotheses. Table 5-1 represents a summary of the evidence in support of the four hypotheses linking education with the life chances of poor and minority students. The educational strategies and the measures of educational outcome that are consistent with each hypothesis are shown in this table. But beyond this, the important concern is whether certain specified educational outcomes have been produced successfully by the corresponding educational strategy. The extent to which the desired educational outcome is linked to such adult attainments as income and occupational status is of substantial concern as well. These aspects are essential to determining the degree to which we can expect a particular educational strategy to produce enhanced income and occupational positions. Accordingly, the summary of the evidence linking the educational strategy to a specified educational output, and the educational output to measures of life attainment is also provided in Table 5-1. It is important to observe that a lack of evidence for the impact of any particular strategy does not mean that the approach is without merit. It simply means that existing research—which may be quite minimal on the subject—has not provided sufficient empirical support for such a strategy.

Measures of Educational Outcome

The cognitive skills hypothesis has as its measure of educational outcome standardized test scores. Despite the fact that there are many and diverse measures of the broad range of cognitive skills, the evidence, as indicated below, is remarkably consistent whether IQ tests, achievement tests, reading tests, mathematics tests, or others are used. In order to raise the level of cognitive performance of low income and minority youngsters, the educational strategies usually invoked are the provision of greater resources for compensatory education and racial and socioeconomic integration. The evidence is weak that either of these policies has significant impact on test scores. For example, neither the *Coleman Report*[25] nor subsequent studies, some of which used the data collected for the *Coleman Report*, found that differences in the level of educational resources have any major impact on test scores.[26] An analysis based on the statistical results of a

Table 5-1
Summary of Evidence in Support of Four Hypotheses Linking Education to Life Chances of Low Income and Racial Minority Students

	Hypotheses			
	Cognitive Skills	*Noncognitive Work Characteristics*	*Sorting and Selection*	*Reduction of Racial and Class Frictions*
Educational Strategy	Compensatory Education & Integration	Compensatory Education & Integration	Changes in Selection Mechanisms	Integration & Multi-cultural Environment
Measure of Educational Outcome	Test Scores	Values, Attitudes, Behavior	Values, Attitudes Behavior and Test Scores	Attitudes towards Self and Other Groups
Evidence of Strategy's Success for Enhancing Educational Outcome for Poor and Racial Minorities	Weak	Weak	Weak	Inconclusive
Evidence Linking Educational Outcome to Income and Occupational Attainment	Consistent Statistical Tie, but Only Nominal Effect	Strong Inferential Evidence, but Little Direct Support	Not Separable from Cognitive and Noncognitive Results	Very Little Direct Evidence

number of these studies has shown that even major increases of those educational resources most related to test scores would not come close to eliminating the performance gap between white and black students.[27] Evaluations of compensatory education programs carried out under Title I of the Elementary and Secondary Education Act of 1965[28] similarly have been unable to demonstrate any significant relationship between increased resources and improved test scores.[29]

While some studies have suggested that both socioeconomic and racial integration improve the test scores of minority and low-income students,[30] these conclusions have been contested in other evaluations.[31] Thus, neither compensatory education strategies nor those related to desegregation show anything other than a weak relationship to cognitive gains. Even when statistical differences in favor of these strategies are reported, the improvement in cognitive skills is generally marginal.

Assuming that strategies other than compensatory education and racial and class integration could be found which did improve cognitive scores substantially, what would be the impact of such an improvement on income and occupational attainments of poor and minority youngsters? Numerous studies demonstrate a consistent statistical relationship between test scores and these measures of life success.[32] The explanatory significance of this relationship is nonetheless quite weak.[33] At most only about 10 per cent of the differences in income can be explained by test scores, leaving 90 per cent or more to be explained by other factors. Furthermore, relatively large increases in test scores are associated with only modest increases in income. While the apparent effect of test scores on occupational status is somewhat higher, it still only explains—at the most—about 25 per cent of the variance.[34] Differences in test scores, therefore, are not a major factor in explaining why occupational attainments and incomes differ among various cross sections of the population. In summation, the hypothesis that improving the cognitive test scores will raise the adult attainments of children from low-income and minority families shows little promise of success because (1) available educational strategies have not demonstrated much success in improving test scores of these students and (2) increases in test scores show only modest effects on adult income and occupations.

Evidence on Noncognitive Work Characteristics

In contrast with the numerous studies exploring the relationship between test scores and increased resources or integration, there are few research studies devoted to the other hypotheses. Nonetheless, there have been some attempts to explore the noncognitive worker characteristics thesis.

As indicated previously, the measure of educational outcome relating such traits to income and occupation are those values, attitudes, and behaviors which are required for work positions in a hierarchical setting. These include such characteristics as dependability, subordination to authority, respect for rules, and internalization of work norms.[35] Measures of noncognitive work traits have been demonstrated to be related to grades awarded by teachers, more so than are test scores.[36] However, there is apparently no study which has attempted to determine the *degree* to which the worker characteristics of poor and minority students can be altered by compensatory education or integration. Contrariwise, there is a strong presumption that the present approach will resist change because it is functional to the reproduction of the capitalist work hierarchy.[37] Accordingly, the relationship between the educational strategy and the desired educational outcomes must be considered as weak.

There is, however, evidence linking noncognitive outcomes to income and occupational attainments. The amount of schooling a person receives is a more powerful determinant of income and occupation than are test scores. For example, three studies using longitudinal data—permitting prior schooling experiences and test scores to be linked to earnings—have found either a nonexistent or a relatively negligible correlation between test scores and earnings. This is in contrast to the rather pronounced impact that the amount of schooling has on ultimate income.[38] Thus it appears that the amount of schooling a person receives has a considerable effect on adult success, independent of the cognitive skills attained from the educational process.

But there is additional evidence supporting the noncognitive work characteristics hypothesis: teachers tend to award higher grades to students who exhibit personality characteristics functional in the work hierarchy.[39] One study of a sample of workers from three different enterprises found that these personality traits or characteristics are related both to supervisors' ratings and to earnings, even after differences in cognitive skills among employees is accounted for.[40] Obviously, much more research is needed in this area, but the view that noncognitive educational outcomes have more important influences on life attainments than cognitive ones has considerable support. Nevertheless, the lack of evidence indicating that educational strategies can alter the distribution of these traits suggests that the policy implications of this hypothesis are minimal.

Evidence on Sorting and Selection

The difficulty in evaluating the sorting and selection hypothesis is that there is virtually no reliable way to distinguish its effects from those generated by the cognitive and noncognitive socialization hypotheses. Essentially, the difference between the sorting and selection hypothesis and the other two is that the former assumes that schools do not produce the cognitive and noncognitive traits that are reflected in educational attainments and credentials. Rather, schools simply identify and select students according to those traits which they already possessed or acquired outside of the school setting, and bestow upon them differing educational rewards. Whether schools sort according to already-existing characteristics or actually inculcate these characteristics in students cannot be determined without very intensive studies. Possibly both aspects are prevalent but there is no apparent evidence that permits differentiation between the two.[41] Thus, any evidence tending to support the cognitive and noncognitive socialization hypotheses would certainly be consistent with a sorting and selection hypothesis as well.

Evidence on Reduction of Frictions between Races and Classes

Finally, the hypothesis on reducing racial and social class frictions measures educational outcome by the attitudes of representatives of each group towards themselves (self-image and sense of efficacy), as well as by attitudes that connote an understanding and acceptance of members of other groups. Whether the educational strategies of desegregation and multicultural emphasis[42] have long-run effects on attitudes and behavior is questionable. That the evidence in these areas is both controversial and contradictory is reflected in recent debates on the subject.[43] In some instances desegregation of the schools appears to have improved the self-images of racial minorities and racial attitudes of both majority and minority students;[44] in other cases there seem to have been no effects, or even negative ones.[45] One of the basic problems that pervades this research is the questionable reliability and stability of any measure of human attitudes. Given the variable quality of desegregation efforts and multi-cultural educational programs, it is not surprising to find such a divergence of results.

There is at least some empirical evidence supporting the view that socioeconomic integration improves the life chances of low-status children. An analysis of data collected for a sample of youngsters then in the ninth grade, supplemented by follow-up information on their subsequent schooling, occupational attainments, and income nine years later, indicates that students who had similar test scores and social class backgrounds as well as educational attainments had higher incomes if they had attended secondary schools with other students from high socioeconomic backgrounds.[46] A particularly interesting aspect of this study was that low-status individuals appeared to "gain" more than twice as much income from this effect as did the high-status individuals. However, even this finding applies only to the young adults in this particular sample. Furthermore, it is not clear why socioeconomic composition per se should lead to higher incomes.

Social Science and the Choice of a Strategy

The difficulty of using social science research to determine how different educational strategies can be used to affect the future life chances of low income and minority students is clear. While virtually all of the four hypotheses discussed above have some support, the results are ambiguous and inconclusive. Advocacy of any particular approach, therefore, is not based so much upon its general acceptance in the scientific community as it is upon the predilections of researchers and policy makers. The fact that they as well as the courts have not been neutral among competing ideas suggests that it is useful to explore the reasons that particular strategies are selected.

At the outset, one may very well ask how social science researchers can commit themselves to a particular hypothesis or approach on the basis of ambiguous, fragmented, and often contradictory findings. The answer, seemingly, is that researchers often have commitments based upon deeply ingrained social experiences that affect their understanding of how society functions. The natural consequence of these experiences encourages the social scientist to accept the evidence which reinforces his own experience and to be skeptical of that which does not.[47] As Polanyi has noted:[48]

I start by rejecting the ideal of scientific detachment. In the exact sciences, this false ideal is perhaps harmless, for it is in fact disregarded there by scientists. But we shall see that it exercises a destructive influence in biology, psychology and sociology and has falsified our whole outlook far beyond the domain of science.

To a substantial degree the social scientist is himself a product of the very forces he wishes to study. Long before he has received his professional training he is exposed to such phenomena as class, race, family structure, money, prices, religion, industry, politics, work, the messages of the media on all of these subjects, and more. His perspective of the world is largely a cumulative result of his role as a child, student, sibling, husband, consumer, professor, rich man, black, woman, mother, and so on. All of these roles have defined the boundaries of experience which in turn mold his social reality.[49] In a more specific sense, the social scientist who studies the effects of schooling on achievement has been socialized to a large degree by his own particular experiences during his education. His knowledge about the determinants of poverty is influenced by his own class origins and experiences. His image of political reality is conditioned by his own interactions with the political system and other institutions that inculcate political attitudes. Interacting with these influences is his professional training which emphasizes particular metaphysical and epistemological frameworks for viewing the world.

Moreover, since researchers are not randomly assigned to studies, the effects of the researcher's commitment and ideology on the interpretation of research findings is not a chance event. To the contrary, there is a self-selection of problems by researchers according to their predilections, as well as the selection by government and other decision makers, based upon the "outlook" of the researcher and the sponsoring agency. Social science investigators choose those problems that interest them and to which they feel they can contribute something of value. Of course, research support is also a prerequisite, but most social science analysts— particularly in the academic setting—have a choice of problems on which to focus. Public policy-oriented research has a substantive or topical component that may or may not be of interest to potential investigators. Such motives as a sincere wish of the individual to improve government decision-making are often strong factors in the choice of problems, but they also coincide with a deep personal involvement in the outcome of the study. That is, the researcher is likely to have relatively strong viewpoints about what proper policy should be in advance of his research.

The agencies that support research are just as likely to select a researcher on the basis of his values as on his "scientific" competence. As Paul Samuelson has remarked:[50]

The leaders of this world may seem to be led around through the nose by their economic advisers. But who is pulling and who is pushing? And note this: he who picks his doctor from an array of competing doctors is in a real sense his own doctor. The Prince often gets to hear what he wants to hear.

It would be inconceivable to think of the United States Commission on Civil Rights hiring a researcher for his neutrality on the desegregation issue. Indeed, we expect that government decision makers seek out those investigators who are sympathetic to the agency's own orientation.

Obviously, these phenomena dovetail very closely with the use of social science evidence in the courts. Legal proceedings are endeavors in advocacy, each side seeking that "evidence" which will support its own position. There is always some social science evidence on virtually any phenomenon, so one must ask what types of evidence are likely to be drawn into the courts. I assert that the social science evidence which courts are likely to receive has the following attributes: (1) It tends to be based upon complex, statistical methodologies that are generally beyond the experience and the competence of the court to question. (2) It directly supports or refutes the matter under consideration. (3) It is based upon a theory which is credible and understandable to the court. (4) And, finally it implies a remedy that is readily within the court's power and is politically feasible.

The first requirement evolves from the image that the laymen has of science. "Good" social science is characterized by large data sets, complicated statistical methodologies, and an aura of technical competence. While the researcher has made many personal judgments with respect to his formulation of the problem—selection of a framework for the analysis, definition and measurement of variables, technique of data analysis and interpretation of results—all will tend to be obscured by what appears to be a strictly technical analysis. The greater the methodological sophistication, the more difficult it is to demystify the analysis and the more tempting it becomes to see "the emperor's new clothes." The bias in favor of sophisticated empirical studies also rules out the consideration of hypotheses that are not conducive to empirical evaluation.

The second requirement suggests that ambiguity in research findings will be shunned. Alternative interpretations of the results can obviously be dangerous to the advocate who uses the evidence to support his client's case. Thus, the social science research that is utilized must unequivocally support the particular objectives of the advocate. This tends to eliminate any opportunity for a thoughtful analysis of all of the competing hypotheses.

The third requirement, that the social science evidence presented to the court be based upon a credible hypothesis, is illustrated by the fact that while social science research in the Marxian tradition may be both extremely sophisticated and unambiguous, the theory upon which it is based may not be acceptable to those heavily indoctrinated with the capitalist viewpoint.

Another example: no evidence has been presented in either the desegregation or the school finance cases that argues in favor of the noncognitive worker characteristics hypothesis as an explanation of the effects of schools on the life attainments of children from low income[51] and racial minority backgrounds. To the educated layman the cognitive skills theory is much more credible than the noncognitive one.

Finally, the requirement that the social science evidence presented to the court implies a remedy that is both within the court's remedial powers and is politically feasible, is illustrated, for example, by the fact that given the present institutional framework it is not possible for the court to interfere with family child-rearing for educational purposes. Yet studies have shown that such interventions will improve the life chances of students from low-income families.[52]

In light of these principles it is understandable that the courts and other policy makers have focused primarily on the cognitive skills approach.

Firstly, the research in this area, beginning with the *Coleman Report*[53] and the "Racial Isolation" report of The U.S. Commission on Civil Rights the following year,[54] has the aura of being methodologically sophisticated and empirical. Enormous data sets (about 650,000 students and 70,000 teachers comprise the *Coleman Report* data), sophisticated methodologies such as multiple regression analysis, and quantification of educational outcomes as reflected in test scores, create a strong image of valid scientific endeavor. Secondly, these studies purport to show unambiguously that socioeconomic and racial integration as well as certain school resources improve the test scores of low income and minority students. Thirdly, educated men tend to believe that cognitive test scores are important determinants of life chances because they are likely to attribute their own educational and occupational success to their relatively high levels of knowledge and skills rather than to "less rational" factors such as those related to family socioeconomic origins. Cognitive skills are an attractive basis for constructing the meritocracy.[55] Finally, implementation of the desegregation and compensatory education strategies implied by the cognitive hypothesis are within the powers of the courts and educational decision makers.

Effects of Social Science Evidence

Thus far, it has been argued that the social sciences cannot produce conclusive results that would support a particular educational strategy for improving the life attainments of students from low-income and minority families. Also, it has been asserted that the evidence that does enter the courts or policy arena is considered and utilized on the basis of factors other than its scientific "validity." What are the implications of these assertions for the evolution of public policy and the law?

There are three possible cases. The first is the happy one where the evidence presented is somehow the "best" that is available. In other words, the evidence is based upon the clearest attainable picture of the world and is unequivocally better than that which supports alternative hypotheses on the subject. It is not clear how this would happen but to the degree that it does occur, it can be viewed as advancing the wisdom of the legal system. The second case is a less benevolent one in which the social science evidence, while representing just one among competing views on the subject, nonetheless carries the day. To the degree that the results of the research are erroneous, the use of social science may be harmful.

But in many ways it is the third case that is most interesting. Here social science evidence is used to support both sides of a legal dispute.[56] In educational finance litigation, the constitutionality of state school finance systems was challenged on the ground that they provided lower quality education for children in low property wealth districts than for those in more affluent districts. The defense relied upon social science research which, they asserted, indicated no relationship between the level of expenditures and the quality of an education program. The defense arguments were buttressed by the *Coleman Report*[57] and other research,[58] tending to show that there was little or no causative effect between educational expenditures and other measures of school quality and student achievement. The plaintiffs countered with witnesses and research that disputed the methodologies and data employed in the studies cited by the defense, and which indicated a correlation between increases in educational resources and improved pupil achievement.[59] In some cases the plaintiffs won the argument;[60] in others, the courts were unpersuaded.[61]

Even where both sides draw upon social science evidence and the court decides between the two competing presentations, there is a possibility that use of such evidence will tend to redefine the issue itself. Presentation of evidence on the relationship between educational expenditures and cognitive achievement implicitly narrows the context within which the effects of unequal expenditure patterns will be considered. While the two sides of this debate disagree on the effect of school resources, both have accepted the view that standardized achievement scores are the appropriate focus for exploring educational outcomes. Since courts and policy makers generally find it easier to understand a point of agreement than of contention, such points of accord have more influence on the assimilation of the policy implications of research than the conclusions of the research itself. Thus, much of the legal debate surrounding the challenge to present methods of financing education does not address the basic unfairness reflected by state arrangements to spend more on the education of children in rich districts than in poor ones. Rather, the prima facie inequalities are ignored as the courts are tortured with the convoluted arguments provided by social scientists about whether money makes a difference for "poor kids."[62] It is unfortunate that the issue has now become framed in terms of whether additional expenditures for children in poor school districts will raise their test scores.[63]

A second example of the tendency of a tacit consensus among litigants having a greater influence on policy formation than the actual research results, is the controversy over the effect of school desegregation. Until the mid-1960's, the case for racial desegregation was one that was based largely upon the type of society one envisioned.[64] For those who equated a fair society with the absence of racial separation, segregation of schools was contradictory. For those who defined a fair society in other ways, racial isolation in the educational system was of little consequence. The argument was primarily a moral one, dealing with normative visions of the world.[65]

With the advent of the *Coleman Report* and the 1967 Report of the U.S. Commission on Civil Rights, *Racial Isolation in the Public Schools,* a new dimension was added. These studies attempted to demonstrate that segregated school environments retarded the test scores of black children and other students from lower socioeconomic backgrounds. By 1972, serious questions were being raised about the validity of the earlier findings. Reanalysis of the Coleman data did not support the hypothesis that the test scores of black students were a function of the racial composition of the schools.[66] A subsequent analysis of several longitudinal studies of the effects of busing argued that the data do not support the conclusion that racial integration of schools in itself will improve the achievement levels of racial minorities and that there is at least some evidence that harmful changes in attitudes take place.[67]

The results of this study were shocking[68] due to the fact that heretofore there seemingly had been one point of agreement in the social science studies on desegregation—that "[i]ntegrated education will enhance the academic achievement of minotority groups, and thereby close (or at least substantially reduce) the achievement gap."[69] Despite the very contradictory literature on school desegregation, the case for desegregation was seen as hinging *primarily* on whether it improves the achievement test scores of minority students. Rather than considering what kind of educational policy regarding school racial patterns is consistent with our democratic ideals, the issue seems to be whether or not blacks and other minorities gain a few more points on a vocabulary or reading test. This standard is far removed from the declaration of the Supreme Court of 1954 that the separation of black children "because of their race generates a feeling of inferiority as to their status in the community that may affect their hearts and minds in a way unlikely ever to be undone."[70] At this stage, the issue has thus been cast in terms of the achievement scores of blacks rather than in terms of the larger moral and human dilemmas raised by segregated public institutions. There is little doubt that the research agenda has framed the issue.

Conclusion

What is the proper role of social science in charting educational policy for improving the life chances of low income and minority students? The answer to that question is not clear. The question of the relationship between educational influences and actual adult status addresses a very complicated area of social and individual behavior. In particular, little is known about the effects of different school environments on human behavior, about underlying theories of human productivity and its determinants in a particular social setting, about the myriad of other influences that can intervene between the educational strategy and the adult outcomes many years hence, and about the appropriate measurements of even those factors that do seem relevant. Further, the fact that experimentation as an empirical investigating tool is politically and practically infeasible limits severely our ability to uncover the true relationships.

Some observers may react to these conclusions by suggesting the social science evidence in these complicated areas is likely to be so misleading and value-laden that we ought to ignore it.[71] In contrast, some technocrats will argue that the case *against* the ability of social science to validate the relationships between education and life chances has been overstated and that rapid scientific advances in research methodology will even nullify those anomalies which have arisen. Both of these views assume that the social sciences must play a deterministic role in contributing to policy or that they can play no role at all. Yet, it may be the heuristic aspects of social science research which are most useful.

Alice Rivlin has suggested that we acknowledge the development of a "forensic social science," rather than pretending "to be part of the tradition of balanced, objective social science in which the scholar hides (or claims to hide) his personal biases, and attempts to present all the evidence on both sides of a set of questions so that the reader may judge for himself."[72] Using the notion of a forensic social science for addressing policy issues,[73]

scholars or teams of scholars take on the task of writing briefs for or against particular policy positions. They state what the position is and bring together all the evidence that supports their side of the argument, leaving to the brief writers of the other side the job of picking apart the case that has been presented and detailing the counter evidence.

The problem with such an approach is that it assumes that all of the sides will be fairly represented. But adversary proceedings normally are based upon only two conflicting points of view.[74] Moreover, the fact that the epistemology of the social sciences itself limits the analysis to a specific set of hypotheses (particularly ones that have readily identifiable empirical consequences) suggests that the issue might be framed in an erroneous manner. Of course, this type of bias can be avoided by permitting non-social scientists to enter the forum to present their views and argue their evidence. It is not clear what criteria would be used to select such witnesses nor is it obvious how one could determine how many points of view should be permitted. It is also not clear that the courts would attach great weight to "non-scientific" presentations. Finally, the court lacks expertise in selecting among alternative presentations that are grounded in complex statistical procedures and highly technical language.[75] Of course, the court could hire its own experts for examining and interpreting the evidence, but what guarantees the objectivity of the "wise men" who advise the court?

Social science research can best be used to frame the issues and their consequences rather than to obtain conclusive evidence on what is right and what is to be done. This approach requires a recognition that while many aspects of the world cannot be quantified or analyzed in a social science setting, such factors should be considered along with the results of social science research.[77] It is not clear that utilization of social science research in this manner is consistent with an adversary framework. Further, if social science findings increasingly are used to create what appear to be technical issues out of essentially moral dilemmas, this presents a potential social danger. The apparently increasing reliance of the courts on social science evidence suggests that intensive debate on these issues should be given high priority.

Notes

1. *See generally* D. Kirp & M. Yudof, *Educational Policy and the Law* chs. 4, 6, & 7 (1974).

2. A recent summary of these strategies is contained in Staff of Senate Select Comm. on Equal Educ. Opportunity, 92d Cong., 2d Sess., Report: Toward Equal Educational Opportunity (Comm. Print 1972). *See also* J. Coons, W. Clune III, & S. Sugarman, *Private Wealth and Public Education* (1970); J. Owen, *School Inequality and the Welfare State* (1974); Wise, "School Desegregation: The Court, the Congress, and the President", 82 School Rev. 159 (1974).

3. D. Kirp & M. Yudof, *supra* note 1.

4. For the best discussion of the experimental and quasi-experimental approaches in a related context see D. Campbell & J. Stanley, *Experimental and Quasi-Experimental Designs for Research* (1966). For a more skeptical statement on the ability of social science research to provide "proof" for a theory see Address by D. Campbell, before the Society for the Psychological Study of Social Issues meeting with the American Psychological Association, New Orleans, La., Sept. 1, 1974 (to be published in *J. Social Issues*). *See also* J. Katz, *Experimentation with Human Beings: The Authority of the Investigator, Subject, Professions and State in the Human Experimentation Process* (1972).

5. It is very difficult to explain the experimentation in such precise terms that a layman will understand the full implications of the testing and thus be able to provide an effective waiver. Compare the requisite standards for valid consent in the area of medical experimentation and re-

search. *See* Kaimowitz v. Department of Mental Health, Civil No. 73-19 434-AW (Mich. Cir. Ct., July 10, 1973) for a judicial response to the legal and medical issues posed by experimental psychosurgery. In that case, the court determined that the consent must be competent, voluntary, and knowledgeable. *Id.* at 31-32. *See also* Herch & Flower, "Medical and Psychological Experimentation on California Prisoners," 7 *U. Cal. Davis L. Rev.* 351 (1974).

6. A creative attempt at using experimental methodology to ascertain the effects of intervention on racial interactions is found in Cohen & Roper, "Modification of Interracial Interactions Disability: An Application of Status Characteristic Theory," 37 *Am. Sociological Rev.* 643 (1972).

7. *See* D. Campbell & J. Stanley, *supra* note 4.

8. *See generally* Levin, "The Social Science Objectivity Gap," 55 *Saturday Rev.* no. 46, at 49 (1972).

9. *See* Address by D. Campbell, *supra* note 4.

10. In addition to programs under Title I of the Elementary and Secondary Education Act, 20 U.S.C. § 241 (1970), several states provide funds for compensatory programs. *See, e.g., Cal. Educ. Code* §§ 6499.230-6499.238 (West 1975); *Wis. Stat. Ann.* §§ 115.90-115.94 (Supp. 1974).

11. Project Head Start, instituted under authority of Title II of the Economic Opportunity Act of 1964, 78 Stat. 516 (1964), *as amended* 42 U.S.C. § 2781 (1970), offers a variety of health, social and educational services to enable pre-school children from deprived families to enter kindergarten or first grade.

12. *See* Coleman, "Toward Open Schools," 9 *Pub. Interest* 20 (Fall 1967).

13. *See* R. Edwards, "Alienation and Inequality: Capitalist Relations of Production in a Bureaucratic Enterprise," July 1972 (unpublished Ph.D. thesis, Department of Economics, Harvard University).

14. Bowles, "Understanding Unequal Economic Opportunity," 63 *Am. Econ. Rev.,* 346, 353 (1973).

15. Gintis, "Education, Technology and the Characteristics of Worker Productivity," in "Proceedings of the Eighty-Fourth Annual Meeting," 61 *Am. Econ. Rev.* 266 (1971) [hereinafter cited as Gintis].

16. *Id.* at 274.

17. *See* Levin, "A Conceptual Framework for Accountability in Education," 82 *School Rev.* 363 (1974).

18. *See* I. Berg, *Education and Jobs: The Great Training Robbery* (1970); Hall, "On the Road to Educational Failure: A Lawyer's Guide to Tracking," 12 Inequality in Ed. 1 (1970); Kirp, *Schools as Sorters: The Constitutional and Policy Implications of Student Classification,* 121 *U.*

Pa. L. Rev. 705 (1973); Sorgen, "Testing and Tracking in Public Schools," 24 *Hastings L.J.* 1129 (1973). Use of the term "filter" is adopted from Arrow, *Higher Education as a Filter,"* 2 *J. Pub. Econ.* 193 (1973).

19. *See generally* Bowles, "Unequal Education and the Reproduction of the Social Division of Labor," in *Schooling in a Corporate Society* 36 (M. Carnoy ed. 1972); Karabel, "Community Colleges and Social Stratification," 42 *Harv. Ed. Rev.* 521 (1972).

20. *See* Arrow, *supra* note 18; Spence, "Job Market Signaling," 87 *Q.J. Econ.* 355 (1973).

21. *See* Thurow, "Education and Economic Equality," 28 *Pub. Interest* 66 (Summer 1972); L.I. Berg, *supra* note 18.

22. *See* D. Gordon, *Theories of Poverty and Underemployment* (1972). *See also* Harrison, "Education and Underemployment in the Urban Ghetto," 62 *Am. Econ. Rev.* 796 (1972).

23. Contacts that bring knowledge and acquaintance are likely to engender sounder beliefs about minority groups. . . . Prejudice . . . may be removed by equal status contact between majority and minority groups in the pursuit of common goals. The effect is greatly enhanced if this contact is sanctioned by institutional supports (i.e., by law, custom or local atmosphere), and if it is of a sort that leads to the perception of common interests and common humanity between members of the two groups. G. Allport, *The Nature of Prejudice* 268, 281 (1954); *see* M. Deutsch & M. Collins, *Interracial Housing: A Psychological Evaluation of a Social Experiment* (1951); J. Dollard, *Caste and Class in a Southern Town* (1937); G. Myrdal, *An American Dilemma* (1944). *But see* Armor, "The Evidence on Busing," 28 *Pub. Interest* 90, 102-05 (Summer 1972); Armor, "The Double Double Standard: A Reply," 30 *Pub. Interest* 119, 127-29 (Winter 1973).

24. *See* Address of D. Campbell, *supra* note 4.

25. J. Coleman, *Equality of Education Opportunity* (1966).

26. *See, e.g.,* C. Jencks, *Inequality* 93-95, 255 (1972) [hereinafter cited as Jencks].

27. Carnoy, "Is Compensatory Education Possible?," in *Schooling in a Corporate Society* 175 (M. Carnoy ed. 1972).

28. 20 U.S.C. § 241 (1970).

29. *See, e.g.,* M. Wargo, G. Tallmadge, D. Michaels, D. Lipe, & S. Morris, "ESEA Title I: A Reanalysis and Synthesis of Evaluation Data From Fiscal Year 1965 Through 1970, March 1972" (unpublished document on file at American Institute for Research, Palo Alto, Cal.): Levin, "Effects of Expenditure Increases on Educational Resource Allocation and Effectiveness," in *School Finance in Transition* 177 (J. Pincus ed. 1974). A study prepared by the Rand Corporation acknowledges that

"[v]irtually without exception, all of the large surveys of the large national compensatory education programs have shown no beneficial results on average." The Rand Corporation, *How Effective is Schooling?* 124-25 (1971). The study, however, is quick to note that "the evaluation reports on which the surveys are based are often poor and research designs suspect." *Id.* at 125. The caveat points to such factors as non-random assignment of children, bias in project selection, "continuation" of the questionable evaluation procedures. *Id.* at 106-07. Consequently, "no . . . assurance is possible . . . that the survey evaluations used in arriving at such a verdict were themselves an accurate description of the real world. . . ." *Id.* at 105.

30. *See* J. Coleman, *supra* note 25; U.S. Commission on Civil Rights, *Racial Isolation in the Public Schools* (1967); Pettigrew, Useem, Normand, & Smith, "Busing: A Review of 'The Evidence,'" 30 *Pub. Interest* 88 (Winter 1973).

31. *See* Armor, "The Evidence on Busing," 28 *Pub. Interest* 90 (Summer 1972); Bowles & Levin, "The Determinants of Scholastic Achievement—A Critical Appraisal of Some Recent Evidence," 3 *J. Human Resources* 3 (1968); Cohen, Pettigrew, & Riley, "Race and the Outcomes of Schooling," in *On Equality of Educational Opportunity* 343 (F. Mosteller & D. Moynihan eds. 1972); Hanushek & Kain, "On the Value of *Equality of Educational Opportunity* as a Guide to Public Policy," in *id.* at 116; St. John, "Desegregation and Minority Group Performance," 40 *Rev. Ed. Research* 111 (1970); Smith, "Equality of Educational Opportunity: The Basic Findings Reconsidered," in *On Equality of Educational Opportunity, supra* at 230.

32. *See, e.g.,* D. Duncan, D. Featherman, & B. Duncan, *Socioeconomic Background and Achievement* (1972); Jencks; T. Ribich & J. Murphy, "The Economic Returns to Increased Educational Spending," 1974 (to be published in *J. Human Resources*); P. Wachtel, "The Effect of School Quality on Achievement, Attainment Levels and Lifetime Earnings," May 1974 (unpublished paper at the New York University Graduate School of Business Administration); Griliches & Mason, "Education, Income, and Ability," 80 *J. Pol. Econ.* 574 (1972); Sewell & Hauser, "Causes and Consequences of Higher Education: Models of the Status Attainment Process," 54 *Am. J. Agric. Econ.* 851 (1972); Taubman & Wales, "Higher Education, Mental Ability, and Screening," 81 *J. Pol. Econ.* 28 (1973).

33. *See* Bowles & Nelson, "The Inheritance of IQ and the Intergenerational Reproduction of Economic Inequality," 56 *Rev. Econ. & Statistics* 39 (1974).

34. *See generally* O. Duncan, D. Featherman, & B. Duncan, *supra*

note 32; Jencks; Bowles & Nelson, *supra* note 33; Griliches & Mason, *supra* note 32; Sewell & Hauser, *supra* note 32.

35. *See, e.g.,* R. Edwards, *supra* note 13; Bowles, *supra* note 14; Bowles & Gintis, "IQ in the U.S. Class Structure," 3 *Social Policy* 65 (Nov./Dec. 1972, Jan./Feb. 1973); Gintis.

36. *See* Gintis.

37. *See* Bowles, *supra* note 14; Bowles, *supra* note 19.

38. *See* T. Ribich & J. Murphy, *supra* note 32; P. Wachtel, *supra* note 32; Sewell & Hauser, *supra* note 32. Even when test scores are included in the analysis, the effect of schooling alone on earnings is not significantly reduced. *See* Bowles, *supra* note 14; Gintis; Griliches & Mason, *supra* note 32.

39. *See* Gintis.

40. *See* R. Edwards, *supra* note 13.

41. A related question is the degree to which educational credentials reflect differences in productivity as opposed to their role in screening employees for particular occupational positions without regard for productivity. *Compare* Taubman & Wales, *supra* note 32, *with* Layard & Psacharopoulos, "The Screening Hypothesis and the Returns to Education," 82 *J. Pol. Econ.* 985 (1974).

42. *See* text at _____ .

43. *See* Armor, *supra* note 31; Armor, *supra* note 23; Pettigrew, Useem, Normand, & Smith, *supra* note 30.

44. *See* G. Allport, *supra* note 23; M. Deutsch & M. Collins, *supra* note 23; J. Dollard, *supra* note 23; G. Myrdal, *supra* note 23. *See also* Epps, "The Impact of School Desegregation on Aspirations, Self-Concepts and Other Aspects of Personality," 39 *Law & Contemp. Prob.* no. 1, at (1975) for a review of the research on the impact of desegregation on self-esteem, and Cohen, "The Effects of Desegregation on Race Relations," 39 *Law & Contemp. Prob.* no. 1, at _____ (1975) for a review of the research on the impact of desegregation on interracial relations.

45. *See* Armor, *supra* note 23.

46. *See* T. Ribich & J. Murphy, *supra* note 32.

47. *See generally* P. Berger & T. Luckman, *The Social Construction of Reality* (1966); T. Kuhn, *The Structure of Scientific Revolutions* (1962); K. Mannheim, *Ideology and Utopia* (1936); R. Merton, *Social Theory and Social Structure* (1949); R. Merton, *The Sociology of Science* (1973); M. Polanyi, *Personal Knowledge* (1958); K. Popper, *Objective Knowledge: An Evolutionary Approach* (1972); Y. Elkana, "Rationality and Scientific Change," 1972 (unpublished manuscript at Department of History and

Philosophy of Science, Hebrew University, Jerusalem); Y. Elkana, "The Theory and Practice of Cross-Cultural Contacts," 1972 (mimeograph at Hebrew University, Jerusalem).

48. M. Polanyi, *supra* note 47, at vii.

49. *See* P. Berger & T. Luckman, *supra* note 47.

50. Samuelson, "Economists and the History of Ideas," 52 *Am. Econ. Rev.* 1, 17 (1962).

51. *But cf.* Serrano v. Priest, Civil No. 938,254 (Cal. Super. Ct., Apr. 10, 1974). In that case, conflicting evidence was introduced on the proper test to be applied in determining the quality of education existing within a school district, defendants urging the "pupil-achievement standard" while the plaintiffs urged a "school-district-offering standard." *Id.* at 52. The controlling dispute did not focus on the relationship between noncognitive theories of education and life attainment, and much of the opinion *was* cast in terms of the skills and cognitive achievement hypothesis. *See, e.g., id.* at 89. By holding for the plaintiffs, however, the court accepted the testimony that "Standardized achievement tests . . . are not appropriate for measuring the degree of attainment of many of the educational goals of the State. . . ." They "do not measure for progress in the affective domain—a pupil's personality characteristics, interests and attitudes, interpersonal skills and socialization skills." *Id.* at 91. In concluding that standardized test scores are not determinative of the quality of an educational program, the court also adverted to the parties' stipulation to the following:

That a child's self-concept can be improved by the educational process; that the educational process can reinforce a child's negative self-concept; that schools can, do, and should, play a role in providing a child with acceptable social values and behavior norms; that schools can, do, and should, play a role in equipping children with what it takes to get along in a technological society; that schools can, do, and should, play a role in making children better future citizens; that many components of a good education are not measured by pupil performance on achievement tests; that many aspects of a student's capabilities and progress are not measured by performance on achievement tests; and that the scope of skills measured by achievement tests is limited.

52. *See, e.g.,* Bowles, *supra* note 14; Bowles, *supra* note 19; Hess, Shipman, & Jackson, "Early Experience and the Socialization of Cognitive Modes in Children," 36 *Child Development* 869 (1965); Olim, Hess, & Shipman, "Role of Mothers' Language Styles in Mediating Their Pre-School Children's Cognitive Development," 75 *School Rev.* 414 (1967).

53. *See* J. Coleman, *supra* note 25.

54. *See* U.S. Commission on Civil Rights, *supra* note 30.

55. *See* R. Herrnstein, *IQ in the Meritocracy* (1973); M. Young, *The Rise of the Meritocracy* (1958); Bowles & Gintis, *supra* note 35.

56. In Hobson v. Hansen, 327 F. Supp. 844 (D.D.C. 1971), Judge J. Skelly Wright commented on the utilization of expert social science evidence in an adversary proceeding:

Plaintiffs' motion for an amended decree and for further enforcement has now been argued and reargued via a series of motions and written memoranda for one full year. During this time the unfortunate if inevitable tendency has been to lose sight of the disadvantaged young students on whose behalf this suit was first brought in an overgrown garden of numbers and charts and jargon like "standard deviation of the variable," statistical "significance," and "Pearson product moment correlations." The reports by the experts—one noted economist plus assistants for each side—are less helpful than they might have been for the simple reason that they do not begin from a common data base, disagree over crucial statistical assumptions, and reach different conclusions. Having hired their respective experts, the lawyers in this case had a basic responsibility, which they have not completely met, to put the hard core statistical demonstrations into language which serious and concerned laymen could, with effort, understand. Moreover, the studies by both experts are tainted by a vice well known in the statistical trade—data shopping and scanning to reach a preconceived result; and the court has had to reject parts of both reports as unreliable because biased. Lest like a latter day version of Jarndyce v. Jarndyce this litigation itself should consume the capital of the children in whose behalf it was brought, the court has been forced back to its own common sense approach to a problem which, though admittedly complex, has certainly been made more obscure than was necessary. The conclusion I reach is based upon burden of proof, and upon straightforward moral and constitutional arithmetic.

Id. at 859.

57. *See* J. Coleman, *supra* note 25.

58. *See generally,* Jencks; *On Equality of Educational Opportunity, supra* note 31.

59. *See, e.g.,* J. Guthrie, G. Kleindorfer, H. Levin, & R. Stout, *Schools and Inequality* (1971); E. Hanushek, *Education and Race* (1972); Bowles & Levin, *supra* note 31; Hanushek & Kain, *supra* note 31.

60. *See, e.g.,* Serrano v. Priest, Civil No. 938,254 (Cal. Super. Ct., Apr. 10, 1974); Robinson v. Cahill, 62 N.J. 473, 303 A.2d 273 (1973).

61. *See, e.g.,* Jensen v. State Bd. of Tax Comm'rs, Civil No. 24,474 (Ind. Cir. Ct., Jan. 15, 1973).

62. It seems inconceivable that prior to the *Coleman Report* a state would defend its arrangements to spend more money for the education of children in wealthy districts than in poor ones by arguing that dollars do not affect educational outcomes. I believe that this assertion would seem incredulous to a court. Common sense suggests that if higher expenditures

make a difference for children in wealthy districts, they also make a difference for pupils in poorer districts. At the least, a court should question why a state sanctions such high expenditures in wealthy districts if such resources are "wasted." *Cf.* Hobson v. Hansen, 327 F. Supp. 844 (1971), where the court stated that the defendants "cannot be allowed in one breath to justify budget requests to the Congress and to the District of Columbia City Council by stressing the connection between longevity and quality teaching, and then in the next breath to disavow any such connection before the court." *Id.* at 855.

63. *See* Carrington, "Financing the American Dream: Equality and School Taxes," 73 *Colum. L. Rev.* 1227 (1973).

64. *See generally* Clark, "Social Policy, Power, and Social Science Research," 43 *Harv. Ed. Rev.* 77 (1973).

65. *Compare* Cahn, "Jurisprudence," 30 *N.Y.U.L. Rev.* 150 (1955), *with* Clark, "The Desegregation Cases: Criticism of the Social Scientists' Role," 5 *Vill. L. Rev.* 224 (1960).

66. *See* Cohen, Pettigrew, & Riley, *supra* note 31, at 439-50, 356.

67. Armor, *supra* note 31.

68. The critics moved in quickly to question the criteria, statistical procedures, choice of studies reviewed, and other aspects of the Armor analysis. *See* Pettigrew, Useem, Normand, & Smith, *supra* note 30. The reply to this criticism also quickly followed. *See* Armor, *supra* note 23.

69. Armor, *supra* note 23.

70. Brown v. Board of Educ., 347 U.S. 483, 494 (1954).

71. In *Rodriquez* Justice Powell noted that in view of the division of opinion among "scholars and educational experts . . . [on] the extent to which there is a demonstrable correlation between educational expenditures and the quality of education," the judiciary should refrain from deciding the issue. 411 U.S. at 42-43. *See also id.* at n.86.

72. Rivlin, "Forensic Social Science," 43 *Harv. Ed. Rev.* 25 (1973).

73. *Id.*

74. While in most school litigation expert testimony is offered by both parties to the dispute, see, *e.g.,* Serrano v. Priest, Civil No. 938,254 (Cal. Super. Ct., Apr. 10, 1974); in Robinson v. Cahill, 118 N.J. Super. 223,287 A.2d 187 (1972), only the plaintiffs introduced expert witnesses on the relationship between expenditures and achievement.

75. *See* note 56 *supra.*

76. And even if the court's own expert is "objective," by what criteria, for example, is he to choose between two competing economic theories?

77. *See* Address by D. Campbell, *supra* note 4.

6

Education of the Disadvantaged: A Problem of Human Diversity

Edmund Gordon*

Once again, we find ourselves considering problems of educating low-income and low-status persons, with a sense of *déjà vu* and an even greater sense of embarrassment which borders on shame. I feel *déjà vu* because I know that we have done this before. I sense embarrassment in part because of the contrast between the affluence of the resort area of this conference and the conditions of life in which the people we have come to talk about struggle hour after hour, day after day. That embarrassment changes to shame as I recall that it was fifteen years ago when I first started attending meetings like this and more than twenty years ago that I began professionally to try to do something about changing the life chances of the children of the poor. In those fifteen, twenty, twenty-five years my life circumstances have greatly improved—as have yours, largely as a result of the fact that helping the poor has become a respectable professional and research pursuit. Yet the life chances of the people we are supposed to be helping have changed very little. In the early 1960s we did not know what needed to be done to make school achievement independent of social class and social caste. Most of us thought that more money, extra effort, improved technology would solve the problems of educating the minority poor. Here in the mid-1970s most of us agree that to the extent that these things have been tried, they have not solved the problems. Despite cumulative appropriations of what must be nearly $30 billion and an enormous amount of sometimes misdirected effort and equivocal research, we still don't know how to make school achievement and developmental opportunity independent of social position. Our best general predictor of success in school is successful birth into a middle- or upper-class Caucasian family.

I am ashamed that our efforts have been so futile. I am not so much ashamed that we have not succeeded but that we have not sufficiently tried. Ten years ago I predicted that we might not succeed, that we might not try hard enough, and that some of us would try to blame the victims for our lack of success. Permit me to be so immodest as to quote from my own writing, "Help for the Disadvantaged," published in the *American Journal of Orthopsychiatry*, vol. 35, no. 3, April 1965.**

*Columbia Teachers College

It is tempting to anticipate that the current outbreak of enthusiasm will produce results consistent with the quality of time, energy, money and concern being expended. However, in dealing with problems for which solutions are based upon significant social and scientific advances, popularity and productivity do not necessarily go hand in hand. In the present situation there is grave danger that work with the unfortunate may, unfortunately, become a fad. So great is the danger, that it may not be out of place to suggest that the appropriate attitude at this time for those truly concerned with the long-range goal of significantly improving the life chances of disadvantaged populations, is one of restraint and considered action. It is obviously not the quantity of effort that will solve the problems here involved. Work of high quality which more correctly reflects scientific and social reality finally will give this result.

Having recently reviewed much of the research and most of the current programs concerned with the disadvantaged, I am impressed by the pitifully small though growing body of knowledge available as a guide to work in this area. The paucity of serious research attention to these problems has left us with little hard data, many impressions and a few firm leads. What is distressing, however, is the slight representation of even this research in the rapidly proliferating programs. Much of what is being done for and to the disadvantaged seems to be guided by the conviction that what is needed is more of those things we feel we know how to do. Despite the fact that much of our knowledge and techniques of behavioral change have proved to be of dubious value in our work with more disadvantaged populations, these same procedures and services now are being poured into the new programs. Although service to the disadvantaged has become popular, there remains a serious lack of basic research on the developmental needs of such children as well as on the applicability of specific techniques of behavioral change to their directed development.

It is not intended to suggest that the extension of known techniques to these previously neglected populations is entirely negative. Humanitarian concern calls for the use of all possible resources to relieve human suffering. What is suggested is that there may be vast differences between what we feel we know how to do and that which must be done. To settle for what we ''know'' while we ignore new concepts and the exploration of new leads renders us less humanitarian, less scientific and less professional. Unfortunately, our society has permitted us to place the burden of proof of the worth of our services on the beneficiaries of these services rather than on the professional worker or the system in which he functions. This has permitted us to ignore or rationalize our failures. If real progress is to be made, we as professionals must assume greater responsibility for the success of our work, recognizing that it is our role to better understand these problems and to design techniques and measures more appropriate to their solution. It must be clear to all of us that more counseling is not going to solve the problems of a population we have defined as nonverbal. Reading texts in technicolor are not going to solve the reading problems of youngsters who we claim are deficient in symbolic representational skills. Reduced demand curricula and work-study programs are not going to advance the conceptual development of youth whose conditions of life may have produced differential patterns of intellectual function which are so frequently interpreted as evidence of mental retardation rather than as challenges to improved teaching. Occupational information and aspirational exhortation are not going to provide motivation for youth who have yet to see employment opportunities or employed models with whom they can identify and accessible routes to achievement. Intensive psychotherapy is going to have little impact on the neurotic mother whose energies are consumed by the struggle to meet the minimum physical needs of herself and her children. Similarly, preschool programs which capture the form but not the content of some of the more advanced models are doomed to failure. Nor will good programs which are not followed by greatly strengthened primary, elementary and secondary school programs make a major difference in the lives of these children. Improved and expanded mental health services will mean little unless our nation comes to grips with the problems of economic, political and social opportunities for masses of disfranchised and alienated persons.

To honor our traditional concern and for the sake of the disadvantaged, it is essential to recognize the limitations of the current effort. If the products of serious research were as well represented in this effort as the good intentions, the enthusiasm, the "band-wagon hopping" and the grant hunting, we could be more hopeful that meaningful solutions would be found to the problems of the disadvantaged. Unfortunately, some of us viewing the current efforts are left with a nagging suspicion that the net result of many of these programs will be to provide (for those who choose to interpret it so) empirical evidence of fundamental inferiority in these populations we are trying so hard to help. When five or ten years from now the populations we now call disadvantaged are still at the bottom of the heap, those who only reluctantly acceded to the current attempts to help may revive their now dormant notions of inherent inferiority to explain why all the money and all the effort have failed to produce results. The more likely fact will be that we shall have failed to produce the desired results simply because we shall have failed to develop and apply the knowledge and the skill necessary to the task. Unless the issues are more sharply drawn, we may not even then recognize the nature of our incompetencies. We see in retrospect that bleeding was an ineffective cure for the plague, not because the barber-surgeons did not know how to draw blood, but because they did not sufficiently understand the nature of the disease with which they were dealing.

To honor our commitments to science and professional service, we must understand the limitations of our knowledge and our practice. Much of what we do is based on the hopeful assumption that all human beings with normal neurological endowment can be developed for participation in the mainstream of our society. We believe this because we have seen many people from a great variety of backgrounds participate and because we want to believe it. But we do not yet have definite evidence to support our belief. We operate out of an egalitarian faith without knowing whether our goals are really achievable. Yet it must be our aim, not only as scientists and professional workers, but as humanitarians as well to determine the potential of human beings for equality of achievement. If in the light of our most sophisticated and subtle evaluations, we conclude that such equality is not generally achievable, if in spite of the best we can do it seems likely that some of our citizens will remain differentiated by their own biology, then we shall merely have answered a persistent question. We will still have no evidence that group differences per se imply any inability on the part of particular individuals to meet the demands of society. We will then be able to turn our energies to helping individuals meet those demands. And if, on the other hand, as we believe, true equality of opportunity and appropriate learning experiences will result in equality of achievement, then we must so organize our professional services and our society that no person is kept from achieving that potential by our indifference to his condition, by the inadequacy or inappropriateness of our service, or by the impediments society deliberately or accidentally placed in his path. It is not an unhopeful paradox that the only way we shall ever know whether equality of human achievement is possible is through providing for all our citizens, privileged and underprivileged, the kind of service and society that assumes it is possible and makes adequate provision for the same. As we pursue the "Great Society" let us not be misled by the plethora of activity or companions in the cause.**

A great deal has happened in the U.S. since 1965. Even though we do not have final answers, we know somewhat more in 1975 than we knew in 1965. Now, as then, it may be beneficial to think more about what we know and to try to generate better conceptions of what needs to be done.

Research related to the education of the disadvantaged has covered a wide variety of approaches and issues. However, most of the work can be classified under two broad categories: (1) the study of population characteristics and (2) the description and evaluation of programs and practices. In the first category, investigators have focused on eliciting deficits in the conditions or behaviors of the target population—the ways the groups studied differ from alleged "normal" populations. In the second category, which is only now beginning to build a body of theoretical and descriptive material, investigators have attempted to describe what goes on in the schools and to relate such variables as school structure, teaching methods, or a myriad of special services to student achievement. While the first type of study has been conducted largely by educational psychologists, specialists in testing and measurement, and developmental psychologists, the second has been the product of anthropologists, sociologists, social psychologists and, on a more informal level, teachers who have worked in the school system. Studies in the former group precede those in the latter and have tended to place responsibility for failure on the children and their background. Although studies in the latter group grew out of the same philosophy and were developed with the goal of designing compensatory experiences for identified deficiencies, newer research in this group has begun to emphasize the role of the educational experience in producing the observed dysfunctions in performance.

Population Characteristics

Studies within this category can be further divided between investigations of performance and life conditions. The largest body of research concerns what is called "intellectual performance." Most studies in this area have concentrated on IQ test results and consistently support the hypothesis that high economic, ethnic, or social status is associated with average or high IQ scores, while the reverse—low economic, ethnic, or social status—is associated with low IQ scores relative to the other group.[1]

** Reprinted with permission of the *American Journal of Orthopsychiatry* (New York: Orthopsychiatric Association, Inc., 1965).

A by-product of descriptions of the relationship between socio-economic status (SES) and/or ethnic groups and intellectual performance has been the attempt to interpret results with speculations as to causes. On the one extreme, investigators have seen their work as supporting genetic determinants of intelligence;[2] at the other end of the spectrum, researchers have viewed their findings as support for environmental determinants of intelligence.[3] However, the majority of investigators now interpret the data as reflecting a complex and continuous interaction between hereditary and environmental forces.[4]

In contrast to the huge body of statistics and analyses concerning intellectual status as judged by standardized tests, only limited effort has been directed at differences in cognitive style. There has been some attempt to factor-analyze standardized tests,[5] and one substantial investigation deals with differential strengths and deficits in the intellectual functioning of different ethnic groups.[6]

Another area of considerable research is that of the plasticity of intellectual development. This work has been conducted by both those investigators who would support the dominance of genetic determinants of intelligence and those who adhere to the importance of environmental factors in determining the quality of intellectual functioning.[7] Building upon Binet's early concern with the trainability of intellectual functioning and Montessori's efforts to modify intellectual performance in children with subnormal performance levels, investigators have worked with all but the most gifted children.[8] There is only one major longitudinal study which attempts to relate intellectual development to differences in environmental conditions: this investigation traces the development of a sample of twins reared in dramatically different environments over a period of 25 years and shows significant variations in their level of intellectual functioning.[9]

Short-term studies dealing with the plasticity of the intellect have led to mixed feelings. Some reports show intervention to be associated with no significant change in intellect as measured by intelligence test scores.[10] Others have shown only modest change, and many of these results have been interpreted as reflecting a normal fluctuation in intellectual function from one test period to another.[11] On the other hand, some studies have demonstrated significant increases when pretreatment and posttreatment scores are compared.[12] Unfortunately, these improvements have not yet been tested in large populations, and no follow-up studies have been made after a long enough time period to justify the conclusion of permanent change.

However uncertain these data may be, there remains among many researchers the conviction that intelligence is largely a trainable function. A number of studies have attempted to relate trainability to age.[13] One of the more pessimistic positions is that, due to the lack of powerful and positive environments, the processes underlying intellectual functioning rapidly lose their plasticity after three years of age.[14] More optimistic reports show typical IQ gains of 10 points with adolescents; however, such gains are still only half as much as can be generated with younger subjects.[15] Studies of such programs as Harlem Prep and Upward Bound support the hypothesis that big changes in achievement, if not in intellectual functioning, can be effected in adolescence.[16]

In general, the data lead one to conclude that, as measured by standardized tests, significant changes in the quality of intellectual function are more likely to occur to the extent that there are powerful positive changes in environmental interactions, and that these changes occur early in the life of the individual. The fact that malleability may decrease with age, however, may not reflect a recalcitrant character of intellectual functioning. Rather, what may be operating is the tendency to rely on earlier patterns of stimulus processing in the absence of exposure to powerful and different environmental input. It has been suggested, for example, that the decreasing malleability of intellectual functioning among the urban disadvantaged may be the result of prevailing school practices, which do not provide new positive inputs and which may even reinforce previous maladaptive patterns of functioning.[17]

As measured by grades, standardized tests, and high school attrition, there is an abundance of data showing that disadvantaged populations do not perform as well academically as do more advantaged populations. Their lower achievement and higher dropout rates have been related to such environmental factors as low income (resulting from limited education and occupational level of parents);[18] health and nutritional deficits;[19] childrearing patterns which do not prepare the children for school;[20] cultural differences between disadvantaged students and their teachers;[21] and racial isolation and discrimination as well as other school-related variables.[22]

Demographic studies have fallen into several categories. The more traditional type has concentrated simply on economic, employment, and educational levels of the family as they relate to the children's school performance.[23] A newer type attempts to go beyond a strictly economic kind of data and, centering its interest around what has become known as the "culture of poverty," examines various aspects of family disorganization such as consensual marriage, out-of-wedlock children, divorce rates, broken homes, and matriarchal or female-dominated households.[24] One or more of these configurations are then related to children's performance in school. However, the concept of the "culture of poverty" has recently been highly criticized, and a few investigators have begun to focus on those patterns which may be adaptive within the school in a depressed environment, even if they are not totally adaptive within the school environment.[25]

The relationship between specific childrearing practices and academic achievement has been copiously studied. Concentrating particularly on mother-child interaction, investigators have identified maternal influences which may create such characteristics as language behavior, task orientation, and value commitment in the disadvantaged child. Implicit in these studies is the assumption of a middle-class norm, and most studies compare interactions in disadvantaged families with those in more privileged households.[26] So far there has been little attempt to describe the variations in childrearing practices among lower-class or minority-group families, and there has been scant research on those elements in these families which lead to academic success.[27]

A neglected area in educational research has been the investigation of the relationship between health status and school performance. Data on the effects of poverty on health and nutrition are substantial, all showing that disadvantaged populations suffer from poorer health care, a greater proportion of premature deliveries, higher mortality rates, poorer nutrition, etc.[28] There is also some research indicating the possible effects of the health of the pregnant mother on the intellectual functioning of the developing child.[29] However, there are scant data on the relationship between the individual's own health and nutritional condition and his/her cognitive development or academic performance in school. There is also little research showing the mechanism by which poor health affects performance. Most investigators assume this to be the case, however, and conclude that poor health may result in lowered performance through impaired efficiency or reduced energy levels, or, in more serious conditions, through impairment of the nervous system.[30]

With the concentration still on demographic characteristics, racial and economic segregation of a disadvantaged population as it relates to school performance is one of the most heavily researched areas.[31] Investigations have consistently led to the conclusion that low school achievement is associated with the concentration of low-income and minority-group students in separate school situations (the one possible exception being Oriental students in segregated situations).[32] A small group of studies focused on separating out the effects of economic from racial or ethnic isolation, and the predominating view has been that economic segregation is even more deleterious to school performance than is racial segregation. However, the point has often been made that it is impossible to draw strictly comparable socioeconomic groups across racial or ethnic lines.[33]

Related to this research on economic and racial isolation have been those investigations which focus on the effects of desegregation on school achievement. Studies in this area take two forms: those which measure achievement before and after desegregation, and those which examine the relationship between the degree of ethnic or economic mix and the level of achievement. Research in the former group has arrived at the conclusion that differential response to desegregation is based on such factors as the reasons for desegregation, students' expectations of how they are going to be evaluated in the integrated setting, and the degree of organization or disorganization in the integrated as compared to the segregated setting.[34] Studies in the latter group, which are usually based on larger populations than the former, show that desegregation is more likely to be associated with heightened achievement for the minority-group child when the receiving school population is predominantly white and middle-class.[35] However, caution is often expressed about applying these findings to smaller populations and individual cases because of the intervening variables, such as student expectations or school disorganization.[36]

An area of research which is crucial to the interpretation of any results on population characteristics is that of testing and measurement. Most of the effort in this area has been directed toward validation of the content and construction of existing standardized tests and the predictive value of test scores.[37] Research on testing and measurement of disadvantaged populations had been largely concerned with the relative predictability of specific tests for minority-group versus white students, the efficacy of traditional as opposed to culture-fair and other innovative tests, and the problems inherent in testing minority-group populations.[38] More recently, there has been interest in factorial analyses of test data; the aim of this research is to identify specific patterns of functioning in different populations in order to understand variations in skills as well as deficits.[39] A small group of investigators has also begun to research the effects of intelligence and achievement tests on such variables as teacher attitudes, student expectations, and school administrative policy.[40]

Programs and Practices

In contrast to the rather well-designed and detailed research into the characteristics of disadvantaged groups, the description and evaluation of educational programs and practices for these children have generally been superficial. There has been little effort at matching treatment efforts with the nature and needs of the subject population. Programs are often designed on the basis of long-standing theoretical models or the special biases of researchers. Program evaluations stress little more than the fact or the magnitude of the intervention and a general assessment of the impact. What is lacking are detailed descriptions of the nature of the intervention, the interaction between the intervention and the learner, and the outcome of a particular treatment or intervention program when used with specific kinds of learners.

Research on programs and practices can be grouped into four types on the basis of the scope of the subject treated. Most prominent are studies which report on large-scale projects such as Head Start, Title I, More Effective Schools, Project Talent, and Upward Bound. A second group of studies reports on specific programs and services in the schools. A third attempts to relate administrative and organizational change to student progress. Changes in attitudes and orientations of school personnel are the subject of the fourth type.

Large-scale projects run the gamut from preschool to college. The aim of these programs has been to provide intensive compensatory education—school readiness, remediation of lagging achievement levels, or supply of the necessary skills for success in higher education—to disadvantaged students. With the exception of preschool projects, where centers have developed experimental programs, most of the large-scale programs have been more intensive versions of standard curriculum and teaching methods.[41] The projects have been evaluated by pretreatment and posttreatment test scores and subjective evaluations of student progress; little research has focused on describing the exact nature of program input or on following the subjects' longitudinal development once the treatment is completed.[42]

Project evaluations in general indicate that compensatory education has failed. In those cases where positive findings are reported, it has been difficult to identify or separate treatment effects responsible for the result from Hawthorne effects (the impact of a changed situation itself) or from Rosenthal effects (the result of changed expectations). However, recent reviews of the research criticize evaluation methods and indicate that the tests used may be insensitive instruments for tapping whatever progress might be made.[43]

Evaluations of specific programs and services in the schools include studies of such elements as counseling programs, tutoring projects, special service personnel (bilingual teachers, reading specialists, paraprofessionals, etc.), curricular innovations (such as bilingual or ethnically oriented studies and teacher-student developed materials), and changes in teaching techniques (individualized instruction, teaching machines, team teaching, etc).[44] Here too, much of the intervention has been a continuation of traditional programs and services, and little effort has been given to matching the specific needs of the population with the intervention instituted. Only projects focusing on curriculum relevance and individualized instruction have been directed toward matching learner and the learning experience.[45] Adequate evaluations of these programs have also been scarce. Programs tend to introduce a number of services simultaneously, and it has been difficult to identify, even in successful programs, the element or elements which are most instrumental in causing change.[46]

Until recently, studies of administrative and organizational change in the schools have been directed primarily at desegregation. Research on desegregation in Southern school districts describes the politics and process of desegregation, including the implementation of federal guidelines and community resistance to change.[47] Literature on Northern desegregation deals with the same issues, but also describes the development and implementation of specific desegregation plans such as bussing and transfer programs, school zoning, or the creation of the middle-school and education parks.[48] As reported earlier, findings on the effects of desegregation tend to show that the single most important school factor influencing academic achievement for black and other minority-group children (as well as low-income students) is that the classroom be made up predominantly of white middle-class students.[49]

More recent organizational and administrative changes in the schools include experiments with homogeneous and heterogeneous groupings, changes in pupil-teacher ratio, and the implementation of parent and community involvement. Major research on ability grouping shows that it has no measurable effect on student achievement.[50] When homogeneous grouping causes de facto segregation, it may, in fact, lower the achievement of minority-group and low-income students.[51] Changes in pupil-teacher ratio have been studied by a number of investigators with differing viewpoints; and as might be expected, the conclusions reached vary according to the point of view of the researcher.[52] Since extensive parent and community involvement are still relatively new areas for investigation, there is no definitive work on this subject. However, a number of researchers have hypothesized that the influence of parent and community forces in the schools may provide a powerful force for instituting needed changes in both the children and the schools.[53] Several investigators have linked the "sense of fate control," which has been found necessary for school achievement, with parental involvement in the schools.[54] One major research project concludes that the only hope for narrowing the spatial, cultural, and emotional gap between school personnel and school children is through introducing parents and other community members into the schools.[55]

There is a rapidly growing body of research which relates teacher attitudes and expectations to student performance. Studies in this area point to the debilitating effect of low teacher expectations.[56] A number of investigations have been aimed at identifying factors which form teacher attitudes and behavior.[57] So far, this research is inconclusive, but indications are that it is not social class background alone, as previously thought, which creates either positive or negative attitudes and behaviors toward disadvantaged children.[58] Without any clear indications of what causes teachers' negative attitudes toward low-income and minority-group children, a few studies have focused on the possibilities of changing teacher attitudes. Research in this area is difficult to interpret, since positive changes are usually measured by answers to a questionnaire[59] and thus indicate little more than the fact that teachers have learned more "acceptable" responses. It has been hypothesized that artificially changing teachers' expectations of student performance can create measurable change in student achievement; but data on this subject also remains inconclusive.[60]

A brief examination of the work which has been done over the past few years indicates that many investigators are turning their attention to the vitally important problem of quality education for the many disadvantaged youngsters in our society. These concerned educators are directing their efforts to a variety of problems. But the variety of questions to be answered only serves to indicate the complexity of the problems, and there remain, in addition to the many unanswered questions, many problems with the answers we have and the methods used in obtaining them.

1. A common fault among those investigators concerned with population characteristics among disadvantaged groups has been the tendency to view all the many groups involved as constituting one homogeneous population, with a common set of problems and deficits and a common set of needs. The *real* problem may lie in the degrees and types of differences between groups.

2. A result of this hasty attitude on the part of one set of researchers has been the tendency of those educators concerned with compensatory program design to search for *the* program or *the* remedial approach which will prove to be the magic answer to this problem which is called "the disadvantaged learner." Attention is diverted from the problem of designing specific approaches to benefit specific learner characteristics.

3. The tendency in past research has been to concentrate on quantitative data to the neglect of those qualitative analyses and process variables which may provide more useful keys to successful individual treatments.

4. Much of the research evaluation has simplistically tended to relate single variables, avoiding the more realistic conclusion that the complex process of behavior determination must be the result of complicated interactions of many variables and conditions.

5. In a failure to maintain the traditional research stance of objectivity, investigators too often have yielded to the assumption that those variations from the assumed norm which their research discovers constitute deficits to be overcome in the education of the groups being studied. There has been an almost general neglect of the possibility that

these differences, once carefully defined and determined, may be used as helpful features in the design of new educational treatments which are more appropriate for the children to whom they are applied.

6. Far too frequently, evaluators of specific programs or practices have gone no further than to look for certain improvements in the program's subjects; when these changes are not noted, the immediate assumption is that the compensatory practice does not work; some have even gone so far as to assert that compensatory education as a whole cannot work. These kinds of assertions have been made with no attempt to determine the quality of the program used, or even if the program as described was actually implemented. Often the *fact* of intervention is assumed to be sufficient effort to merit results, and when those results are not forthcoming, the tendency is to place the blame on the pupils, not on those responsible for assuring the quality of the program.

7. Sloppy experimental design is a frequent fault in research to date, and with the increasing complexity of our society, improvement in the use of controls cannot be expected unless a great deal of expert attention is turned to this problem.

8. Too much of educational research has been turned to the purpose of proving a hypothesis, and too little research effort has been spent in that kind of systematic observation which leads to theory generation. Given our lack of success so far in this vital field, all our efforts should be bent toward the fostering of new ideas, instead of the reworking of old and tired arguments and failures.

In reviewing briefly, as we have done here, the progress to date in research on the disadvantaged, I think we find in our list of weaknesses several important insights which not only apply to future research, but also have valuable implications for those of us who are more concerned with practice. Although it is certainly important to bring increased technical competence to research issues, improved research design simply cannot compensate for the lack of programs or material available for study. This is the problem we cannot avoid facing: if we can gain any general impression of the field, it is that not one program of demonstrated effectiveness has yet been successfully implemented on a large scale.

Two basic problems lie behind this disturbing failure. The first is the crippling lack of funds for meaningful large-scale innovation. In a report prepared for the Civil Rights Commission recently, Jablonsky and I estimated that the cost of an effective effort would be $100 billion per year, which is just about double what we are presently spending on education in the United States.[61] In a more modest estimate, prepared for the same body, David Cohen suggested that it would be necessary to spend $10 billion more each year than we now are spending. Even this lower figure contrasts dramatically with the $1 to $2 billion yearly which is in actuality allotted to the effort to bring about quality education for disadvantaged children and youth.

However, even when money is available, we face another critical shortage: a lack of effective ideas for the best utilization of available funds. By 1966, when I worked with Wilkerson on a national survey of compensatory education programs, we found very little that was substantially different from traditional approaches to education. In 1968, conducting a similar survey with Adelaide Jablonsky, I did observe a few programs with promise, but their reflection in widely accepted practice was minimal. Still another study, conducted by Hawkridge in 1969, found few programs associated with significant changes in the level of achievement. In review of his data, it becomes clear that he was no more successful than my colleagues and I in identification of substantive innovations in this field that is so desperately in need of change.

Obviously, then, we are not putting high creative conceptions or the necessary national resources into this task. I am not impressed that we are utilizing the valuable research information which is available to us. What are some of the conceptions and research leads which we can use immediately to improve the outlook for the attainment of a higher level of effort?

Upon completing the study with Wilkerson, I concluded that more effort was needed to improve technical educational procedures designed to change cognitive function. I felt then that we greatly needed to improve formal teaching behavior. I am certainly not ready to back away from this position now, but I do think there is increasing evidence that this cognitive emphasis may not really be the most productive pursuit at this time; the field of education and its supporting sciences may not be able to move quickly enough to make meaningful modification in cognitive functions a viable goal. Zigler has suggested that affective processes may be more malleable and that we may better be able to modify affective than cognitive functions. In addition, we have good reason to believe that appropriate changes in affective state are likely to result in significant changes in the quality of cognitive function. I must emphasize that I do not mean to abandon a concern for understanding and improving teaching. I do believe that most aspects of the teaching-learning process can be identified and refined, that this process can be systematized, and that educability is primarily a function of the quality of the learning experiences to which pupils are exposed. However, although I believe that teaching may become scientifically based, I think we may not at present be able to identify sufficiently and apply those underlying scientific principles to the task at hand. However, we do seem to have better leads toward levers for involving ourselves and pupil environments in the changing of attitudes, feelings, motivation, and task involvement.

Without demeaning the cognitive aspect, I think we may still conclude that effort directed at better understanding and more appropriately designing and controlling the social-psychological conditions in which learning occurs may, in the present period, be a more appropriate strategy. The rationale, viewed in light of the current sociopolitical scene, is obvious and lends additional support for this position. Many argue that formal education, divorced from the main currents of the life experiences of our pupils, is perceived by them as irrelevant and retards academic development. As a result, such issues as ethnic studies, participatory democracy, and decentralization are seen as possible levers for making the learning experience more relevant to the conditions of life, and more conducive to success for greater numbers and varieties of students.

Once we have conceded the importance of social and psychological conditions to success in learning, we will find ourselves with a valuable tool if we extend our use of it far enough. In the past, our concern with analysis of pupils has been characterized by a heavy emphasis on identification of levels of achievement. What we need now is greater qualitative analysis of learning behaviors, combined with the matching of this broader range of characteristics to the design of appropriate learning environments and experiences. Of course, this is not a simple task, since we know very little about the ecological or psychological environments of our pupils. Clinical psychology has at least provided us with models for investigating psychological environments, that is, the way in which individuals perceive their effective environment; but this expertise has not yet been systematically applied to education. The study of ecological environments, that is, the physical, social, and political conditions of the surroundings in which learning occurs, is still in its infancy. Yet it is increasingly clear to me that differences in achievement are more related to the circumstances and conditions in which learning occurs and the extent to which the environment supports the mastery of the learning task than they are a function of variations in measured intelligence. Looking at these variations in intelligence, we don't see a sufficient relationship between alleged potential and actual performance to say that intelligence, as we know how to measure it, is the sole or most important factor; but the conditions under which learning occurs, the degree of support they provide for learning—these appear to be very important indeed.

Now if we agree that there exists wide variance in the character and quality of the learning behaviors that children bring to school, and if we agree that the conditions under which learning and development occur can influence the quality of achievement, then it is possible to conclude that relationships between quality of learning behaviors and quality of learning conditions may be of importance as determinants of quality of achievement. If this somewhat complex statement of a rather simple concept holds, it has critical significance for conceptualizing the central issue in the education of the poor or disadvantaged.

For more than a score of years the concept of "equal educational opportunity" has dominated our thinking. The concept grew out of court litigations around issues related to ethnic segregation in public education. As a nation, we have affirmed our commitment to equality of educational opportunity for all and have translated this to mean equal access to the educational resources provided to the populus through public funds. But if my little paradigm is permitted to stand, equal opportunity may not adequately reflect the implicit commitments of a democratic, diverse, and pluralistic society. If what we are committed to is to make educational and other achievements independent of ethnic group, social class, sex group, religious group, or geographic origins, concepts such as diversity and justice may be more worthy of our tradition. Diversity focuses our attention on those aspects of difference or variance in human characteristics which have relevance for pedagogical and developmental intervention. Justice moves beyond a concern for distributive equality to a concern for distributive sufficiency. When we speak of distributive sufficiency, we are immediately forced to look to questions of need rather than share. The functional education question becomes, "What do the special characteristics of this person suggest that the intervening institutions of society do to enable this individual to function with adequacy and satisfaction?" The answer to that question should dictate the quality and quantity of the educational or developmental intervention. The program indicated may violate our more narrow conceptions of equality, but given the compelling facts of diversity in our people, it may be the only way in which we approach justice. For the next period in the history of our nation, let us build on our commitment to equality of opportunity with a new commitment to the nurturance of human diversity and the achievement of social justice.

Notes

1. Kennedy, W.A., Van De Riet, Vernon, and White, James C. *A Normative Sample of Intelligence and Achievement of Negro Elementary School Children in the Southeastern United States.* Chicago, Ill.: Society for Research in Child Development, Serial No. 90, 28 (6), 1963.

2. Jensen, Arthur R. "Social Class, Race, and Genetics: Implications

for Education," *American Educational Research Association Journal,* 5: 1-42, 1968.

Jensen, Arthur R. "How Much Can We Boost IQ and Scholastic Achievement?" *Harvard Educational Review,* 39: 1-123 1969. (ED 023 722)

Shuey, Audrey M. (ed.). *The Testing of Negro Intelligence.* 2d ed. New York: Social Science Press, 1966.

3. Hunt, J. McVicker. *Intelligence and Experience.* New York: Ronald Press, 1961.

Hunt, J. McVicker. "Black Genes—White Environment," *Transaction,* 6: 12-22, June 1969.

4. *IRCD Bulletin,* 5(4), Fall 1969. [See especially "Behavior-Genetic Analysis and Its Biosocial Consequences" by Jerry Hirsch (pp. 3-4: 16-20). This article also appears in the February 1970 issue of *Seminars in Psychiatry,* Henry M. Stratton, Inc., publisher.]

5. Cleary, T. Anne, and Hilton, Thomas L. "An Investigation of Item Bias," *College Entrance Examination Board Research and Development Report 65-6, No. 12.* Princeton, N.J.: Educational Testing Service, 1966. (ED 011 267)

Cleary, T. Anne. "Test Bias: Validity of the Scholastic Aptitude Test for Negro and White Students in Integrated Colleges," *College Entrance Examination Board Research and Development Report 65-6, No. 18.* Princeton, N.J.: Educational Testing Service, 1966. (ED 018 200)

6. Stodolsky, Susan S., and Lesser, Gerald S. *Learning Patterns in the Disadvantaged.* New York: Yeshiva University, ERIC Information Retrieval Center on the Disadvantaged, 1967. (ED 012 291)

7. Bloom, Benjamin S. *Stability and Change in Human Characteristics.* New York: John Wiley, 1965.

8. Examples of this research are:

Schwebel, Milton. *Who Can Be Educated?* New York: Grove Press, 1968.

Bereiter, Carl, and Englemann, Siegfried. *Teaching Disadvantaged Children in the Preschool.* Englewood Cliffs, N.J.: Prentice-Hall, 1966.

Hurley, Rodger. *Poverty and Mental Retardation: A Causal Relationship.* New York: Vantage Books, 1969.

9. Skodak, M., and Skeels, H.M. "A Followup Study of Children in Adoptive Homes," *Journal of Genetic Psychology,* 66: 21-58, 1945.

10. Granger, R.L., et al. *The Impact of Head Start. An Evaluation of the Effects of Head Start on Children's Cognitive and Affective Development.* Vol. 1. Report to the U.S. Office of Economic Opportunity by the Westinghouse Learning Corp. and Ohio University, 1969.

11. Thorndike, Robert L. *Head Start Evaluation and Research Center*

Annual Report, September 1966-August 1967. New York: Teachers College, Columbia University, 1967. (ED 020 781)

12. Smilansky, Sarah. "Promotion of Preschool, 'Culturally Deprived' Children through Dramatic Play," *American Journal of Orthopsychiatry,* 35: 201, 1965.

13. Thorndike, E.L. *The Measurement of Intelligence.* New York Teachers College, Columbia University, 1927.

14. Bloom, *Stability and Change*, 1965.

15. Smilansky, Moshe. "Fighting Deprivation in the Promised Land," *Saturday Review*, 82: 85-86, 91, October 15, 1966.

16. Hawkridge, David G., et al. *A Study of Selected Exemplary Programs for the Education of Disadvantaged Children: Part II, Final Report.* Palo Alto, Calif.: American Institutes for Research in the Behavioral Sciences, 1968. (See especially the evaluation of the New York City College Bound Program.) (ED 023 777)

Guerriero, Michael A. *The Benjamin Franklin High School Urban League Street Academies Program. Evaluation of ESEA Title 1 Projects in New York City, 1967-68.* New York: Center for Urban Education, 1968. (ED 034 000)

17. Leacock, Eleanor B. *Teaching and Learning in City Schools: A Comparative Study.* New York: Basic Books, 1969. (ED 033 989)

Jensen, Arthur R. "Cumulative Deficit in Compensatory Education," *Journal of School Psychology*, 4: 37-47, Spring 1966.

18. For a collection of this literature see:

Goldstein, Bernard. *Low Income Youth in Urban Areas, A Critical Review of the Literature.* New York: Holt, Rinehart and Winston, 1967. [The "Annotated References for Chapter One" (Family of Orientation) are especially relevant.]

19. Birch, Herbert G. *Health and the Education of the Socially Disadvantaged Children.* Presented at the Conference on "Bio-Social Factors in the Development and Learning of Disadvantaged Children," Syracuse, N.Y., April 1967. (ED 013 283)

Birch, Herbert G., and Gussow, Joan D. *The Disadvantaged Child— Health, Nutrition and School Failure.* New York: Harcourt, Brace and World, 1970.

20. Goldstein, *Low Income Youth*, 1967.

21. A recent conference sponsored by the U.S. Office of Education addressed itself to the question "Do Teachers Make a Difference?" The papers which were presented which soon will be available as conference proceedings discuss this topic along with other teacher influences. The

relevant papers are by: James Guthrie, Stephen Michelson, Eric Hanushek, Henry Levin, George Mayeske, and Alexander Mood.

22. U.S. Commission on Civil Rights. *Racial Isolation in the Public Schools*. Washington, D.C.: U.S. Government Printing Office, 1967. (Vol. I: ED 012 740: Vol. II: ED 015 959)

23. Goldstein, *Low Income Youth*, 1967.

24. Several examples are:
Moynihan, Daniel P., and Barton, Paul. *The Negro Family: The Case for National Action*. Washington, D.C.: U.S. Office of Policy Planning and Research, 1965.
Lewis, Oscar. *La Vida: A Puerto Rican Family in the Culture of Poverty—San Juan and New York*. New York: Random House, 1966.
Valentine, Charles A. *Culture and Poverty: Critique and Counter-Proposals*. Chicago, Ill.: University of Chicago Press, 1968. (ED 035 707)
The latter, while covering the concept of the culture of poverty, is critical of its usage.

25. See, for example:
Lewis, Hylan. "Culture, Class, and Family Life among Low-Income Urban Negroes," in *Employment, Race, and Poverty*. New York: Harcourt, Brace and World, 1967.
Valentine, *Culture and Poverty*, 1968.

26. The work of Robert Hess and his associates done at the Urban Child Study Center at the University of Chicago should be noted. A representative piece is:
Hess, Robert D., and Shipman, Virginia C. *Maternal Attitudes toward the School and the Role of Pupil: Some Class Comparisons*. Paper presented at the 5th Work Conference on Curriculum and Teaching in Depressed Urban Areas, Teachers College, Columbia University, 1966.

27. An exception to this is:
Davidson, Helen H., and Greenberg, Judith W. *Traits of School Achievers from a Deprived Background*. New York: City University of New York, City College, 1967. (ED 013 849)

28. For a comprehensive overview of a wide variety of studies in this area, see:
Scrimpshaw, Nevin, and Gordon, John. *Malnutrition, Learning and Behavior*. Cambridge, Mass.: M.I.T. Press, 1967.

29. The work of Lilienfeld and Pasamanick during the 1950s is still among the best concerning possible effects of various pregnancy experiences. Two of the best references include:
Pasamanick, Benjamin, and Lilienfeld, A.M. "Association of Maternal and Fetal Factors with the Development of Mental Deficiency, I: Abnor-

malities in the Prenatal and Perinatal Periods," *Journal of the American Medical Association*, 159: 155, 1955.

Lilienfeld, A.M., Pasamanick, B., and Rogers, Martha. "The Relationship between Pregnancy Experiences and the Development of Certain Neuropsychiatric Disorders in Childhood," *American Journal of Public Health*, 45: 637-43, 1955.

30. No investigator has been more critical of the lack of research in this area than Birch, who recently published a comprehensive and incisive volume emphasizing which specific mechanisms actually affect performance. The book's particular strength is its inclusion of references to research which substantiates what has been assumed for some time. See:

Birch, Herbert G., and Gussow, Joan D. *The Disadvantaged Child: Health, Nutrition and School Failure*. New York: Harcourt, Brace and World, 1970.

Cravioto, J., Delicardie, E.R., and Birch, H.G. "Nutrition, Growth and Neurointegrative Development: An Experimental and Ecologic Study," *Pediatrics*, 38: 319, 1966.

31. For the most complete review of the research in this area, see:

St. John, Nancy H. *Minority Group Performance under Various Conditions of School Ethnic and Economic Integration: A Review of Research*. New York: Teachers College, Columbia University, ERIC Clearinghouse on the Disadvantaged, 1968. (ED 021 945)

32. Coleman, James S., et al. *Equality of Educational Opportunity*. Washington, D.C.: U.S. Office of Education, 1966. (ED 012 275)

33. St. John, *Minority Group Performance*, 1968.

34. Three sources offer a comprehensive discussion of these three factors:

Katz, Irwin. *Desegregation or Integration in Public Schools: The Policy Implications of Research*. New York: Teachers College, Columbia University, ERIC Information Retrieval Center on the Disadvantaged, 1967. (ED 015 974)

McPartland, James. *The Segregated Student in Desegregated Schools: Sources of Influence on Negro Secondary Students: Final Report*. Baltimore Md.: Center for the Study of Social Organization of Schools, Johns Hopkins University June 1968. (ED 021 944)

St. John, Nancy. *Minority Group Performance under Various Conditions of School Ethnic and Economic Integration: A Review of Research*. New York: Yeshiva University, ERIC Information Retrieval Center on the Disadvantaged, 1968. (ED 021 945)

35. Coleman et al., *Equality of Educational Opportunity*, 1966.

36. St. John, *Minority Group Performance*, 1968.

Weinberg, Meyer. *Desegregation Research: An Appraisal*. Bloomington, Ind.: Phi Delta Kappa, Commission on Education and Human Rights, 1968.

[Also see articles by Meyer Weinberg in *Integrated Education* from Volume 4 (6), 1966 to Volume 6 (6), 1968.]

37. For example:

Testimony of Dr. Roger T. Lennon as Expert Witness on Psychological Testing in the Case of Hobson, et al. vs. Hansen, et al. (Washington, D.C. Schools). New York: Harcourt, Brace and World, 1966.

38. The Educational Testing Service, Princeton, N.J. has done much work in this area. See:

Campbell, Joel. "Testing Culturally Different Groups," *College Entrance Examination Board Research and Development Report 63-4, No. 14*. Princeton, N.J.: Educational Testing Service, 1964.

39. Stodolsky and Lesser, *Learning Patterns in the Disadvantaged*, 1967.

Minuchin, Patricia. *Patterns and Correlates of Achievement in Elementary School Children*. New York: Bank Street College of Education, 1965.

40. Rosenthal, Robert, and Jacobson, Lenore. *Pygmalion in the Classroom: Teacher Expectation and Pupils' Intellectual Development*. New York: Holt, Rinehart and Winston, 1968.

41. A notable exception to this is the work Susan Gray and her associates have done at George Peabody College.

Gray, Susan W., and Klaus, Rupert A. "An Experimental Preschool Program for Culturally Deprived Children," *Child Development*, 36: 887-898, 1965.

Another exception is the Perry Preschool Project in Ypsilanti, Mich. See:

American Institute for Research in Behavioral Sciences, Palo Alto, Calif. *Perry Preschool Project, Ypsilanti, Michigan. One of a Series of Successful Compensatory Education Programs*. 1969.

42. References to preschool projects which are exceptions to this generalization include:

Wolff, Max, and Stein, Annie. *Six Months Later, A Comparison of Children Who Had Head Start with Their Classmates in Kindergarten—A Case Study of Kindergartens in Four Public Elementary Schools, Study I*. New York: Yeshiva University, Ferkauf Graduate School, 1966. (ED 015 025)

Wolff, Max, and Stein, Annie. *Long Range Effects of Preschooling on Reading Achievement, Study III*. New York: Yeshiva University, Ferkauf Graduate School, 1966. (ED 015 027)

Klaus, Rupert, and Gray, Susan W. *The Early Training Project for*

Disadvantaged Children—A Report after Five Years (Monograph), Vol. 33(4). Chicago, Ill.: Society for Research in Child Development, 1968. So far no one has studied longitudinal development after treatment at the primary, intermediate, secondary, or college levels.

43. Scrimpshaw and Gordon, *Malnutrition, Learning and Behavior*, 1967. (See especially Part VIII, pp. 464-542.)

44. A cross section of studies which discuss these elements includes:

Channon, Gloria. "The More Effective Schools: An Evaluation," *Urban Review*, Vol. 2, February 1967. (ED 013 845)

Khanna, J.L. *Human Relations Training Program*. 1969. (ED 032 965)

Rigrodsky, Seymour. *Speech Therapy for Disadvantaged Pupils in Non-Public Schools: An Evaluation of the New York City Educational Project 1966-67*. New York: Center for Urban Education, Committee on Field Work and Evaluation, Sept. 1967. (ED 026 756)

Shaw, Merville C., and Rector, William. *Influencing the Learning Environment by Counseling with Teachers*. Monograph #6, July 1968. (ED 022 233)

American Institutes for Research in the Behavioral Sciences, Palo Alto, Calif. *Diagnostically Based Curriculum: A Compensatory Program; An Evaluation*. Washington, D.C.: Superintendent of Documents, U.S. Government Printing Office, 1969.

Jablonsky, Adelaide. *A Selected ERIC Bibliography on Individual Instruction, ERIC-IRCD Urban Disadvantaged Series #2*. New York: Teachers College, Columbia University, ERIC Information Retrieval Center on the Disadvantaged, January 1969. (ED 027 358)

45. Glasser, Robert. *The Education of Individuals*. Penn.: Learning Research and Development Center, University of Pittsburgh, 1966. (ED 014 785)

Glasser, Robert. *Objectives and Evaluation: An Individualized System*. Penn.: Learning Research and Development Center, University of Pittsburgh, 1967. (ED 015 844)

46. For example, in the Title I, ESEA project in Camden in 1966-67, a number of global variables including class size, teaching conditions, corrective reading, medical services, audio-visual programs, and teachers aides were introduced simultaneously, preventing isolation and evaluation of those specific variables which actually had impact. See:

Camden City Schools, New Jersey. *Title I: E.S.E.A., 1966-67, Projects of the Camden City Board of Education—Evaluative Report*. 1967. (ED 018 473)

47. Orfield, Gary. *The Reconstruction of Southern Education. The Schools and the 1964 Civil Rights Act*. New York: Wiley-Interscience, 1969.

48. Weinberg, Meyer. *Integrated Education: A Reader*. Beverly Hills, Calif.: Glencoe Press, 1968.

49. Coleman et al., *Equality of Educational Opportunity*, 1966.

50. Passow, A Harry, Goldberg, Miriam, and Tannenbaum, A.J. *Education of the Disadvantaged: A Book of Readings*. New York: Holt, Rinehart and Winston, 1967.

51. Esposito, Dominick. *The Relationship between Ability Grouping and Ethnic and Socioeconomic Separation of Children*. New York: Teachers College, Columbia University, ERIC Information Retrieval Center on the Disadvantaged (in press).

52. For example, the Center for Urban Education did an evaluation of New York City's "More Effective Schools" program which criticized it.

Kravetz, Nathan, et al. *The More Effective Schools Program*. New York: Center for Urban Education, 1966.

The United Federation of Teachers responded with a criticism of the Center for Urban Education's report.

Schwager, Sidney. *An Analysis of the Evaluation of the More Effective Schools Program Conducted by the Center for Urban Education*. New York: United Federation of Teachers, 1967.

Hawkridge, 1968. (Hawkridge named "More Effective Schools" an exemplary compensatory program.)

53. For a recent and complete discussion see:

Lopate, C., Flaxman, E., Bynum, E., and Gordon, E.W. "Some Effects of Parent and Community Participation on Public Education," *Review of Educational Research*, February 1970. (ED 027 359)

54. Coleman et al., *Equality of Educational Opportunity*, 1966.

55. Leacock, Eleanor B. *Teaching and Learning in City Schools: A Comparative Study: Psychosocial Studies in Education*. New York: Basic Books, 1969.

56. Rosenthal, Robert, and Jacobson, Lenore. *Pygmalion in the Classroom: Teachers' Expectations and Pupils' Intellectual Development*. New York: Holt, Rinehart and Winston, 1968.

57. Look for the future publication entitled:

How Do Teachers Make a Difference? by the Division of Assessment and Coordination, Bureau of Educational Personnel Development, U.S. Office of Education, Washington, D.C.

Two more references should also be helpful:

Webster, Staten W. (ed.). *The Disadvantaged Learner: Knowing, Understanding, Educating*. San Francisco, Calif.: Chandler, 1966. (ED 013 266)

Flaxman, Erwin. *A Selected Bibliography on Teacher Attitudes:*

ERIC-IRCD Urban Disadvantaged Series #1. New York, Teachers College, Columbia University, ERIC Clearinghouse on the Urban Disadvantaged, January 1969. (ED 027 357)

58. Webster, *The Disadvantaged Learner*, 1966.

59. Flaxman, *A Selected Bibliography on Teacher Attitudes*, 1969.

60. Rosenthal and Jacobson, *Pygmalion in the Classroom*, 1968.

61. Gordon, Edmund W., and Jablonsky, Adelaide. "Compensatory Education in the Equalization of Educational Opportunity," report commissioned by the United States Commission on Civil Rights, November 1967. *The Journal of Negro Education*, Vol. 37, No. 3 (Walter C. Daniel, ed.), Howard University, Washington, D.C., Summer 1968.

7

Equality and Diversity in Education

*Arthur R. Jensen**

Gordon's long and complex chapter, which I have been asked to discuss, touches upon so many of the important problems of the current educational scene that a comprehensive discussion of all its points would require a work at least as long. Since that is impossible here, I shall try to focus my discussion on only a few of the main points that seem to most warrant further attention.

At many conferences on the problems of education, we often emphasize points of disagreement more than points of common agreement. It would be worthwhile if educators and behavioral scientists could spend some time discussing their points of agreement. We need more consensus as to (1) what precisely the problems are that we should be most concerned with, (2) what is known about the conditions and causes underlying these problems, and (3) what is known that can feasibly contribute to a solution. Each of us is more qualified, by experience and interests, to contribute to one of these facets more than to the others. There may well be a sizable area of disagreement among professionals concerning each of these points. Yet, unless educators and behavioral scientists can find some common core of agreement about some of the problems and the relevant facts, we haven't even taken the first step toward a solution.

Technological advances of any kind depend upon a hard core of agreed-upon facts, principles, and theories. Our physicists and engineers could never have harnessed the energy of the atom or put a man on the moon without a tremendous common core of agreement among all those involved in these achievements. One of the chief aims of behavioral scientists today should be to determine just how large a core of agreement there exists as a basis for discussing educational problems. If there is not some substantial body of knowledge upon which we can agree at this point, then one might justifiably demand to know just what social scientists and educational researchers have been doing in their heyday of multimillion-dollar grants from federal research funding in the years since 1960. It would be most interesting and important to know just what is the lowest common denominator of agreement among researchers and educators concerning educational problems, their nature, causes, and solutions. If the areas of

---

* University of California, Berkeley.

agreement are scant, then it is about time we found out why, and proceeded to obtain the crucial factual information that must compel agreement among all rational persons. A most important property of scientific investigation is that it can compel agreement despite philosophic, ideological, or political differences—that is, unless science itself is corrupted by politics, as was so well exemplified by Lysenkoism in the U.S.S.R. Are there realities of human psychology that exist independently of our differing political and social philosophies and upon which all must agree that need to be taken into account if we are to find ways for public education to serve better the whole society?

Big problems like "educational inequality" have to be greatly subdivided even to be discussed, to say nothing of being solved.

Dividing the problem should be a basic principle, and we need to keep on dividing the problem until we get down to the raw specifics about which we can determine just what can or cannot be done in quite concrete terms. It can be likened to troubleshooting in repairing machinery or electronic equipment—a progress through a branching tree, going from recognition of a general problem ("for some reason this car doesn't run"), through various diagnostic branches to specific causes ("the fuel line is clogged"). At this point possible or probable solutions can be evaluated in terms of the *reality principle*—that is, in light of known resources, costs, and social and political conditions. Problem solution must take into account the gap between utopia and the U.S. in 1975. In the real world, such as it is, public education is the art of the feasible.

A first step in dividing the problem of educational inequality can be shown as follows:

	Individual	Group
Input	II	IG
Conditions	CI	CG
Output	OI	OG

Now, instead of one problem—inequality—to talk about at a high level of generality and abstraction, we have six problem areas to talk about, some more crucial than others. Of course, each of these could be further subdivided, as would be necessary if we are to come fully to grips with them, which we can't do at this broad-gauge conference.

What does the above table mean? It can be likened to an industrial manufacturing process, as unappealing as this may seem in talking about the education of children. But the analogy is useful up to a point.

Input refers to the raw materials with which the school must deal. It is the total nature of the children (whatever the causes of that nature) the day they enter school; also it is the extraschool influences that shape the children when they are outside of school, influences over which the school itself has virtually no control, and which the children bring with them every day that they attend school.

Conditions refers to what the school itself is and does, in terms of physical plant, curriculum, quality of teachers, staff morale, instructional facilities, management of instruction, pupil-teacher ratio, special services, and so on.

Output refers to scholastic achievement in the strict sense of the term (How much of what was taught did the children actually learn?) as well as to other benefits of the school experience to the individual, in terms of overall personal development and self-realization.

Inequalities in each of these factors—input, conditions, and output— can be viewed and studied from the standpoint of *Individual* differences or *Group* differences. The meaning of "individual differences" is obvious— differences between persons as individuals. "Group differences" refers to statistical differences between various racial, ethnic, or social class groups in the school population. Such groups are aggregates of individuals who happen to be classified together because they share some features in common—the income bracket of their parents, their neighborhoods, or their racial or national origins.

The statistics of groups have properties of their own which do not inhere in individuals as such. Means and standard deviations and correlations and heritability coefficients and percentage overlaps are group statistical phenomena with no referents to any given individual. A most important lesson that must be taught to everyone is that none of these statistics inhere in the individual and that no one's fate is determined by his or her particular group mean or any other statistic computed from aggregations of persons. Statistics can describe groups. They do not determine individual fates.

About the input factors we can ask whether the problems of inequality are better dealt with as individual differences or as group differences, or if the inequalities need to be classified in ways that make some of them better dealt with as individual differences and others as group differences.

Cultural difference and perhaps some personality, attitudinal, and value differences may best qualify for consideration in the group input (GI) cell. But these factors, in my opinion, are minor contributors, among all the input variables, to variance in the output, particularly scholastic achievement in the traditional sense.

What we identify as cognitive ability differences are the input factor which is undoubtedly the most highly correlated with output. Two fundamental things can be said here on which I believe the evidence is so overwhelming as to command practically universal assent among all who

128

conscientiously study and understand the evidence. If I am wrong in supposing this, then we are not as far ahead as I had imagined, and we'll have to go back to our spadework in basic psychology.

First, there is the *fact* that there is a factor of general cognitive ability which accounts for the largest part of individual differences in all tests or measurements involving complex cognitive processes. A tremendous diversity of tests tap this general factor. It underlies the positive correlations among all tests of complex mental functions. The general factor, traditionally called "general intelligence," is not the whole of mental ability, but it is more important than any other single ability identified by the factor analysis of mental tests. Technically, this general factor is the first principal component in any large battery of diverse, complex mental tests. Standard intelligence tests measure individual differences in this general factor, although they do so imperfectly and some tests do a better job than others. A number of these various tests (so as to achieve as much diversity as possible) given at, say, yearly intervals from ages 6 to 18, and averaged (preferably in the form of a factor score on the first principal component) would provide a very reliable and valid measure of the individual's standing, relative to others, in "general intelligence."

Second, there is the *fact* that objective measures of scholastic achievement (i.e., how much and how well the child learns of what is specifically taught in school) show a large general factor. The most reliable measure of this general scholastic achievement factor for an individual is obtained by averaging a large number of assessments taken at regular intervals over the entire course of schooling.

Even if the cognitive ability tests consist of nothing that is a part of the school curriculum, and if the achievement tests measure only what is actually taught in school, the first principal component or general factor of the ability tests and the first principal component of the scholastic achievement tests are so highly correlated in a population which has had more or less the same scholastic experience as to be regarded as virtually the same factor. This one general factor, however, usually accounts for slightly more of the total variance in the ability tests than in the scholastic achievement tests, since other factors involving motivation, personality, special aptitudes for particular subjects, and the like, enter more into scholastic achievement than into performance on cognitive ability tests. But the largest source of variance (i.e., individual differences) is essentially the same general factor of cognitive ability.

Thus, this general factor is the single most important input variable as far as scholastic performance is concerned. All the large-scale studies of the correlates of scholastic achievement, both in Europe and in the United States, are consistent in showing very much greater correlations between *input* and *output* (as defined above) than between *conditions* and *output*.

Table 7-1

Percentage of Total Variance and Average IQ Difference in WISC-R Full-scale IQs Attributable to Each of Several Sources

Source of Variance	Percent of Variance	Average IQ Difference
Between *races* (independent of SES)	14 ⎫ 22	12
Between *SES* groups (independent of race)	8 ⎭	6
Between families (within race and SES groups)	29 ⎫ 73	9
Within families	44 ⎭	12
Measurement Error	5	4
Total	100	17

For our present purpose it seems unnecessary to go into the *causes* of input differences. The school takes input differences as given. Whatever their causes, we know they are complex, they are not the same for all individuals or all groups, and, as we have so well learned from the innumerable researches of the 1960s, they are not superficial or easily changed. They have to be reckoned with.

In discussing input problems, it has become almost habitual to focus on *group* differences. Racial and social class differences are a reality, of course, but we are too apt to lose sight of the fact that the largest part of the problem of input differences would remain even if all the group differences to which we have given so much attention were completely eliminated.

I have recently analyzed some data on the newly revised Wechsler Intelligence Scale for Children (WISC-R) (Wechsler, 1974), which is one of our best measures of the general cognitive ability factor. The data are based on a perfectly random sample of all California school children, ages 6 to 12, except that the sample was drawn in such a way as to equalize the numbers of black and white children (622 of each). (All other minority groups were omitted from this analysis.) We can divide up the total variance in WISC-R IQs to show what percentage of the total variance (i.e., the mean squared differences among all individuals) is independently attributable to each of several sources. The results, shown in Table 7-1, will be surprising to many.

We see that race (white-black) and socioeconomic status (a 10-point scale of SES) together account for only 22 percent of the total variance. Average differences *between* families within each race and SES group account for 29 percent, and differences among children *within* families account for 44 percent. Thus, even in a school with 50 percent whites and 50 percent blacks (any other split would yield a lower racial variance), the race plus SES differences would contribute less than one-fourth of the total cognitive abilities variance that the schools have to deal with.

The last column in Table 7-1, headed "Average IQ Difference," means that the average IQ difference found by averaging the IQ differences between all possible pairs of children, e.g., all possible pairs of black versus white children, would show an average difference of 12 IQ points—which is just the same as the average IQ difference found between pairs of children—full siblings—from the same family. The average difference between children (all of the same race) selected from different SES groups is only 6 IQ points, which is less than the average difference between families in the same SES category! The average difference between the IQs of the same individual tested on two occasions is 4 points. The average difference between pairs of persons selected at random from the total population is 17 IQ points.

What all this means is that if we are concerned with input differences in the variable that counts the most in schooling, we should probably be more concerned about individual differences than about group differences—*unless* it could be shown that the group differences are in some way essentially different from individual differences. If they are not essentially different, then differences between individuals classified as members of different groups can be treated as individual differences.

In fact, it is very hard to find differences between groups that do not behave just like individual differences as far as abilities and schooling are concerned. Though there are average group differences on cognitive ability tests, we find it impossible either by direct inspection or by fine-grained statistical analyses to discriminate between the intelligence test protocols of black and white children. There is just nothing you can find in the child's test performance itself that will tell you whether a child with an IQ of, say, 100 is black or white. The same is true of scholastic achievement tests.

Moreover, the correlations among various tests are the same for black as for white children, and tests of cognitive ability predict scholastic performance the same for black children as for white (Jensen, 1974a, 1974b; Humphreys, 1973). In dealing with individual children, race and social class per se seem to make no difference. I have never seen any demonstration that individual prescription for any educational purpose need take race into account at all.

Group differences in the distribution of scholastic aptitudes and attitudes, however, may take on an importance of their own under two main sets of conditions: (1) when low aptitudes or poor attitudes for schooling become heavily concentrated in certain schools, as we have seen in some urban ghetto schools, and (2) when "representative equality" becomes the main criterion of the school system's effectiveness.

The two problems, (1) and (2), I believe are related. Much of the first problem is a result of frustration leading to aggression and demoralization due to insistence on a more or less uniform, lock-step curriculum throughout the grades in every school of the system, regardless of the input differences. This, in turn, is fostered by a misguided emphasis on representative equality of educational treatments. The notion of representative equality in education, when applied to the input and output factors, is based on the false premise that the observed group differences in input and output are merely signs of discrimination, racism, or social injustice. I advocate focusing on individuals in education, and evaluating educational programs in terms of their effectiveness in maximizing individual potential rather than in terms of equalizing group differences. However, I would not ignore group identity in research to evaluate school outcomes, because if, say, black and white children equated on key input variables showed up as significantly different on the output variables, I would want to find out why and see what might be done about it.

Now we come to the *conditions* part of our table. Here is where educational equality can be most clearly assessed and inequalities most easily remedied, given the will and the resources to do so. The main point concerning equality of conditions that most educators and behavioral scientists now agree on is that equality shouldn't be interpreted as *uniformity* of curriculum, instruction, services, and facilities, but *equality of opportunity for a diversity of conditions suited to the diversity of individual abilities and needs of the pupils*.

It seems quite justified to pay attention to group differences in the category of *conditions*. Equality of educational opportunity will not become a reality until all groups in society enjoy equality of conditions as here defined. The *quality* of education should be the same for all. This is largely what Gordon means when he speaks of achieving "justice in a diverse society."

One point that we don't understand well enough is the interaction of conditions and input and output. Parents generally view poor output as poor conditions. There is some truth in this. When *output* is poor and is associated with a demoralized school atmosphere, the conditions for learning are adversely affected for all children, regardless of the objective equality of those conditions which are directly under the school's control. The input and output aspects of a school seem to carry more weight with parents than the school conditions per se. This is in large measure the basis of public resistance to bussing and enforced racial integration of the schools. It is largely responsible for the "white flight" from the schools and neighborhoods when these measures are instituted. But one of the most cogent arguments for bussing, etc., is that in some cases it has proved to be the only way of getting equality of conditions. As long as schools are de facto segregated, it is argued, the system under white majority control will not grant equality of conditions. This whole issue has never been sufficiently examined and discussed publicly. The problems of racial integration of schools are problems more of differing values and attitudes and the public's perception of these, than of differing academic abilities per se.

Problems in this realm are whitewashed by school people so often that it is difficult to obtain much objective evidence, and the largely sub rosa discussion of these problems consists mostly of word-of-mouth personal anecdotes of teachers, children, and parents who have had experience in forcibly integrated schools. A thorough description and diagnosis of these conditions may prove painful, but it may be a necessary step toward improving the situation. The U.S. Senate Committee report on school vandalism, headed by Senator Birch Bayh, is an important though disturbing attempt to describe and diagnose a part of this problem in the schools. Again, it is not a racial problem per se, but neither is it uncorrelated with school input and output variables.

The overriding question among educators today is how to manage conditions so as to improve output. We are getting away from thinking of this as *equalizing* output and are now thinking more in terms of trying to make the outcomes of education *beneficial* to every child, even though this may explicitly mean quite different outcomes for different children. This goal, which seems to me very realistic, runs into direct conflict with the goal of representational equality of output, which I consider inappropriate (not necessarily unrealistic) as an *educational* goal. If group differences are diminished as a by-product of attempting to maximize the benefits of education to all individuals, all well and good. But educational programs should not be evaluated on that basis.

Concern with representational equality—i.e., the same percentage of every group meeting a given criterion—*exaggerates* group differences. Because of the nature of the normal or Gaussian distribution of abilities and achievements, a relatively small difference in group averages can make for enormous differences in the *percentage* of persons in each group who fall above or below some given selection cutoff. It will be much less fruitful educationally to go on emphasizing these statistical percentage differences than to focus on the scholastic progress made by individual children.

Three classes of educational conditions have been proposed for increasing the benefits of education to all children. These are: (1) the "problem of the match" or "readiness," (2) aptitude × training interaction, and (3) computer-assisted instruction.

(1) Gordon emphasizes first the "problem of the match," an old concept first labeled by Piaget and popularized in education circles by Hunt. It simply means matching the instruction to the child's "readiness" or "entry skills." It amounts to teaching the child what he or she is able to learn under the prevailing instructional procedures. Children differ greatly in readiness for various school learning tasks. Good teachers have always taken account of this, but our past emphasis on equality of conditions, I fear, has led us to neglect readiness factors. Much that we struggle to teach in the

primary grades could well be postponed to later grades for many children, entirely to their benefit. A great deal of early failure experiences in school could be cut down by more attention to readiness.

There are dangers in this, too, of course. Putting off instruction in, say, reading or arithmetic, because of a supposed lack of the pupil's readiness, can be used as an excuse for not teaching at all. So the readiness factor requires a great deal of thought and planning to avoid abuse. But if intelligently managed, it could have considerable consequences in the economy of teaching and in final achievement levels.

Preschool programs are of dubious value in terms of cognitive development because so much of what constitutes development at that age is a matter of maturation. What early cognitive development programs have concentrated on teaching children are things they all will learn to do spontaneously a year or so later in any case, and there seem to be no residual effects of the early instruction in these cognitive skills (Jensen, 1973, pp. 72-102; Kohlberg, 1968).

(2) The *aptitude × training interaction,* called "ATI" for short, is another possible means for coping with individual differences. What it means is that we can get better achievement from everyone by using different teaching methods for different persons than by teaching everyone in the same way. By varying instructional techniques, the teacher can presumably optimize each pupil's scholastic achievement and greatly reduce the wide range of individual differences that results with more or less uniform instruction for everyone.

So far in educational research, the fruits of ATI are a mere hope, not a demonstrated fact. Unreplicated examples involving very narrow parts of the school curriculum can be pointed to, as well as subjects × methods interactions in the very limited tasks of the experimental psychology laboratory, but as yet no broad effective instructional program involving ATI for scholastic subject matter has been demonstrated. No one has yet found a way of appreciably reducing the achievement differences predicted by IQ differences, which, as I pointed out earlier, contribute the largest part of the variance in scholastic performance (Jensen, 1975, pp. 69-70).

Since rote learning and memory abilities have been found to show rather low correlations with IQ, it has been suggested that perhaps greater use can be made of these abilities in school learning; and in fact the few instances of ATI that have been demonstrated as in the learning of arithmetic, have consisted of rote learning versus conceptual learning of the subject matter. Low-IQ children were somewhat more successful with rote learning instruction while high-IQ children did better under instruction emphasizing a more abstract and conceptual approach (Anderson, 1941; Cronbach, 1967). Bereiter's suggestion** of making the instruction less

** Editor's note: See "IQ Differences and Social Policy" by Carl Bereiter in Chapter 8 of this volume.

cognitively loaded for some children with below-average IQs, while making more use of their rote learning and memory abilities, which are not highly tied to IQ, is in the same vein.

(3) *Computer-assisted instruction*, called "CAI," has permitted a greater diversity of instructional techniques that can be managed by a single classroom teacher charged with teaching some twenty or thirty children. In fact, some CAI programs have used as many as 70 different program variations per 100 pupils, in order to deal with the problem of individual differences in learning styles and learning rates. But what this research has consistently shown is that while it raises the average level of achievement for all children, it also increases the spread of individual differences. It seems to be impossible to maximize the overall mean and minimize the variance (i.e., individual differences) at the same time. Differences still are highly related to IQ.

Nevertheless, CAI is beneficial. With it, more children acquire essential scholastic skills and knowledge than would do so in the same amount of time in ordinary class instruction. Also, CAI greatly reduces certain motivational barriers for slow-learning children. Since each child works individually at a program that best suits his or her own pace and level of readiness, differences in performance are visible only to the teacher and do not act as stigma and punishment to the pupil's self-esteem, as so often results when the pupil's performance in class is visible to all the other classmates.

A third approach now being seriously discussed in educational circles is a much greater diversification of school curricula and organization after the elementary grades, at about 12 years of age. The range of abilities and interests is too great for all to benefit from continuation in academically oriented curricula. European school systems have long recognized this fact, but unfortunately in Europe the educational diversification after age 12 or so has been more closely associated with social class differences than we know is warranted in terms of the wide distribution of academic talent in all social classes.

A greater diversity of curricula and educational goals, involving more vocational education, work apprenticeship programs in industry, and the like, could be tolerated in the United States only if selection for various programs were highly flexible and based on frequent and continuing assessment of the child's progress through the first several years of school. At age 10 there should be a comprehensive assessment of the child's level of mastery of basic scholastic skills needed for coping in an industrialized society. For those who fall below a certain reasonable standard, the school should make special provisions for bringing children's mastery of the basics up to a functional standard between the ages of 10 and 12. The techniques of "mastery learning" seem most appropriate in this context.

The years between 12 and 15 could be a period of increasing diversity of programs in which pupils could find what path is best suited to their abilities and aspirations. After age 15 no one would be required to attend school in the traditional sense. It would be optional for those who wish to prepare for college or pursue technical training. A wide variety of options should be available for further specialized training outside the usual high school setting. At present, public high schools have become prisons for many youths who all too clearly realize they are failing to benefit in any way from the narrow academic program the school has to offer. Beyond the acquisition of functional skills in the three R's, many children simply do not find further "book learning" or lectures and class discussions of topics at an abstract level at all in line with their interests or ambitions. They are simply turned off by it, and when it is repeatedly forced upon them, they react with frustration and finally apathy or aggression. Not all persons can be made to fit the same mold. A traditional, scholar-oriented kind of education has been oversold and overvalued in America, and this value system is the root of many of the present problems of compulsory universal public education.

Equality of educational opportunity—by all means. But we may question the dogma of compulsory school attendance for the many who fail to benefit beyond the elementary grades or who are forced to stay in the system merely to obtain formal credentials, often amounting in fact to no more than a certificate of attendance, needed to gain entry into the job market. What we see, as a result, is an inflation of educational credentials. It can be counteracted only by "decredentializing" the job market and insisting that hiring and promotion of personnel be based strictly on job-related skills and aptitudes. Selection procedures should be made more job-specific and not be based upon formal educational credentials remotely, if at all, related to the particular job or training program applied for. Objective job-validated tests and work-sample assessments are much preferable to general educational credentials, and their wider use would give greater incentive for the acquisition of functional job-related skills.

The schools should not be charged with solving all the social and economic problems of society. Yet they must mesh with the economic system in ways that can benefit in some degree all who are required by law to spend a decade or more of their lives in school. A growing youthful population, a shrinking job market, the technologizing of many forms of work, and the increasing variance in scholastic abilities in the population associated with markedly differential birthrates among population groups differing in scholastic aptitudes—such factors can be expected to add to the problems of the schools in the near future. Either universal compulsory education will have to evolve rapidly into something quite different from the traditional pattern, or we can expect future historians to look back upon it as the greatest dinosaur among our public institutions.

References

Anderson, G.L.A. "A Comparison of the Outcomes of Instruction under Two Theories of Learning." Unpublished doctoral dissertation, University of Minnesota, 1941.

Cronbach, L.J. "How Can Instruction Be Adapted to Individual Differences?" In Cagné, R.M. (ed.), *Learning and Individual Differences.* Columbus, Ohio: Merrill, 1967, p. 23-39.

Humphreys, L.G. "Implications of Group Differences for Test Interpretation," *Assessment in a Pluralistic Society.* Proceedings of the 1972 Invitational Conference on Testing Problems. Princeton, N.J.: Educational Testing Service, 1973, p. 56-71.

Jensen, A.R. *Educability and Group Differences.* New York: Harper & Row, 1973.

————. "Ethnicity and Scholastic Achievement," *Psychological Reports,* 1974a, 34, 659-668.

————. "How Biased Are Culture-loaded Tests?" *Genetic Psychology Monographs,* 1974b, 90, 185-244.

————. "The Price of Inequality," *Oxford Review of Education,* 1975, 1, 59-71.

Kohlberg, L. "Early Education: A Cognitive Developmental View," *Child Development,* 1968, 39, 1013-1062.

U.S., Congress, Senate, Committee on the Judiciary, *Our Nation's Schools—A Report Card: "A" in School Violence and Vandalism*, 94th Cong., 1st sess., 1975, p. 1.

Wechsler, D. *Manual of the Wechsler Intelligence Scale for Children—Revised.* New York: Psychological Corporation, 1974.

8

IQ Differences and Social Policy

Carl Bereiter*

The argument of this chapter consists of qualifications to four well-established propositions:

(1) While it is probably inevitable that modern societies will demand higher levels of intellectual ability in the future, it does not follow that other kinds of human abilities must fade into relative uselessness. Human intelligence can and should be directed toward making success and productivity less dependent on general intelligence.

(2) Although general intelligence will probably continue to be the main factor determining scholastic achievement, schooling too can be carried out in ways that depend less on this factor.

(3) Although there is little chance that education can substantially reduce individual differences in intelligence, there is much to be gained from trying to raise the overall level of intelligence in society through education.

(4) Although methods of substantially increasing the intelligence of normal people are practically nonexistent, there is justification for continued basic research to discover such methods.

It is impossible, within the scope of this chapter, to discuss these propositions in much depth. In particular, I have to ask the reader to take the first part of each proposition on authority, in order to proceed with a consideration of the second and more controversial part.

Making Work Less Dependent on IQ

As technology advances, the work that a person can accomplish comes to depend less and less on physical and sensory abilities. In the process, of course, accomplishment comes to depend more and more on the higher intellectual abilities that are a uniquely human possession. While this is on the whole a benefit to people, the benefit is not shared equally by all. People who have less than the normal endowment of intellectual abilities find themselves cut off from many avenues to achievement and status, even though they possess abilities which in another time might have held them in good stead.

---

*The Ontario Institute for Studies in Education.

Intelligence is by no means the only factor determining occupational status—overall it accounts for only a small part of the variation in attainment—but it appears to be a necessary condition for many occupations. There are indications that between World War I and World War II the number of occupations that exclude people of low intelligence increased (Freyer, 1922; Harrell and Harrell, 1945),[a] and there is little doubt that this trend continues.

This increasing dependence on IQ is wasteful of human resources.[b] Because of the scarcity of high IQs (and because high IQ is never a sufficient qualification by itself) much of society's work is done by people intellectually incompetent to do it, while other kinds of human abilities are underutilized. Dependence on IQ also has the effect of elevating IQ as a criterion of human worth. People of low IQ are thought to deserve their lowly status (a view often shared even by those handicapped by low IQ). The extraordinary alarm raised by Jensen's suggestion that one race may have a genetically determined lower average IQ than another only makes sense on the presumption that having a low IQ makes one a fundamentally inferior human being. That does seem to be the presumption in our society. Once you have said that someone has a low IQ, there is not much more you can say that does not sound condescending.

Can the tendency toward increased dependence on IQ be reversed? Not entirely, it is safe to say. In part it follows from the continuing discovery of new ways to use human intelligence. But surely part of human intelligence could be directed toward finding ways of making work less intellectually demanding.

Human-factors engineering is a field already concerned with designing tools and work processes so as to conform to human limitations. A concerted effort to reduce the IQ demands of all kinds of jobs, and not just those that currently draw people from the lower IQ ranges, could have the effect of greatly increasing the employment options open to people of low IQ, allowing them to excel on the basis of other abilities.

Another step in the direction of reducing IQ-dependence, oddly

---

[a] The two studies cited provide Army intelligence test score data on men from different civilian occupations, in World War I and World War II respectively. In several important ways the two sets of data are not comparable, but the following weak generalizations can be made. In all occupations a substantial proportion of men had scores above the normal range (hence the low correlation between intelligence and occupational status), but in some occupations few, if any, men had scores below the normal range (hence the inference that IQ is a necessary condition for certain jobs). The number of such occupations appears to have about doubled between the two world wars.

[b] In this discussion I use "IQ" and "intelligence" interchangeably. The term "intelligence" has a number of legitimate meanings. One of the more limited, but nevertheless legitimate, meanings is "that which IQ tests measure." That is the meaning I use here, out of necessity, because the data do not support any broader interpretation. I see no harm in this, as long as we remain aware of the limitation and recognize that "intelligence" means other and broader things in other contexts."

enough, would be to require employers to use tests of relevant competence, instead of educational credentials as means of selecting employees. As it is, the crucial abilities involved in getting a job are often not the abilities needed to do the work but the abilities needed to complete the schooling required for employment, and it is schooling that makes the strongest demands on IQ.

Any move toward equalizing the rewards and prestige of occupations would also probably have the effect of creating more opportunities for people of lower IQ. As it is, the more attractive fields can demand and get people of higher intellectual abilities than the work minimally demands, while less attractive fields have to adjust to what comes along. It is doubtful, for instance, if the large difference in average IQ between doctors and school teachers can be justified by the intellectual demands for the work.

None of this is to deny that for most jobs a higher IQ is a valid asset. But it would seem that in a wise approach to human resources, high intelligence should be recognized as a scarce resource and efforts should be made to make maximum use of other available ability resources so as to obtain maximum social benefit from all of them.

Differentiated staffing is a move in this direction. Few jobs require full use of one's mental abilities continuously; large parts of the work could be done by people of lower IQ or done better by people with different abilities. Thus one of the most promising ways for creating new opportunities for people of lower IQ would be to "unpackage" existing jobs, making several different jobs, in the place of one, that could be performed by people of different abilities. Instead of twenty teachers doing much the same thing, there could be twenty people with different assignments drawing upon different abilities, performing the same total set of functions with more effective use of varied skills. Ideally, such differentiated staffing would not mean that a few professionals were in charge and that the other people perform routine subordinate chores. Rather, there would be a number of different jobs of equal or nearly equal status that allowed for different kinds of excellence.

Making Learning Less Dependent on IQ

Scholastic achievement is determined more by IQ than by any other known factor. It is most unlikely that any reasonable way of teaching could be found that would produce a substantial *relative* improvement in the achievement of low-IQ students. Improved teaching methods tend to raise the performance of high-IQ students as much as or more than they raise the performance of low-IQ students. But substantial gains could be made in the *absolute* levels of achievement of low-IQ students, and this would be most beneficial from both a human resources and a humanitarian standpoint.

There is nothing about the basic skills of reading and arithmetic that intrinsically requires high levels of intellectual ability. Both have been effectively taught to young children of less-than-average potential (Engelmann, 1970; Becker, 1974). The reason, I believe, that higher levels of IQ are normally required is not because of the difficulty of the skills but because of the difficulty of the teaching methods.

The point I am making is a very simple one. If a subject is taught badly, then only very intelligent students can learn it. Confusing explanations, misleading examples, large gaps in the instructional sequence, faulty timing, failure to establish prerequisite skills—all these pedagogical errors will have the effect of causing low-IQ students to fail while high-IQ students will be able to learn in spite of them because of their superior ability to figure out things for themselves. Also, teaching that relies on the "discovery" method or that presents material at a high conceptual level, like some of the "new math," while it may be well suited to the high-IQ student, places unsupportable burdens on the student of low IQ. According to the current fashion, "making students think" is considered a pedagogical virtue. So it may be, but when this policy is converted into "making it impossible for students to learn unless they can think," it becomes cruelly discriminatory against the student who is not blessed with an aptitude for thinking.

If the last two decades of educational experimentation have shown us anything, however, it is that there is no simple recipe for improving the effectiveness of instruction. Some of the work has been misdirected, of course. As a result of noble efforts supported by the National Science Foundation, we now know a lot about how to make mathematics and science more difficult; it remains to find ways to make them easier. There are some promising developments—the low-literacy version of the Biological Sciences Study Committee materials (Grobman, 1969), Mathematics for the Majority (McHale and Witzke, 1971), and an operational cost-effective computer-assisted program in remedial mathematics for postsecondary students developed at the Ontario Institute for Studies in Education (Olivier, 1973), not to mention several promising programs at the elementary level.

It is clear that if we are to make significant progress in helping low-IQ children to learn, we must stop looking for panaceas like performance contracting, contingency management, open classrooms, instructional "systems," and the like. We must invest heavily in the much slower and less glamorous process of engineering, subject by subject and step by step, instructional programs that methodically remove difficulties and fill the gaps so that students of low aptitude can make steady progress. The programs must be enjoyable for students and teachable by ordinary teachers. It is a large undertaking, and it has scarcely begun. What is most discouraging is that the great bulk of the educational community has neither commitment to nor talent for the task.

Jensen has suggested that we try to design instructional methods that draw on different abilities than those represented by the IQ. This parallels the suggestion made in the preceding section of this chapter that we redesign jobs so that they draw on different abilities. In principle, the idea is an excellent one, but I am less optimistic about applying it in education than I am about applying it in the world of work, at least in the foreseeable future. Differentiation of methods makes sense only after technique has reached a certain level. Technique in teaching is at such a primitive level that to begin looking now for different methods for different kinds of students can only serve to retard overall progress, which is already slow to the point of being imperceptible. The search for one method of teaching that is best for student A and another that is best for student B is actually, in the present state of the art, an investigation to find which of several bad methods is least bad for A and which is least bad for B.

Raising the Overall Level of Intelligence

The early literature on experience and intelligence (Hunt, 1961) raised hopes that IQ gains on the order of 30 points could be achieved through feasible kinds of educational intervention. There is now ample evidence that these hopes were mistaken. Evidence from genetics suggests that IQ gains of this magnitude, while not outside the range of variation due to environment, could be achieved only by the most extraordinary improvement in all the environmental factors known to influence IQ. In order to achieve such gains, we would have to have heaven on earth, in which case we would probably no longer be interested.

If we stop thinking about making everyone equal or making everyone a genius, however, we can begin to recognize that there is exciting promise in working toward IQ gains that lie within the bounds of reasonable expectation. It is well within reason, for instance, to think of raising the mean IQ of the population by 2 points through such conventional and benign means as improved prenatal and postnatal care, better nutrition, and generally greater intellectual stimulation throughout the years of growth. Such a small gain would be imperceptible in small samples such as one would encounter in daily life, but for the population as a whole it would have results of potentially enormous consequence. Assuming that the shape of the IQ distribution remained the same, it would mean there would be only three-fourths as many mental retardates (IQs below 70) as there are now. The number of people with IQs above 130, on whom we depend for most of our professional and highly technical work, would increase by a third. The number of people with IQs above 145, on whom we depend for highly creative intellectual achievements, would increase by more than half.[c] It might be more realistic to expect, however, that environmental improvements would have a greater effect on lower ranges of IQ than on higher. If so, an average rise of 2 points might produce only something like a 16 percent gain in the number of IQs above 130 but a 40 percent reduction in the number of retardates.[d]

We must recognize that IQ improvements of this magnitude or even greater magnitude would have no material effect on the spread of individual differences in IQ. The bottom fourth would still be as far away from the top fourth as they are now, and there is no guarantee that they would not be just as badly off. If an upward shift in the IQ distrubution were accompanied by an upward shift in the IQ demands of school work, there would be no change in the distribution of social advantages, even though society as a whole might function to the better advantage of everyone. Thus the effort to raise IQ through environmental improvement must not be seen as a panacea but only as one part of a larger program to meet the need for human resources and raise the quality of life.

I don't think we are in a position to make any but the crudest estimate of the costs of producing a small mean gain in general intelligence, and I am not competent to make even that crude estimate. It is clear that the improvements in health are worth making on other grounds, even if they do not prove to have an effect on IQ. Efforts to increase intellectual stimulation are also worth making on other grounds. We are talking about directly enhancing the quality of life over a span of years that amounts to one-fourth of an average lifespan. This is surely worth something even if it has no effect on later years. It should be recognized that the expected tangible benefits are sufficient to justify a fairly ambitious effort on that basis alone. Assuming that the added educational and welfare costs of the average mental retardate are between $500 and $750 a year, then the expected

[c] Many people seem to find this argument quite implausible. Their objection is that a 2-point gain in IQ does not magically transform a mental retardate into a normal person or a normal person into a gifted one, even if it results in crossing some arbitrary numerical boundary. They also argue that IQ scores are not that exact, that the gains may be meaningless, and so on. It is important to realize that what we are talking about is a change in the environment that produces a 2-point *average* difference between IQs in the present population and IQs in the future population. Whatever an IQ of 70 or 130 implies now in terms of real mental abilities, it means then. The implication is that by whatever real-life standards of performance we might categorize people as retarded or gifted, if we apply the same standards on both occasions, we should have fewer retardates and more gifted in a population that had a 2-point higher mean IQ, given the same shape of IQ distribution.

[d] These results assume that the 2-point mean increase is accompanied by a 3.33 percent decrease in standard deviation, as a result of the distribution's being compressed upward instead of simply shifted upward.

savings from reductions in the number of retardates of the magnitude indicated above would lie between $0.6 and $1.4 billion per year.

To produce a moderate increase in intellectual stimulation lies well within the present state of art. Much could be done in the way of television programing and infusing school curricula with thinking games and exploratory activities, although not without sizable developmental costs. Perhaps the most problematical task is to alter teacher and parent behaviors, although much could probably be accomplished through a massive public information push. The danger is that in rallying the public to support a drive toward greater intellectual stimulation of the young, we might be encouraging a further ascendancy of IQ as a human value. For this reason it would be well if a drive for intellectual stimulation were joined with a more comprehensive emphasis on the development of human abilities.

Searching for Heredity-Environment Interactions

Those who wish to deny the importance of heredity as a determinant of intelligence reiterate the fact that heritability is only a description of the current state of affairs in a population and tells us nothing about the potential susceptibility of a trait to environmental influence (Hirsch, 1972). This is a slender twig on which to hang an egalitarian platform, in the absence of any promising leads to environmental changes that might produce large IQ changes, but it should not be entirely discounted.

It is reasonable to suppose that the customary ways to rearing children that have evolved over the ages are ones that work fairly well on the average, but that they are not necessarily the most favorable ways for all children. There may be special kinds of treatments for certain children that would release unrecognized potentials for intellectual attainment. It is safe to assume, however, that we will not discover those ways by looking at what is normal or even exemplary. If the magic keys existed there, we would no doubt already have found them.

What is needed is an extensive and penetrating search for what are known as heredity-environment interactions, carried out at much the same level as the search for cancer cures. The search is similar in that the primary problem is "where do you look?" One possibility, mentioned only for purposes of illustration, is that some of the critical determinants of IQ may be motivational. Some children may inherit the neural structures for high intellectual ability but may lack hereditary dispositions toward certain kinds of mental activity that are necessary in order for these abilities to develop (Hayes, 1962). It might be possible to compensate for the lack of these hereditary dispositions if we knew precisely what they were, but then again it might not. It might require a kind of treatment that was inhumane or that required such radical changes in parenting behavior that no one was capable of them. Or it might be easy and harmless, and not done at present simply because no one has recognized the need, just as no one recognized for a long time the need of children with the PKU syndrome to have special diets in order to develop normally.

One of the ironies of the environmentalists' opposition to research on the genetics of human intelligence is that they thereby block efforts that might eventually lead to discovery of environmental ways to treat intellectual deficits. There is a great need for genetic research to go beyond study of global IQ and tease out single-gene components of intelligence, some of which might be susceptible to specific compensatory treatment. It is our present state of ignorance that makes "heredity-environment interaction" a futile banner to carry.

It is certainly wrong to regard low intelligence generally as a disease to be cured (Zigler, 1967). I am suggesting, however, that for exploratory research purposes this may be a valuable working hypothesis. Some of the intellectual differences that appear normal to us because they are not associated with any biological defects—and which are in fact normal from the standpoint of genetic variation—may nevertheless be treatable. Low intelligence, like far-sightedness, hyperactivity, and distractability, is one of those normal variations that becomes a disease only as a result of modern cultural demands.[e] In the modern world, low intelligence is certainly a far more serious problem than cancer, and yet there is no comparison in the amount of research effort that is being invested in finding something to do about it.

Conclusion

I have suggested several ambitious undertakings that address the problems

[e] Hyperactivity and distractability are particularly clear cases of "normal" traits that have become defects. In the kinds of environments in which most of human evolution took place, it was no doubt advantageous to the species to have considerable variations in activity level and distractability. It was good to have some people who could concentrate on tasks and to have others who were more easily distracted and thus more likely to detect the approach of enemies. It was good to have steady plodders and others whose level of physical activity was such that they ranged about more widely. But in a school classroom or a sedentary occupation, hyperactivity and distractability are grave handicaps and they must either be cured or ways must be found to restructure situations so that they are less of a handicap. It does not seem as if wide variations in general intelligence could have had similar advantages for the species in the past, but it is clear that a diversity of abilities was and still could be advantageous; and it is reasonable to suppose that such diversity would entail variations in the particular set of abilities that we identify with IQ. Thus variations in general intelligence that were once compensated for by other abilities become a serious problem as those other abilities diminish in significance.

of intelligence in the modern world. Together they constitute a program with the following components:

(1) Redesign occupations and work methods so that fewer kinds of work demand high levels of IQ.

(2) As much as possible, eliminate educational requirements for employment and base employment instead on competence directly relevant to the work to be done.

(3) Work to reduce the differences in status, income, and work satisfaction between occupations of high and low IQ demand.

(4) Invest heavily in the design of instructional methods and materials that make the learning of basic academic subjects less intellectually demanding.

(5) Undertake a massive, continuing effort to provide more intellectual stimulation for children and youth and to mobilize public interest in the development of human abilities of all kinds.

(6) Provide ample support for basic research on the genetics of intellectual abilities and for extensive exploratory research aimed at discovering factors in intellectual ability that are amenable to treatment.

No doubt to many people this program, even if it were accepted as constructive, would be seen as having a low priority in light of the immediately pressing problems of society. To be sure, this program does not offer immediate solutions to any problems. Yet all social problems relate in some way to individual differences, and as people become more aware of the genetic bases of individual differences, there is a danger that they will develop a defeatist attitude toward social problems. There does indeed seem to be a growing defeatist attitude.

I have tried to show that there are many hopeful things that can be done even if the most pessimistic conclusions from genetics are true. Even if we cannot do much to modify people's intelligence, we can do quite a bit to modify the intellectual demands of schooling and work. Even if we cannot eliminate the vast individual differences in intelligence, we have a reasonable likelihood of producing small gains in the overall intelligence of the population that would have major social benefits. And there remains the largely unexplored possibility that some normal variations in intellectual abilities can be treated by practical and humane, though presently unforeseen, means.

The greatest obstacle to constructive action on problems of individual differences is the belief that the problems will go away if we only change our attitudes—if, for instance, we "stop putting so much emphasis on IQ." To me this is an entirely wrong-headed view. "Putting less emphasis on IQ" is something that can only be done within limits and only by painstaking development of new structures and processes of education and work.

Changes in attitudes toward IQ may well follow such material changes; they cannot be expected to precede them.

There is a strong tendency to deny the existence of problems related to individual differences. Jensen's statement, which I have echoed, that the differences in intelligence between social groups are real (that, whatever the cause, they are not merely an illusion created by false tests) has caused us to be branded as racists. The movement to abolish the use of IQ tests is a further illustration of the urge to kill the messenger who brings bad news. My position is that the news, though unpleasant, is far from hopeless, and that we had better study the news carefully, analyze its implications, and start doing something about it.

References

Becker, W.C. Aptitude and treatment from the point of view of the teacher. In W.R. Green (ed.), *The aptitude/achievement distinction.* Monterrey, Calif.: CTB/McGraw-Hill 1974.

Engelmann, S. The effectiveness of direct instruction on IQ performance and achievement in reading and arithmetic. In J. Hellmuth (ed.), *Disadvantaged child 3.* New York: Brunner/Mazel, Inc., 1970, 339-361.

Freyer, D. Occupation-intelligence standards. *School and Society,* 1922, *16,* 273-277.

Grobman, A.B. *The changing classroom: The role of the Biological Sciences Committee Study.* Garden City, N.Y.: Doubleday, 1969.

Harrell, T.W., and Harrell, M.S. Army General Classification Test scores for civilian occupations. *Educational and Psychological Measurement,* 1945, *5,* 229-235.

Hayes, K.J. Genes, drives, and intelligence. *Psychological Reports,* 1962, *10,* 299-342.

Hirsch, J. Genetics and competence: Do heritability indices predict educability? In J. McV. Hunt (ed.), *Human intelligence.* New Brunswick, N.J.: Transaction Books, 1972, 7-29

Hunt, J. McV. *Intelligence and experience.* New York: Ronald Press, 1961.

McHale, T.J., and Witzke, P.T. *Milwaukee Area Technical College mathematics series.* Reading, Pa.: Addison-Wesley, 1971.

Olivier, W.P. Computer-assisted mathematics instruction for community college students. *International Journal of Man-Machine Studies,* 1973, *5,* 385-395.

Zigler, E. Familial mental retardation: A continuing dilemma. *Science,* 1967, *155,* 292-298.

9 IQ Tests and the Handicapper General

Thomas R. Pezzullo *

IQ testing, a principal area of concern for those who search for equality, is steeped in great controversy. This chapter will attempt to bring some sharper focus on this issue in American education and suggest some direction for future policy. This author maintains that the controversy is largely misdirected. Before exploring this misdirection, however, some stage-setting is necessary.

Equality: Public Policy and Educational Practice

Kurt Vonnegut satirized our endless search for equality through the short story character "The Handicapper General." In that story the Handicapper General assigns handicaps to all men and women in order to bring them down to a common denominator of mediocre but equal circumstances. Those with outstanding physical attributes are required to wear weights around their waists and wrists and ankles, those with outstanding mental attributes have electronic devices implanted in their skulls which buzz, tingle, and shock whenever a complicated thought enters. The result is equality—guaranteed and enforced. In fact, in his 1984-like setting, removing one's handicap even for a moment is a capital crime against the state.

It is important to note, however, that Vonnegut's satire is satire on the bureaucratization of the means of achieving equality and not of the ideal itself. Unfortunately, public policy has often materialized as a bureaucratization of a philosophical ideal. All too often we have created policies and practices which are no more reasoned than the Handicapper General's. For example, in one California school district where there was an accelerated class for exceptionally bright students—eight in all—*egalitarian* policies mandated that an equal number of minority students be placed in the class. Numerical equality was achieved and presumably a feeling of victory for those responsible, but in terms of educational results their effort produced a deleterious effect. Eight minority students selected on the basis of relaxed criteria subsequently had to struggle along performing tasks for which they were not prepared. Had they remained in their former high-level classes

---

* University of Rhode Island.

they would no doubt have performed very well rather than facing incessant frustration just to ensure *representative* equality. (There are, of course, highly defensible arguments against using criteria which do not admit minority students, but the point of the anecdote is to illustrate the effect of a wrong-headed insistence on a superficially defined equality. This author is no more comfortable than the most liberal reader with the suggestion implicit in the preceding illustration that only majority students can or should be selected in "gifted" programs.)

In an area where social science data seem to be relevant to policy and practice but also somewhat ambiguous, the data can often become a political tool to be bent to the motives of the majority. Those responsible for policymaking must, of course, make the conscious or unconscious choice of whether policy is to flow principally from facts or from moral and philosophical principles. The following excerpt from H.J. Eysenck's "I.Q., Social Class and Educational Policy"[1], aptly sums up the situation:

It is widely agreed that social policy should be governed by the interplay between philosophical and ethical ideals on the one hand and scientifically ascertained facts on the other. Facts by themselves are neutral. Even if we could be certain, for example, that intellectual differences between whites and blacks were wholly determined by heredity (a position not maintained by any serious psychologists who have studied the literature) we could argue from that either for a policy of segregation or a system of positive discrimination in favor of blacks. One's philosophical and ethical ideals, one's political orientation and the like, govern the way one deals with facts.

One such clear philosophical value permeating our history is the ideal of equality. All overt American traditions, beginning with the Constitution, subscribe to the ideal of equality—a history of slavery, social injustice, child labor abuse, and racial and ethnic discriminatory patterns not-withstanding. Public policy, as reflected in legislation, judiciary decisions, and Congressional appropriations, particularly with respect to education, has at least nominally subscribed to the special role of education as equalizer. The decision of *Brown vs. Board of Education of Topeka* in 1954, a unanimous decision which maintained that separate-but-equal schools were inherently unequal and unconstitutional, reflected the belief, by both the judiciary and civil rights advocates, that schools were an effective way to achieve equality. The Congress was similarly disposed in the passage of the 1965 Elementary and Secondary Education Act and the Civil Rights Act in 1964 when it directed the Commissioner of Education to conduct a nationwide assessment of the equality of educational opportunity. The results, published in 1966 by James Coleman as *Equality of Educational Opportunity,* were sometimes distressing for those who argued first that schools are inherently unequal, and second, that these inequalities in schools produced inequalities in achievement and ultimate social and economic success. These findings gave pause to those who advocated schools as economic and social mobilizers.

Coleman's findings lent considerable empirical evidence to the belief that integrated education, under the right circumstances, seemed to be associated with greater achievement by blacks. The special limitations on those circumstances were disappointing to the proponents of school integration, but not nearly as disappointing as his other general conclusions. These suggested that while the average black student attended a predominatly black school, the difference on the average between predominatly black and predominatly white schools was not nearly so great as had been imagined. Further, school characteristics did not contribute very much to the differences in IQ and achievement in those schools. Rather, home and community characteristics seemed to bear far more heavily on intelligence and achievement. These findings left the egalitarians cold. Confirmation of these findings was published by Christopher Jencks and a team of researchers at the Cambridge Center for Policy Research in 1972, as *Inequality: A Reassessment of the Effect of Family and Schooling in America*. So much of inequality, Jencks concluded, results from inherited inequality both in ability and in social and economic condition, that nothing short of socialism can overcome economic inequality.

In other words, most of what children do in schools is attributable to factors outside the schools' influence; further those lifetime effects we'd believed attributable to school—earning power, social status, and the like—were more likely a consequence of the child's forebear's earning power and social status than of the school's intervention. *Marginal institutions* were what he called the schools—marginal in the sense that they seemed associated with effects on social and economic mobility, but not on the order of magnitude that we had formerly attributed to them.

To say that these challenges to the traditional role of education were staggering would be a monumental understatement. But an even more far-reaching challenge to our basic assumptions was made public in the interim between these reports. This work, challenging a key policy and operating principle of the Great Society, was published in 1969 in the *Harvard Educational Review*. In one of the longest articles ever published in that review, and easily the most controversial, Arthur Jensen undertook a substantive challenge to environmental theories of intelligence, aptitude, and educational progress. To those more familiar with the controversy than with the work, the title is apparently misleading: "How Much Can We Boost IQ and Scholastic Achievement?" The most widespread impression left by that article is that Jensen asserted that IQ differences between blacks and whites are largely genetic, that the available gene pool for blacks is inferior to the gene pool available for whites, and that blacks have little hope that equality of condition can be attained by conventional means because of this inherent difference. His article, of course, dealt with a great deal more. He argued, sounding much more egalitarian than most people give him credit for, that differential treatment should be offered to people of different abilities and that since some of these abilities are no doubt inherent, compensatory education efforts through conventional means are doomed to failure.

Jensen took great pains to define the *single* factor to which his 80 percent heritability thesis applied. He described at length a constellation of other abilities which are important to success and survival but which are not valued or rewarded by schools as they are constituted today. In the long run, one of his most important messages was obscured by the dust from the race issue, namely: people should be treated as individuals and in ways which are likely to equalize opportunity and condition, but the individual should not be considered so highly malleable that through environmental manipulation each person will ultimately be equal to every other person. (Either Vonnegut reads Jensen or Jensen reads Vonnegut!)

Most of those who challenged his work focused on either the genetic model he applied or his reliance on the IQ as a single, stable measure of scholastic aptitude. An examination of the efforts to discredit the genetic model is too technical for consideration in this work. IQ testing, however, can be considered on a less technical level and is a far more productive area of discussion since it is of more general interest in the search for equality, and most challenges to the IQ test are themselves technically unsophisticated.

The IQ Test: The Misdirected Search for Equality

Much has been written and circulated through the media on abuse of the IQ test, its use, and the general concept of predictive tests. The IQ testing movement had its rather innocent origins in the work of Binet in France at the turn of the century. Binet merely attempted to establish a series of criterion tasks which would help determine which students were, in today's sense, retarded, and those for whom ordinary schools would be inappropriate. What he and his successors in the testing movement discovered was that the same criterion tests, when appropriately scaled, correlated with overall success in school, not only among the retardates, but in the whole range of ability and experience. The following sixty years spread the concept around the Western world with many technical refinements and increasing efforts to remove the cultural saturation found in earlier forms.

Most psychometrists today agree that IQ tests depend a great deal on individual cultural and experiential readiness to take tests. Enough cultural factors can be shown to be related to IQ to cast doubt as to whether any test can be independent of experience and cultural bias. Were this the only data on the subject, the IQ testing movement would have dried up long ago. The principal reason that it has not is that the IQ test score is *highly* correlated with success in school. Possibly, and probably, it is more highly correlated with success than with these cultural factors that have been used to describe its inherent unfairness. When one extracts, as Jensen has done, a common factor among all intelligence, aptitude, or IQ tests, correlations tend to be reduced with respect to cultural factors, and correlations with achievement tend to become more specific rather than general. What this means is we have an "impure" measure, tainted (in a manner of speaking) by the culture, background, education, and experience of the subject of measure. Although a number of measures show differing degrees and kinds of taintedness, the one common factor that can be detected among all these measures is quite independent of the measure and somewhat independent of these cultural factors. More simply, culture bias is most apparent from test to test and least apparent in the general factor that all the tests appear to have in common.

Spearman, a pioneer in psychometrics, first discovered that this general factor was present in all aptitude tests, regardless of the medium through which they purported to measure aptitude. He called the factor "g," or "general factor." Jensen was referring to "g" in his 80 percent heritability hypothesis.

All the foregoing becomes rather immaterial if one attends to the most significant issue of culture bias: *the school's focus on culturally biased modes of behavior, language models, experience prior to schooling, and entering attitudes and behaviors,* which are measured only covertly by IQ tests, and upon almost all of which beginning school experience depends heavily.

When psychologists cite IQ test differences between ascriptive groups, the champions of equality seek to discredit the psychologists, their data, their analysis, their test, or all four. The greatest effort has been focused on discrediting the tests. In order to properly discredit, or at least disregard, the IQ test (whether culture-biased or relatively culture-fair), one must set as a goal the reduction of the overall correlation between such test scores and success in school. Since the value of a predictive test is measured by its correlation with the criterion it is designed to predict, eliminating or reducing the correlation would have the most discrediting effect on the IQ test.

There are two obvious approaches: the first facetious; the second sincere. The first is to change the nature of the criterion tasks in the IQ test so that they do not reflect the kinds of activities necessary for success in school. Many people, who have written on the subject of establishing a counterbalanced or culture-biased *minority* IQ test, have done this. Little research literature on the use of these tests exists, but it seems obvious that such scores will not be correlated with the general success of the American majority *or* minority populations in school.[2] The tasks presented just don't reflect what goes on in school.

The second approach is to so substantially change schooling's expectations of aptitudes and interests of individuals and refocus those primary media through which learning and teaching take place in our schools that the tasks or skills in the IQ test are made unrelated to tasks and skills required in school. Jensen[3] stated in his 1969 article:

> If diversity of mental abilities, as of most other human characteristics, is a basic fact of nature, as the evidence indicates, and if the ideal of universal education is to be successfully pursued, it seems a reasonable conclusion that schools and society must provide a range of diversity of educational methods, programs, and goals, and of occupational opportunities, just as wide as the range of human abilities.

While Jensen has argued, in that and subsequent articles, that the culture bias in IQ test scores is grossly overstated, he does suggest that these tests represent the cultural bias in our schools. It is interesting that in most essays lamenting the culture bias of IQ tests, scant mention is made of the same inherent cultural bias in our means of teaching and the environment in which we conduct it. That may be a far more relevant area of attack for achieving the ideal of equality of educational opportunity. The "alternative school" and "free school" movements may have some pertinence here, if they seek to teach pupils in culturally relevant ways. T.L. Wilson[4] has written specifically of minority-culture-relevant education plans in a *Harvard Educational Review*[5] volume devoted entirely to the subject of alternative schools. While scant data are available on the cognitive superiority of such schools for their special clientele, prospects seem encouraging, especially with regard to noncognitive outcomes. It will be most encouraging to find that success in them is *not* correlated with IQ.

The fact is, however, that the overwhelming majority of American school children and youth attend a school that can only be considered "conventional." IQ tests predict success in these schools as no other variable can. How then, in the name of equality, equity, or just plain scientific curiosity can one begin to deflate the predictive power of such tests? The necessary background for understanding *predictive* test properties is best described through the following instructional anecdote, told in many educational measurement classes. The story is that a certain insurance company is investing about $25,000 per trainee in their school for new insurance salesmen. They approach a test consulting firm and ask them to develop a short predictive test for success in insurance sales. They hope that by administering a test before investing in training they will screen out those for whom success in the training and subsequent sales will be unlikely. A few weeks later, after testing many, many items and determining those which correlate most highly with ultimate success, it is found that items such as "do you have onions on your hamburgers?" or "do you or does your wife choose your neckties?" turn out to be among the most discriminating. It is clear that there is no logical link between onion on hamburgers or who selects neckties and ultimate success in insurance sales. Yet, they are among the best predictors! And now the point of the anecdote: Predictive tests rest on their predictive power and not on the logical validity of their items. It may be that IQ test scores, like the apocryphal insurance sales test, while possessing predictive power, are inherently unfair, and our nation's educators and psychologists should focus more attention on changing schools rather than tests so that ultimately IQ test scores will have increasingly less and less correlation with success in those schools.

Jensen raised this whole question indirectly, but unfortunately it was obscured by an issue more sensitive and more provocative. Heredity and environment have become an overblown controversy. How important is the hereditary or environmental nature of intelligence in the search for equality if we've only focused on one narrow conception of intelligence? Jensen, as well as Richard Herrnstein, the Harvard psychologist, argued that the reward system makes the IQ important in almost all forms of educational and social success and that familial and educational patterns tend to reinforce that relationship. Even those others who don't accept a high heritability for intelligence take great pains to show the nongenetic but hereditary nature of poverty, unequal conditions, and unequal circumstances in their arguments to support mechanisms for social mobility. One way or another, those wishing to deal with social, educational, and economic inequality have had to ascribe some large measure of each individual's condition to her or his ancestors' condition; whether deemed biological or environmental, it is somewhat *inherited*. This combined inheritance is a fruitful area of inquiry leading toward achievement of equality, but trying to decide which proportions are biological and which sociological contributes little to the search for equality. Jensen's principal message was to divert us from the futile effort to boost IQ and to send us looking elsewhere in the search for equality. It seems, after seven years, to have gone unheeded. Schools and the tests which best predict success in them remain highly culturally biased, and that is simply because the tests reflect the same biases as the schools, which reward and sort according to one's fitting into the school's cultural mold. Whether one construes intelligence to be highly inherited or highly susceptible to environmental manipulation, schools appear to be so limited in the vehicles through which learning takes place as to make the nature/nurture argument far less important than general school reform designed to compensate for existing culture bias.

IQ Tests and a Policy Prescription

What, then, is the policy prescription to be? Let us suppose that the policy prescription for the achievement of equality remains as it is today: conventional schools that operate largely on the cognitive-verbal-abstract level; IQ tests remain cognitive-verbal-abstract. If measures of success for schools and individuals remain the same, and if sorting and rewarding procedures do, too, then the American system of education will always be investing enormous resources in remedial efforts for those who are not highly verbal, abstract, and cognitive in their abilities—whatever the reason for the deficiency. Further, schools will remain *marginal* since they will fulfill only an easy prophecy of finding and rewarding those who have always found success in school. Don't we know of, or suspect the existence of, a diversity of aptitudes through which learning could conceivably take place?

Our next task should be to examine more than the limited, narrow part of that constellation of aptitudes to which educators appeal as the sole vehicle for learning. Jensen's research into a two-level model of learning ability has produced some interesting patterns. While they are still tentative, it appears that one level of learning ability does not show a disadvantage or depression for those from an economic or socially depressed background. Should these tentative findings hold up under further research, then the implications for teaching methods are significant. I don't wish to especially dignify the Jensen research and direction as the only sound vehicle for our future efforts. National policy should continue to support and stimulate research into the basic nature of the learning process, paying particular attention to those other learning modes heretofore unexplored. The search for aptitudes and teaching methods which show no significant differences between ascriptive groups such as race, sex, and social strata is certainly a worthy endeavor; but in addition the search for methods that are positively discriminating in favor of minorities is equally valuable. As S.M. Miller points out in Chapter 2, equality of opportunity often simply advances the majority and minority in equal gains so that relative inequality remains unaffected.

The IQ test cannot and should not be a measure of a person's worth, and even those who have been accused of this in the most villainous way point to the narrowness of the conception of intelligence in our culture, and argue for school reform. When we begin to see IQ as one aptitude among many, rather than a sine qua non, we will have ended a needlessly protracted misdirection in our quest, and put the Handicapper General to rest.

Summary

The success of the culturally biased predictor depends on the degree of culture bias in the criterion measure it is designed to predict. It seems eminently more reasonable to make changes in the criterion variable—in this case, the school—rather than in the predictor. When and if we can accomplish this in American education, the correlation between the IQ test and success in school will be so embarrassingly low as to relegate the IQ to a limited and more realistic role. We can then get about the business of searching for equality, without the inappropriate criterion of IQ.

This chapter has attempted to suggest the futility of attacking the IQ myth head-on. Rather, it seems more fruitful, in the cause of achieving equality, to attack and reform the extreme culture bias in schools, and thus most effectively eliminate the role that IQ tests play.

Notes

1. Eysenck, H.J., "I.Q., Social Class and Educational Policy," *Change Magazine,* pp. 38-42, September 1973.

2. One of the more widely circulated specimens is the Dove Counterbalance Intelligence Test, which is a good example of cultural saturation—See Daigon, A., and Dempsey, R., *School—Pass at Your Own Risk,* Prentice-Hall, Englewood Cliffs, N.J., 1974, pp. 146-149.

3. Jensen, Arthur, "How Much Can We Boost IQ and Scholastic Achievement?" *Harvard Educational Review,* 39, 1, Winter 1969, p. 117.

4. Wilson, T.L., "Notes toward a Process of Afro-American Education," *Harvard Educational Review,* 42, 3, August 1972, p. 374.

5. *Harvard Educational Review,* Alternative Schools, 42, 3, August 1972.

10

Problems Without Solutions: Solutions Without Problems

*Lester C. Thurow** *

A Past of Stable Inequalities: A Future of Rising Inequalities

By now the post-World War II stability of the distributions of income and wealth have become a part of our conventional wisdom. All incomes are rising at approximately the same rate with no group gaining or falling relative to other groups. While this perception is basically true with respect to the distribution of family income, it ignores the fact that stability has been produced by a series of offsetting factors. Relative income stability is not inherent in the economy, but is a byproduct of a number of accidents. Unfortunately, some of the factors leading to greater equality have, or are about, to disappear. Since the factors leading to greater inequalities will remain, we are probably on the edge of a period where strong income redistribution measures will be needed to hold the distribution constant, much less make it more equal.

The distribution of family income is a product of three underlying mechanisms. First, how are incomes awarded to individuals? Second, how are incomes shared among individuals? Third, how are government taxes and transfer payments distributed to individuals and families? In the post-World War II period, the distribution of economic rewards has become increasingly more unequal. But the process of sharing income and distributing government transfer payments has led to more equality and a constant distribution of family income.

Government transfer payments are important since they are the mechanism whereby the incomes of those outside of the labor force (the elderly, female-headed families, the ill, etc.) keep up with the incomes of those in the labor force as productivity and earnings rise. Government transfer payments have risen from $11 billion in 1947 to $113 billion in 1973, but this large increase has mostly gone to preserving the income position of the economically inactive. Very much larger increases would have been needed to equalize the distribution of income.[a] (While taxes have also risen, the U.S. tax system is proportioned. As a result, taxes do not alter the market distribution of incomes.)

---

* Massachusetts Institute of Technology.

[a] This is particularly true since many government transfer payments do not go exclusively to low-income individuals—veterans benefits, social security, farm subsidies, etc.

The family is the basic institution for sharing income since the largest income transfers are made within its boundaries. Individual earners voluntarily combine their incomes and share them with nonearners. In the post-World War II period, the combining and sharing of incomes within the family has been a powerful process leading to more equality in the distribution of income. More and more families have had two earners as labor force participation rates have risen for women. But this process has not occurred equally across the income distribution. Participation rates have risen most rapidly and are highest from women with low-income husbands. With the exception of the very poor, the lower a husband's earnings, the higher the probability that he will have a working wife.

Thus while the incomes of low-income males have fallen relative to the income of high-income males, the earnings of wives of low-income males have risen relative to the earnings of wives of high-income males. The ground lost by low-income males has been made up by sending their wives to work in the paid labor force.

While government transfer payments are at least in principle capable of preserving the economic position of the economically inactive, increases in female participation rates are inherently self-limiting. Technically they cannot rise above 100 percent, but even males do not have participation rates above the low 90's. Realistically, maximum female participation rates are probably well below those of males.

An examination of the participation pattern of women married to low- and middle-income males reveals that those women are already approaching full participation in the paid labor force. Only in the childbearing years is there room for large expansions in participation rates. This means that these families are reaching, or shortly will reach, a time when they are unable to preserve their family's relative economic position by increasing the paid work effort of the wife. When this occurs, an increase in the inequality of male earnings will immediately be reflected in increasing inequality in family incomes.

The problem is compounded by current developments in the labor force participation patterns of women married to high-income males. Their participation rates have now started to rise more rapidly. Regardless of whether this is due to female liberation or not, it is going to have an immense impact on the distribution of family income. While low-income families have little future opportunity to increase their family incomes by increasing female work, high-income families have a large, previously untapped, source of income gains. This is doubly true if you believe in assortive mating (males marry females who could earn what they earn in a nondiscriminatory world) and if you believe that sex discrimination will be eliminated.

While there is almost no doubt that a period of rising inequality will be

Table 10-1
Distributions of Money Income: 1947-1972

| | Families | | Unrelated Individuals | |
	1947	1972	1947	1972
Lowest fifth	5.1%	5.4%	1.9%	3.4%
Second fifth	11.8	11.9	5.8	8.1
Third fifth	16.7	17.5	11.9	13.9
Fourth fifth	23.1	23.8	21.4	24.2
Highest fifth	43.3	41.4	59.1	50.4
Median income (1972$)	$5,665	$11,116	$1,833	$5,144

Source: U.S. Bureau of the Census, *Current Population Reports: Consumer Income, 1972*. U.S. Government Printing Office, Washington D.C. 1973, pp. 34, 45.

visible over the next decade or two, there is also some limited evidence that rising inequalities may already have begun to occur. First, since 1969 the aggregate share of total income going to the bottom 60 percent of all families has been slowly falling. The declines are not yet large enough to be labeled statistically significant, but they are nevertheless persistent and pervasive. Second, black family incomes have begun to fall relative to white. After reaching 63 percent of white incomes in 1970, they have fallen to 58 percent in 1973. Since black female participation rates have reached physical and sociological maximums, black families have little or no opportunity for future income increases from this source. As white females increasingly go to work, white incomes will rise relative to black incomes.

As a result, those interested in obtaining an equitable distribution of economic rewards should be aware that we are probably entering a period of increasing inequality. To increase equality or to maintain the current degree of inequality will require much stronger measures than in the past.

Where Are We?

While the existing distributions of income and wealth are probably familiar to most of, if not all, the participants at this conference, I have been asked to review the data to set a common factual background.

Table 10-1 provides data on the distributions of income for families and unrelated individuals in 1947 and 1972 (the latest year for which complete data are available). As the data indicates, the distributions of income have been basically constant as real incomes doubled. The mean income of the top quintile of all families has remained about 8 times as large as the mean income of the bottom quintile of all families, and the top 5 percent of all

Table 10-2
Family Income Shares: 1966

	Census Money Income	*Adjusted to Reflect Capital Income*
Lowest fifth	4.3%	3.7%
Second fifth	11.3	9.9
Third fifth	17.3	16.1
Fourth fifth	24.5	22.6
Highest fifth	42.6	47.9
Top 5 percent	16.0	22.1
Top 1 percent	4.8	10.5

Source: Joseph A. Pechman and Benjamin A. Okner, *Who Bears the Tax Burden*, The Brookings Institution, Washington, D.C., 1974, p. 46. Reprinted with permission. © 1974 by the Brookings Institution.

families enjoy a mean income more than 30 times as large as that of the bottom 5 percent of all families.

Unrelated individuals have both lower average incomes and a more dispersed distribution of income. While the top quintile of all families have 41 percent of all family income, the top quintile of all unrelated individuals have 50 percent of all their group's income.

While the U.S. Census Bureau collects good, accurate data, it should be recognized that their definitions of income exclude many forms of income from capital. In 1972 wages and salaries accounted for 77.5 percent of total Census income, self-employment income accounted for 8.3 percent, and indirect labor earnings (mostly pensions) accounted for another 8.9 percent—making a total of 94.7 percentage points attributable to labor earnings. Of the remaining 5.3 percentage points, public welfare programs accounted for 1.0 percentage points with 4.3 percentage points coming in the form of dividends, interest, rents, income from estates and trusts, and other forms of capital income. By contrast, capital income accounted for 23 percent of the gross national product in the same year. As a result, Census income data are basically data on earnings.

If the Census data on income are corrected to be made compatible with national income and product account data, the distribution of family income becomes much more unequal than that calculated by Census. As the data in Table 10-2 indicate, the income share of the top 1 percent of all families more than doubles, from 4.8 percent to 10.5 percent. The income gap between the bottom 5 percent and the top 5 percent expands from 30 to 1, to 45 to 1; and the income gap between the bottom 1 percent and the top 1 percent expands from 240 to 1 to 525 to 1.

Adjusting the distribution of income to reflect capital incomes affects only the top of the income distribution for a very simple reason. The

Table 10-3
U.S. Distribution of Family Wealth in 1962

	Percent of Total Families	Percent of Total Family Wealth
Lowest 25.4		0.0
Next 31.5		6.6
Next 24.4		17.2
Top 18.7		76.2
(Top 7.5)		(59.1)
(Top 2.4)		(44.4)
(Top 0.5)		(25.8)

Source: Dorothy S. Projector, "Survey of Financial Characteristics of Consumers," *Federal Reserve Bulletin*, March 1964, p. 285.

Table 10-4
Distribution of Wealth in 1969

Net Assets	Percent of Population with Gross Assets over $60,000	Percent of Total Assets of These with Gross Assets over $60,000
Under $50,000	20.1	6.0
50,000 - 100,000	38.8	19.1
100,000 - 150,000	18.2	14.1
150,000 - 300,000	14.4	18.6
300,000 - 1,000,000	7.1	21.8
1,000,000 - 5,000,000	1.2	13.4
5,000,000 - 10,000,000	0.07	2.8
Over 10,000,000	0.04	4.2

Source: Internal Revenue Service, Statistics of Income 1969: Personal Wealth, Publication 482(10-73), p. 19.

ownership of wealth is extremely concentrated in the U.S. As the data in Table 10-3 indicate, the top 18.7 percent of all families own 76.2 percent of all the privately held wealth in the United States while the bottom 25 percent have no net assets. Although there has not been a comprehensive measurement of wealth since 1962, it is possible to get more current data on approximately the top 7.5 percent of the families shown in Table 10-3. These data (see Table 10-4) indicate that there were no significant changes between 1962 and 1969, but also allow us to examine the very wealthy in greater detail. As the data indicate, the top 0.008 percent of all families own as many assets as the bottom half of all families.

For a brief time in the late 1960s and early 1970s it looked like a breakthrough might have been made on minority incomes. Historically

black family incomes have varied between 60 percent and 50 percent of
white family incomes over the course of the business cycle. In recessions
such as 1957-1958 black family incomes would fall to 50 percent of white
family incomes; in booms such as the Korean War they would rise to 60
percent of white family incomes. As mentioned, black family incomes rose
out of this range to 63 percent of white family incomes in 1970—a year with
a mild recession. Unfortunately the gains that were evident in the late 1960s
now seem to be in the process of being lost. Black incomes were back to 58
percent of whites' in 1973, and they are apt to be much lower when data
become available on the current recession.

The data on women do not as yet indicate any income gains relative to
males. Women who work full-time (35 + hours per week) and full year (50
+ weeks per year) have made approximately 50 percent of the amount
made by full-time full-year males ever since the Great Depression. Female
earnings have gone up since female hours of work have gone up, but there
have been no gains in per-hour earnings. If this problem were to be solved
and women were to both participate and earn equally with men, the distribution of family income would become about 25 percent more unequal than
it now is.

The Pursuit of the Pot of Gold at the End of the Rainbow

The conditions placed upon efforts to alter the distributions of income and
wealth have been such that no change in the distributions of income and
wealth could have been expected to take place. Put crudely, they were as
follows: Some method must be found to alter the distributions of income
and wealth that will be inexpensive (i.e., not require a tax increase), that
will not lower anyone's absolute income, and that will not create a backlash
among those whose relative incomes are to be lowered. As I shall attempt
to demonstrate, there are no social programs for altering the distribution of
income and wealth that meet these conditions.

Before we look at the microeconomic strategies for altering the distributions of income and wealth, it is necessary to recognize a mac-
roeconomic fact of life. The U.S. economy has a gross national income near
$1,500 billion. There is no way to reallocate $1 or even $10 billion that will
cause major changes in the allocation of the remaining $1,499 or $1,490
billion. If you want to design some program to reallocate $1,500 billion, it is
going to have to be a big program even if it is fantastically effective. A very
successful $10 billion program would have little observable effect on a
$1,500 billion economy. If you want to see any results, you have to have
what would be regarded as massive programs. If massive programs are
politically unfeasible, then solutions are unfeasible.

The Education and Training Strategy

The War on Poverty embodied the traditional American reliance on education as the solution to all ills. In theory, the strategy was to reeducate some low-income individuals so that their productivity and income would rise. In addition to raising the income of the retrained individuals, two other equalizing effects would occur. With fewer low-skill workers available, the market wages for low-skill workers would rise. With increased numbers of high-skill workers, the market wages for high-skill workers would fall. Thus there would be a three-pronged effect leading to a more equal distribution of earnings.

This strategy failed for a number of reasons. Most importantly, reeducating and retraining low-income individuals proved to be too expensive for the public's tastes. The Job Corps was only the most publicized example. Costs proved to be around $10,000 per man-year. This was considered absurd since it was higher than the man-year costs at the most expensive universities, but surely it should cost more to educate the most difficult to educate than the least difficult to educate. While it was possible to document changes in the economic characteristics of those in the Job Corps, the public basically said that it was unwilling to support programs with costs in these ranges. Let it be remembered that at no time did anyone seriously charge that the Job Corps was being inefficient or corrupt. The costs were simply too high.

Cheaper programs could be designed, but extensive cost-benefit analysis failed to reveal any that could generate benefits greater than costs and that could be duplicated.[b] Costs typically exceeded benefits since dropout rates were high, many trainees could not find jobs for which they were trained, and many other trainees held the jobs for which they were trained for only short periods of time. It also became evident that the real education problem was not so much one of teaching cognitive job skills, but one of teaching what might be called industrial discipline—good work habits.

With the economic failure of some education programs and the economic unacceptability of other education programs, the strategy shifted from a formal education strategy to an informal on-the-job training strategy. Subsidies were given to employers to hire and train workers from disadvantaged groups. Any such program runs into an immediate problem of what economist's call dead-weight loss.

If you look at any disadvantaged group, you will find that a large proportion of that group is in fact employed. If 30 percent are unemployed, 70 percent are employed. As a result, most workers in disadvantaged groups are already being hired, but given normal labor force turnover, they

___

[b] Occasionally a program with a high benefit-cost ratio can be found, but they seem to depend upon the existence of some charismatic leader that cannot be duplicated.

periodically show up in the labor force looking for work. Thus many employers would agree to be subsidized to hire disadvantaged workers that they would have been hiring anyway. Money given as subsidies to hire workers that would have been hired anyway is dead-weight loss. From this it is clear that most of the on-the-job training funds are dead-weight loss and that they make little or no difference to the characteristics of the labor force hired by different employers. Training subsidies were pumped into the system, but they made little, or no, difference to the observed distribution of earnings in the longrun.

While it is possible to advance many reasons why the education and training strategy did not work to redistribute earnings, an empirical fact of life became increasingly evident. If you want to raise the income of an individual by $1,000 per year for the rest of his or her life, it is cheaper to give that individual $1,000 per year for the rest of his or her life than it is to make the investments necessary to raise that individual's earnings by $1,000 per year. While this unfortunate fact has never percolated into the general public's consciousness, it lies at the heart of the shift in governmental strategy from education to direct income redistribution.

The Direct Income Redistribution Strategy

As the estimated costs of income redistribution via human-capital investments rose, so did the attractiveness of direct income redistribution. At first glance the problem seems simple. Only $12 billion would need to be transferred to bring every family and unrelated individual up to the government poverty lines ($4,512 for a family of four in 1973). Compared to the $113 billion in transfer payments that are already being made, $12 billion is only an 11 percent increase. The problems arise when incentive questions are considered and when attempts are made to integrate new systems of income redistribution with the present systems of income redistribution.

To preserve work incentives, it was thought to be necessary to set up income redistribution programs with implicit tax rates substantially below 100 percent (i.e., when a person earned $1, his or her benefits were not reduced by $1). While the American public is theoretically in favor of work incentives, it does not like to face the fact that work incentives are expensive. For example, if earnings are taxed at 50 percent, the costs of a negative income tax program designed to bring everyone up to the poverty line rises to approximately $45 billion per year. To preserve work incentives, benefits must be given to people that are above the poverty line. If $4,500 is the poverty line for a family of four, benefits will be given to families of four with earnings up to $9,000. A family with $8,000 in earnings would receive $500 in net benefits. As Senator McGovern found out the hard way, it is difficult to sell the idea of $45 billion programs that would place a large fraction of the population on "welfare."

Some people have viewed the 1972 presidential election as a referendum on direct income redistribution. President Nixon repudiated his own family assistance program, and Senator McGovern was perceived as an advocate of more income redistribution and was clobbered as a result. The public voted not to redistribute income. To the extent that this is true, there is no income redistribution problem. Solutions are unnecessary even if they exist.

The other problem with direct income redistribution springs from the multiplicity of federal income support programs and the inconsistency of state income support programs. Put simply, we have reached the point where it is not possible to graft another income support program onto the current system without causing great inequities and without causing implicit tax rates to rise above 100 percent. Imagine a negative income tax system with a 50 percent tax rate servicing an individual in public housing where rents are calculated at 25 percent of earnings, receiving food stamps where stamps costs 30 percent of earnings, and subject to a state welfare tax of 30 percent of earnings. This individual would be paying a 135 percent tax on any earnings.

Direct income redistribution requires the federalization of all income support programs and the coordination or elimination of many federal programs. Politically each of these is defended by its constituency and its bureaucracy. Estimates of the difficulty of bringing about the necessary institutional changes range from difficult to impossible.

What starts as a seemingly simple solution ends up mired in institutional fighting and the necessity to start large or not start at all. There simply is no way to start a negative income tax system small and let it grow in the manner of Social Security.

The net result is two seeming deadends. Both the education and training strategy and the direct income redistribution strategy are unacceptable. But unfortunately these are the only two strategies for altering the distribution of income and wealth. If it is not possible to alter earnings abilities or possible to shift the market distribution of income with taxes and transfers, it is not possible to alter the distribution of income and wealth.

Problems with No Solutions: Bury Them

The easiest way to solve a difficult problem is to discover new, more pressing problems. In the short run this is clearly the solution that we are following. The energy crisis, the inflation crisis, the recession crisis, and the environmental crisis have all served to push the income redistribution problem to a back burner, if not off of the stove altogether. Public opinion polls show a dwindling interest in income redistribution as a major national problem.

Fortunately or unfortunately, more pressing problems are unlikely to provide a long-term solution. The distribution of income and wealth is too fundamental to the rest of the economic system. Civil wars and revolutions arise from maldistributions of income and wealth, not from dirty air or high-priced gasoline. Inflation and recession themselves ultimately rekindle interests in the equitable distribution of economic resources. History indicates that mankind periodically rediscovers the problem of equitably distributing the economic pie.

A Solution: Simple but Difficult

Economic history also provides a guide as to how the distribution of income and wealth can be made more equal. The last major shifts in the distributions of earnings and wealth occurred during the Great Depression and World War II. Compression occurred at both the top and the bottom of the income distribution. The share of the total income going to the bottom 40 percent of the families of the United States rose from 12.5 percent in 1929 to 13.6 percent in 1941 and to 16.0 percent by 1947. The top 20 percent of families saw their income going from 54.4 percent to 48.8 percent from 1929 to 1941 and to 46.0 percent by 1947. The top 5 percent of the population saw its income fall from 30.0 percent to 24.0 percent and then to 20.9 percent over the same period of time.[1] Not only were market incomes becoming more equal, but the only progressive elements of the tax system (the federal income tax and estate and gift taxes) were put in place. These taxes existed before World War II, but the maximum rates and coverage were so low as to preclude any effect on the distribution of income and wealth. World War II rates were much more progressive than those now existing, and many of the now famous loopholes were inserted after World War II.

From the perspective of income redistribution, World War II is more interesting than the Great Depression since the narrowing income differentials were a result of deliberate public policies rather than a result of the pressures of a collapsing economy. As a result of an overwhelming consensus that the economic burdens of the war should be shared relatively equally, the federal government undertook to use its wage and labor controls to equalize market wages and its tax policies to further equalize after-tax incomes. It did not have elaborate education and training programs, and it was politically able to institute large changes in the structure of taxes. Once these new pretax and posttax income differentials were embedded in the economic system, they set a wage and tax framework that has basically existed to this day. They were internalized as part of each individual's and our society's conception of fairness or equity.

The important thing to note about these changes is that they were imposed on the government by changes in the equity norms of its citizens rather than imposed on its citizens by the equity norms of the government. I would suggest that this is a serious lesson to be learned. Income redistribution is easy if there is an overwhelming political consensus in its favor, but it is impossible if such a consensus does not exist.

The basic problem is to bring about a change in the norms of what are regarded as fair. It is at this point that the historian teaches a cynical lesson. Major changes in the distributions of income and wealth only occur in the face of civil revolutions and external threat. Sociologists often maintain that only wars bring about changes in our norms of relative deprivation.[2] If it is true, we clearly have a problem.

The exception that hopefully does not prove the rule is Sweden. Without revolution or external threats they have brought about major changes in their posttax distribution of economic resources. But as yet I have never heard or read a good account of what brought these changes about. Even Swedes do not seem to have a good explanation.

Notes

1. Herman P. Miller, *Income Distribution in the United States*, Bureau of the Census, Washington, D.C., 1966, p. 21.

2. For an example see: Walter Garrison Runcimen, *Relative Deprivation and Social Justice*, Routledge & K. Paul, London, 1966.

11

Equal Opportunity—Some Promise and a Lack of Vision

*Marshall S. Smith**

The first part of this chapter responds to Thurow's discussion of the income distribution; the second part considers the issue of educational opportunity. Neither issue is considered in detail.

Regarding the income distribution, I agree with Thurow that we may be entering a period of increasing inequalities although there is some countervailing evidence to his prediction. Beyond that, three general points are made: (1) many of the families in this country below the "poverty" line are headed by people who, for one reason or another, cannot leave home to work (e.g., they are ill, they are homemakers in single-parent households, or they are retired), (2) the gap between the median incomes of black and white families is strongly determined both by the frequency of different types of families (e.g., single-parent households) and by different incomes of individual black and white families in similar situations, and (3) the opportunity to make a large income may be more equal in the society than most believe. I then consider briefly some policy alternatives directed at reducing poverty and making the income distribution more equal.

In the area of education, I argue two points: (l) the nation's schools are not declining in quality—rather they seem to be doing as well as or better than before, and (2) although compensatory education has not yet succeeded, there are signs of promise.

Income

Increasing Inequality?

Thurow's argument may be summarized in five points:

(l) Since 1945, there has been no systematic national policy toward the redistribution of income. Yet, through a set of "accidents" the distribution

* Harvard University.

The views expressed in this article are those of the author. They in no way represent official positions of the National Institute of Education.

of income has remained fairly stable. This stability may be coming to an end, for we may be entering a period of increasing income inequality.

(2) Increased transfer payments from the federal government has kept the income of nonworking members of the society (the elderly, the handicapped, and single parents with young children) in step with the increase in real income among all members of the society without altering their relative position in the income distribution.

(3) Among male working members of the society there has been an increase in the inequality of the income distribution—"low-income males have fallen relative to high-income males." Thurow sees this as likely to continue.

(4) Since 1945 there has been a relative increase in female workers in low-income, intact families. Taking families as a unit, this increase in earning power of females in low-income families has offset the increasing inequality of incomes among male wage earners, thereby keeping the family income distribution relatively stable.

(5) The number of low-income females who can obtain work may be rapidly approaching an upper limit—this influence may decrease in the future and may not continue to offset the increasing inequality among men. Moreover, a greater number of women from middle-and upper-income families are entering the work force, and the effect of this in the future will also increase income inequality.

Like all predictions, Thurow's are tentative. The increasing disparities among incomes of male heads of households rests in large part on the fact that there has been an increasing percentage of people over the past thirty years in professional and managerial positions, not upon the increasing disparities among the income levels of different occupations. If the percentage of professional and managerial positions has reached a plateau, his prediction may be inaccurate. There is some evidence that this may be happening.[1] And if a national day-care system for the poor evolves, there will be greater opportunity for wives in low-income families to participate in the workforce—a circumstance which would also tend to keep the income distribution stable. Again, there are indications that such a system may be developed.[a]

A key point, however, is that both circumstances which would render Thurow's prediction inaccurate are as problematic as the scenario he describes. In the absence of a systematic policy toward income redistribu-

[a] Once again this year Senator Mondale and Congressman Brademus are sponsoring and holding hearings on a comprehensive child care bill in the U.S. Congress. It is not at all certain when such a bill will be enacted into law—the provisions and priorities which will be built into the law are equally uncertain. Nonetheless there is an increasingly powerful lobby for such a bill and, in my view, an increasing awareness that the bill will first have to address the needs of families where the heads would be unable to work without the opportunities that such legislation would provide.

Table 11-1

Families below the Low-Income Level, by Sex of Head 1959-1967-1970-1974*

	All Families		Families with Male Head		Families with Female Head	
$ in Thousands						
	Black	White	Black	White	Black	White
1959	1,860	6,027	1,309	5,037	551	990
1967	1,555	4,056	839	3,019	716	1,037
1970	1,481	3,708	648	1,606	834	1,102
1974	1,530	3,482	506	2,185	1,024	1,297
Percent below Low-income Level						
1959	48.1	14.8	43.3	13.4	65.4	30.0
1967	33.9	9.0	25.3	7.4	56.3	25.9
1970	29.5	8.0	18.6	6.2	54.3	25.0
1974	27.8	7.9	14.2	4.9	52.8	24.9

*U.S. Bureau of the Census, Current Population Reports, Special Studies, Series P-23, No. 54. The Social and Economic Status of the Black Population in the United States, 1974. U.S. Government Printing Office, Washington, D.C., 1975. From Table 24, p. 43.

tion, we may well be entering a period which will dissolve the advances made during the Depression and World War II. Thurow is pessimistic regarding such a systematic policy. Unlike the policies from 1941 to 1946, which occurred during a period where there was a national "consensus" that the burdens of the war should be equally shared, there is now no national consensus that equity should prevail. Without a national consensus there apparently will not be a systematic government policy. Even the emerging consensus that brought us to the brink of a coherent Family Assistance Plan in the early 1970s seems to have dissipated. One has only to review proposed congressional legislation in this area over the past two years to see the lack of interest—and this is during a Congress of apparently strong liberal persuasion.

For those who believe in some form of income redistribution, times therefore appear bleak. Yet, there are other ways of looking at the income distribution which may suggest relatively inexpensive policies which would at least maintain rather than increase the current level of inequality and which may, indeed, foster some mild form of redistribution.

Decreasing Poverty

Consider the following facts:

(1) Real income has doubled for almost all the population during the last

30 years. Between 1959 and 1974, the percentage of white families below the federally established low-income threshold fell from 14.8 percent to 7 percent. For black families the same percentage fell from 48 percent to 27.8 percent. (See Table 11-1.)

(2) Between 1959 and 1974 the number of white male-headed families which fell below the low-income level decreased from 5.0 to 2.2 million; of white female-headed households the number below the low-income level increased slightly from 1.0 to 1.3 million. Among black male-headed families, the number below the low-income level decreased from 1.3 to 0.5 million, while the number of black female-headed households below the low-income line increased from 0.55 to 1.0 million. Put another way, of the 7.9 million families which were below the poverty line in 1959, 1.64 million, or 21 percent were in female-headed households. In 1974, however, of the 5.0 million households below the low-income level, 2.3 million, or 46 percent, were in female-headed households. (See Table 11-1.)

What do these numbers mean? First, it seems clear that the nation has responded *somewhat* to the plight of low-income people. While their position in the income distribution relative to others has not improved, far fewer now than in 1959 have an income below a basic subsistence level.

Second, in absolute numbers there continue to be more white families in poverty than black families. When we compare white persons with blacks and other races, we find a ratio of absolute numbers of *persons* in poverty families of over 2 to 1. In 1974 the U.S. Bureau of the Census estimated that 16.3 million white persons and 8.0 million persons from black and other races were in families below the poverty guidelines.[3] Poverty is not solely the prerogative of minority families.

Third, the brunt of poverty is becoming more and more centralized in female-headed households. The trends from 1959 are evident, and should they continue at the same rate over the next five years as they have for the past five years, close to 60 percent of all poverty families will be headed by women.

When the characteristics of family heads are looked at, the picture becomes even clearer. As of 1973, approximately 39 percent of the women heads of households held jobs although only 7 percent or so worked full time for the full year. Of the 61 percent who did not work, roughly 75 percent cited "keeping house" as the reason while 17 percent were "ill or disabled." By far, the largest sources of income (in terms of number of families influenced) for all the women-headed households below the low-income line were social security (18 percent) and public assistance (62 percent).

Fourth, of the males who headed households below the low-income level in 1974, roughly 5 percent did not have their wives present. Using data from 1973, 62 percent worked but only 27 percent worked full time for the

Table 11-2

Median Family Income in 1959, 1970, and 1973 for All Black Families and Black Husband-Wife Families as a Percent of Coresponding White Families by Age of Head

	All Families		Husband-Wife Families	
	Total	*Head under 35 Years*	*Total*	*Head under 35 Years*
1959	51	54	57	62
1970	61	65	73	82
1973	58*	62	74	88

*This number may be interpreted as: In 1973 the median income for all black families was 58 percent of the median income for all white families.

Source: U.S. Bureau of the Census, Current Population Reports, Special Studies, Series P-23, No. 54. The Social and Economic Status of the Black Population in the United States, 1974. U.S. Government Printing Office, Washington, D.C., 1975. From Table 19.

full year. Of the 38 percent who did not work, 53 percent were "ill or disabled" and 36 percent retired.[4]

Putting this all together, it appears as if a sturdy 60 percent of the over 5 million families in the low-income group are characterized by family heads who either worked full time but earned less than the low-income level (18 percent) or were unable to work because they (1) were required to be at home as housekeepers (21 percent), (2) were "ill or disabled" (15.2 percent), or (3) were retired (7.5 percent). Greater income for these families will not depend upon more jobs, though better-paying jobs would be some help. In most of these families the head is not presently able to earn more income. This problem will continue and, as the number of single parent families increases, should get worse.

Black versus White Family Incomes

Let us now look at the income distribution in a somewhat different fashion. Table 11-2 indicates the median family income of black families as a percentage of corresponding white family incomes. The first column indicates the continuing strong disparity between the median incomes for all black and white families (as Thurow indicated, the early 1970s showed black family incomes rising from the 1950s to slightly over 60 percent of white family incomes and then dropping as the nation moved into the 1970s to below 60 percent. The same trend is evident when we look at all families where the head is under 35 years of age.

A different picture emerges, however, when husband-wife families are examined. Looking at all such families, the percentage of black to white income increases through the 1960s to 74 percent, an increase which has been maintained through 1973. For husband-wife families under 35 years of age, the level of increase in black percentage of white income during the 1960s has been maintained in the 1970s. In 1973, the median for black families was 88 percent of the white family median. Moreover, there has been a steady relative increase in college-going among young black males—from 1969 to 1973, the percentage of black males 18 to 19 years old attending college rose from 5 to 9 percent of the total male college-going population of the same ages. During that period, black graduate incomes rose by 32 percent while white graduate incomes increased by just 20 percent. (Freeman, 1975). The increased income of these black males will influence the family figures in the near future. Thus, among young intact families racial parity in family income may not be too far in the future.[5]

A major reason for the difference between the family incomes of all black and white families is the difference in the percentage of women-headed households (in 1973, 34 percent of black families and only 10 percent of white families were headed by women). An increase in this percentage from 1970 to 1973 of 3 percent for black families in contrast to only 1 percent for white families also seems to be a chief explanation for the decline from 1970 to 1973 in overall median black income as a percentage of white family income. A second reason is that the percentage of black working wives in intact families decreased from 1970 to 1973 while the corresponding percentage increased in white families; nonetheless, the median income of intact black families, relative to similar white families, remained stable during these years.

Thus, among some parts of the black population there are encouraging signs. There is an indication that black-white disparities may finally be closing, particularly among young intact families. These trends bear careful watching, however, to determine whether the gains accruing among younger families are continued as they get older. Equal employment opportunities must be continued beyond first employment to promotion opportunities and subsequent jobs.

Income Opportunities

A third way of viewing the income distribution borrows from Jencks et al. (1972).

(l) Among white males the influence of family background upon income is far less than many suppose. Jencks estimates that a reduction of all family background influences to a point where the distribution of differences in income among pairs of randomly chosen males would be similar to the income distribution of differences among the incomes of brothers, would reduce average income disparities by less than 10 percent—from an average disparity among randomly chosen white males of $6,200 (1968 estimates) to an average disparity of roughtly $5,600. Something other than family background accounts for most of the variation.

(2) If it is not family background, perhaps differences in educational attainment or in occupational status explain most of the inequalities among incomes. Both do explain some of the inequalities but nowhere near most of those found among white males. Educational attainment explains less than 13 percent of the variation in incomes, and most of the variation in incomes is within occupational groups rather than among occupational groups. In fact, Jencks estimates that "equalizing" family background, cognitive skill, educational attainment, and occupational status simultaneously would explain at most 25 percent of the variation in income. If all white males were "equalized" on these attributes, the average difference among randomly picked individuals would still be roughly $5,300.

(3) This does not mean that individuals cannot enhance their incomes substantially by obtaining more schooling or by entering a different occupation. Rather it suggests that there are also other routes—routes within their own occupations and within their own educational levels that may be equally or more effective.

(4) It also appears as if this situation will continue in the future, particularly for white males. The relative difference between the earnings of white male college and high school graduates has decreased dramatically over the past few years.[6]

Thus, while individual incomes will continue to differ to a large extent, the trends again point toward some reduction of income disparities among selected groups in the population. These data suggest that the society is more equitable with regard to income rewards than many imagine. At least among white males there appear to be substantial opportunities for obtaining rather large incomes that are not dependent upon family background, educational achievement or attainment, or even occupational status. While income is not randomly distributed, at least within this population, it doesn't appear to be perniciously distributed. As Jencks indicates, other factors than those mentioned above may play a major role—perhaps hard work, perceived need, motivation, and abilities such as being able to shoot baskets or sell automobiles may be just as critical.[b]

[b] Such an effort would not increase the median for all families since it is only operating at the bottom end of the distribution. To bring only the families now below the federal poverty line to the psychological line should cost on the order of an addition $8 billion—further additional money would be needed to bring those presently above $5,000 but less than $6,500 to the $6,500 level.

Policy Implications

There is irony in suggesting policy which might redistribute income in almost the same breath as arguing that no policy will be developed in the absence of a national vision—and there seems to be little evidence of such a vision. My personal biases lead me to argue for a general redistributive policy, a policy that has social aims while based on economic actions, for it seems that only through a merging of the nation's economic and social policies will serious redistribution occur. Miller and Rein (1975, p. 18) point out the problems with the traditional separation of such policies:

> To plan for education, training, and cash transfer systems in isolation from economic policies limits severely the effectiveness of these social policies. Actions which determine the level of employment and income obviously shape the possibilities and set the limits of social policy. Growing and sizeable unemployment requires enormous transfers if redistribution is to occur. Low wages make it difficult to provide an adequate level of transfer benefits without promoting fear that welfare is being favored over work. When economic policies fail to move in the same direction as social policies, then transfer, service, and tax systems cannot be large or progressive enough to offset large inequalities in the original distribution of income. Policies must, we believe, be directed at the generators of inequality.

Without doubt serious progress toward redistribution will require a combination of high levels of employment, a more substantial minimum wage, provision for equitable benefits (e.g., health) among all members of society, as well as transfer programs for special parts of the population. It may also require a revamping of the welfare system to provide a more equitable distribution of welfare funds. A reasonable goal for an effort such as this would be to have the ratio of the highest to lowest wage similar to that in the Federal Civil Service (7 to 1). This, however, would require a rather dramatic distribution effort, and there seems little likelihood that such a program will be put together in the near future.

Consequently, it may be less strain on the system to lower the near-term goals. Here it is useful to distinguish between the ultimate goals of dramatic reduction of income inequalities among individuals and the goals (1) of providing all individuals with at least subsistence income and (2) of increasing opportunities for the reduction of disparities between the incomes of white and minority families. Regarding the reduction of income inequalities among individuals, we may again distinguish between the opportunity for earning a large income and general income parity. Opportunities may be more equitable than most imagine—status at birth, academic achievement, educational attainment, and even occupational status appear to have only a small influence on income, at least for white males. In the absence of an overall drive toward reduction of individual income disparities, it seems a reasonable goal to strive for continued reduction of the relationship between income on the one hand and these other characteristics which are essentially unrelated to need, hard work, and motivation.

Regarding the elimination of poverty, I will not pretend to understand the morass of interacting social programs and policies that already exist and that might need restructuring and/or augmenting. Moreover I agree with the position that a criterion for poverty such as that developed by the government and used earlier in this chapter may not address the issue that poverty is both a relative and an absolute condition. Increasing living standards cause an increase in expectations—a family that could "get by" in the 1930s and 1940s with an absolute level of goods may feel in the 1970s that they are badly deprived with the same level of goods, and they are, relative to the living standards of other families. Jencks points out that people have a tendency to classify themselves as poor when their incomes are less than one-half the median income of similarly constructed families in the society. This would suggest in 1974 that a psychological poverty line be drawn somewhere around the $6,500 income level for a family of four—some $1,400 higher than the governmentally constructed line.

Yet even this increase does not appear insurmountable. Thurow argues that it would cost an additional $12 billion or about 11 percent of the $113 billion presently spent for transfer payments to bring all poor families over the government poverty line. An additional $12 billion or so would bring these families to the "psychological" poverty line.

This does not appear to be an outlandish goal or price although it would require careful orchestration of existing programs and policies and some considerable new effort. Within the group of poverty families, moreover, it might be possible to order the nation's priorities or at least to tailor the efforts. I pointed out earlier that a substantial portion (some 60 percent) of the heads of these families do not have the opportunity to earn a larger income than they presently have. The types of programs available to the unemployable elderly and the ill are more limited than those available to others below the poverty line. A national health insurance package that included basic living costs for the poor might help.

An apparently larger effort would be required to ameliorate the condition of financially poor families headed by a single adult. Proposals exist for day-care to free the heads of these families from their need to be home during working hours, but the problem would then arise of finding work for the adults. This may be a difficult task, for some substantial percentage of these adults do not have the skills and experience necessary to enter and compete in the job market. Moreover, the cost of day-care might make such a program quite inefficient at least from the point of view of reducing the poverty of these families (present estimates of day care costs run about $2,500 per year for 8-hour-a-day services for children under the age of 6. It might be far more efficient to realize that mothers work while they take care of their children and to pay them accordingly— even if a mother of two children under the age of 6 were paid only 60 percent of the costs of day-care, the resulting $3,000 might be enough with present welfare payments to allow the family to rise out of poverty.

For other families in the poverty category perhaps the most effective means for ensuring adequate incomes are a reasonable minimum wage and a federally guaranteed job program. Surely there is enough work to go around.

Finally, addressing the differences between white and black family incomes, a continuation of the present policies for equal employment opportunities, increased opportunities for minorities to attend college and postgraduate schools, and attention and (if necessary) action to ensure advancement opportunity would seem to be productive at least for intact families. That part of the disparity created by the differential frequencies of black and white intact families seems far more complex. A simple solution to many of these issues is certainly an adequately funded Family Assistance Plan. Yet in the absence of such a plan the nation could address aspects of the problem. There are substantial technical problems as Thurow and others point out, but I think we all realize they could be solved if the will were present.

Educational Inequality

When we turn to education, a similar lack of will and purpose also seems to exist. Many of the myths of earlier years regarding public schooling as an equalizer have been destroyed. As pointed out in the income section of this chapter, equalizing the schooling of all individuals would do little to change the income inequities in the society. In the absence of support for such an encompassing myth, criticisms of the schools appear to run rampant. Yet hindsight suggests that criticism arising from the destruction of such myths is unwarranted, for clearly schooling is not the sole determinant of individual income. Rather, in this society it might be viewed as enabling people to have the opportunity to compete for higher incomes—an opportunity that appears to exist for many in the society when we consider the low relationships between income on the one hand and schooling, background, and original status on the other.

In this regard, therefore, the schools of America might be viewed as successful at least for a major part of the population. However, it is clear that criticisms of the schools go beyond concern over income opportunities to address issues such as the apparent decline in test scores and the apparent failure of special efforts aimed at children from low-income families. This section addresses both these issues.

Test Scores

We hear a great deal these days about "declines" in test scores, and often the conversations include discussions of the need for schools to restructure themselves—to "return to basics." The issues regarding how our students are doing in school, however, are far more complex than might be represented in a few global scores of the sort that make the headlines. Over the past twenty years, for example, the science and mathematics curricula of high schools have changed and improved to the extent that beginning courses in college have had to be greatly upgraded to match the quality of the incoming students. Moreover, many schools now concentrate more than before on issues relating to the emotional and personal development of the child. Some have even gone so far as to suggest that schools should be pleasant, challenging, and rewarding institutions in their own right. Considering that we spend something on the order of one-fifth of our lifetime in schools, this seems a reasonable goal. Yet test scores often do not reflect such "soft" goals, and in their desire to develop tests that meet the needs of all students, testmakers often have a difficult time assessing the kinds of advanced knowledge that is contained in the new high school courses.

The above is only one way to address the test score issue, however. A second way is to address it directly and to ask ourselves whether we should be greatly concerned about the declines we hear reported. Consider the following information:

(1) Since the early 1900s, there has been an estimated increase in IQ levels in the general population of approximately 0.2 standard deviations per decade. Over a period of fifty years this amounts to a full standard deviation of 15 points. Put another way, a person now at the fiftieth percentile would have scored at roughly the eighty-sixth percentile fifty years ago (see Jencks et al.). Thorndike (1975), discussing the renorming of the Stanford Binet, reports an increase of almost two-thirds of a standard deviation for preschool-level children when comparing scores in the 1930s to scores in the early 1970s. For older children (10 years or older of age) there appears to be much less of a "gain" but certainly no loss.

(2) Farr et al. (1974) surveyed the results of reading achievement and concluded that in the period from 1945 to 1965 substantial increases were found at almost all levels of school. Since 1965 there has been a leveling off and *perhaps* a very slight decline, but the fact is that scores in the mid-1970s are clearly superior to scores in the mid-1940s.

(3) For older age levels the National Assessment of Educational Progress reports slight gains over the past four years in reading achievement and similarly slight losses in science knowledge. And a recent study of the American Institute for Research reports that reading achievement for 17-year-olds appeared to increase between 1960 and 1970.[7]

(4) The most dramatic of the drops in test scores has been reported by the Educational Testing Service. The Scholastic Aptitude Tests given to students wishing to enter college have declined rather sharply over the past ten years. These tests, often called the College Boards, show their greatest decline in the verbal aptitude areas. A somewhat less definitive but still a clear decline has been reported by the American College Testing (ACT) Program on three of the four areas studied (English, mathematics, and social studies). Scores on the ACT natural sciences test have remained constant. These tests generally are administered to students in their senior year of high school and are certainly cause for great concern. Yet on essentially similar tests administered to high school juniors (the Preliminary SATs), scores do not show a decline. The reasons for these mixed results for persons about to enter college are not yet explained, although a great number of plausible and testable hypotheses exist.[8]

My point in listing these findings is not to suggest that they are not cause for some concern. It is rather to highlight two points. *First, looked at in a larger perspective than the past ten years, the evidence seems overwhelmingly to point to substantial gains. Second, even within the past ten years, there is contradictory evidence for general declines.*

Compensatory Education

When we look at the success or failure of compensatory education over the past ten years, a similiar picture of contradictory evidence appears. On the one hand, evaluation reports from federally and state funded compensatory education programs offer little concrete evidence of great success and firm knowledge about what kinds of behaviors and characteristics successful teachers have. On the other hand, we need to remind ourselves that the compensatory programs in this country are still very young and that there are strong and promising prospects for eventual improvement in the system as a whole.

For example, it seems very clear that different curricula produce different outcomes. At the grossest level we certainly know that knowledge of algebra or French is strongly related to a student's having taken a course or courses in these areas. Moreover, most children (upward of 98 percent) do not enter school knowing how to read, and after four or so years in school most children can read basic materials. The fanciful notion that schools do not have an effect—that they do not make a difference—is obviously inaccurate. At a more sophisticated level, critics claim that there are few differences among curricula which intend to teach the same subject matter (e.g., reading). This generally seems to be true, although in regard to short-run effects there is increasing evidence of differential success. The highly structured and parent involvement programs in Follow Through, a federally funded experiment in early elementary schooling for the economically disadvantaged, appear to show substantial achievement gains over conventional classrooms. In addition, the nation is exploring a variety of innovations, including individualized instruction and peer and cross-age tutoring that show promise of influencing ordinary growth in achievement.

Beyond that, the knowledge base concerning how children learn is progressing rapidly. The notion of a passive child responding to teacher stimuli and filling up with information and skills the way a bottle fills with water has been replaced by a much more dynamic notion of the child actively interacting with the environment and moving through stages of rapid growth in skills followed by stages of consolidation and reorganization, only to be followed by further spurts in achievement. Also, the sense that children grow at different rates and have substantially varied abilities is now beginning to influence the curriculum of schools. Finally, our understanding of when and how to intervene to maximally stimulate a child's growth is also growing.

The psychologists among the conference participants at Newport were in complete agreement on two points in this area. First, it seemed reasonable to all of us that the kinds of skills and knowledge presently taught at the preschool level could not be expected to have long-term consequences. While knowledge of such things as letter names, letter sounds, and enumeration should be valued in itself, there is no reason to believe that five to ten years later their earlier acquisition will have an influence on such cognitively different tasks as comprehending written text or solving equations. In this regard the participants also agreed that the conventional wisdom that one-half of a child's potential intelligence is determined by the age of 5 years or so represents a dramatic misunderstanding of the process of growth and maturation. This "wisdom," derived from correlation studies of children's intelligence scores between early childhood and late teens, gives us only information about the similarities between rank orderings of IQ scores at early and late ages. It tells us nothing about the amount or type of knowledge and abilities people obtain at different ages.

Second, the psychologists also agreed that far more exploration of the efficacy of compensatory education programs during early adolesence should be attempted. Belief in the importance of early childhood seems to have played a role in directing the largest percentage of compensatory funds toward the younger years. Yet there is an emerging body of data which suggests the need for compensatory efforts in late elementary and junior high school.**

** Editor's note: Conference participant Gordon Alexander can be credited with helping to shift the emphasis toward the early adolescent period. Based on his work on Senator Birch Bayh's subcommittee to investigate juvenile delinquency, Alexander made a strong case for greater variety and more compensatory effort in these apparently crucial years.

On balance, then, it seems far too early to write off the compensatory efforts in this country. Far more exploration and effort are required to achieve the level of full literacy and enlightened citizenry that most believe the country should aspire to, but there appears to be some promise for success.

Notes

1. In a recent paper prepared for the Aspen Institute, Richard B. Freeman summarizes both the growth of professional and managerial jobs and the opportunities for college graduates to obtain such jobs. He concludes that the percentage of professional and managerial jobs has leveled off during the 1970s and "with the share of high-level jobs steady in the 1970s and continued expansion in the college work force . . . there was a marked worsening in types of jobs obtained by graduates, particularly those starting their careers." R. B. Freeman, "The Declining Economic Value of Higher Education and the American Social System," draft paper for the Aspen Institute for Humanistic Studies Conference on Education in a Changing Society, June 1975, p. 15.

2. The low-income threshold for a nonfarm family of four was $5,038 in 1974, $4,540 in 1973, and $2,973 in 1959. Families and unrelated individuals are classified as being above or below the low-income threshold, using the poverty index adopted by a Federal Interagency Committee in 1969. For a more detailed explanation, see Current Population Reports, Series P-60, No. 98.

3. From Table 23, page 42 of the Current Population Reports, Special Studies, Series P-23, No. 54, U.S. Bureau of the Census, 1975. "The Social and Economic Status of the Black Population in the United States." U.S. Government Printing Office, Washington, D.C., 1975.

4. Ibid., Tables 27 and 29.

5. This picture may not be as rosy as painted here. In intact families where only the male works, black income as a percentage of white income in similiar families has dropped since 1970 from 64 percent to 62 percent. And among families with male heads under 35 years old in which only the male works, black family income is only 72 percent of white family income. Even among families where both husband and wife have earnings, in 1973 male blacks earned only 72 percent of white males. Among intact families, therefore, the movement toward income equality for blacks and whites is dominated by the earnings of the wives—nationally, for example, black working wives in intact families where both husband and wife work earn as much as white wives in similar circumstances, and among the similar families where the head is under 35 years of age black wives earn 111

percent as much as white wives. (These are 1973 figures drawn from Tables 20 and 22 of "The Social and Economic Status of the Black Population in the United States." See note 3 for full citation.) If a much greater percentage of white wives start working, we might see a turnaround from the movement toward equity for these families.

6. See Freeman; full citation is given in note 1.

7. From reports at a recent Conference on Test Score Declines held by the National Institute of Education, June 19-21, 1975 in Washington, D.C. For further information contact Basic Skills Group, National Institute of Education, Washington, D.C. 20208.

8. Ibid.

References:

Farr, Roger, et al. "Reading Achievement in the United States: THEN and NOW." Indiana University, Bloomington, Indiana 1974.

Freeman, R. B., "The Declining Economic Value of Higher Education and the American Social System," draft paper for the Aspen Institute for Humanistic Studies Conference on Education in a Changing Society, Aspen, Colorado, June, 1975.

Jencks, Christopher, et al. *Inequality: A Reassessment of the Effect of Family and Schooling in America*, Basic Books, New York, 1972.

Miller, S. M., and Rein, Martin, "Can Income Redistribution Work?" *Social Policy*, May/June 1975, pp. 3-18. Published by Social Policy Corporation, New York, New York 10010, Copyright 1973 by Social Policy Corporation.

Thorndike, Robert, L. "Mr. Binet's Test 70 Years Later," invited address American Educational Research Association annual meeting, Washington, D.C. April 1, 1975.

Thurow, L. "Problem without Solutions: Solutions without Problems," Chapter 10 of this volume.

12

White Flight Research: Its Importance, Perplexities, and Policy Implications

Gary Orfield*

Social scientists played a visible though modest role in preparing the groundwork for the Supreme Court's 1954 school desegregation decision. With the publication of the 1966 Coleman Report, they became significant participants in the national debate over urban school segregation.[1] In recent years, intense public attention has focused on social scientist David Armor's controversial research suggesting that the courts have been mistaken in their recent decisions requiring desegregation through large-scale busing programs.[2] The most recent controversy had arisen over claims by James Coleman, perhaps the nation's best known sociologist, that urban desegregation is self-defeating because it merely speeds up the departure of a city's remaining white residents. Too often, selective, half-digested reports of preliminary research findings are disseminated by the media and become weapons in the intense political and legal battle being fought in major cities.

Obviously the white flight question has great policy importance. Research showing conclusively that particular actions either enhance or destroy the possibility for a biracial urban future would deserve the most serious attention by public officials. Unfortunately, however, such research has not yet produced. Reaching any kind of firm conclusions on these issues turns out to be an enormously difficult and complex process. This is because there are so many different and powerful forms of change taking place in urban centers that definitively relating changes in white population to particular actions requires analysis controlling a great many factors which are interrelated in decisions to move. Any conclusive analysis would also require a body of national survey data not now available relating the policy changes directly to decisions to move or enter private schools, rather than merely demonstrating a statistical association.

All we have now are preliminary studies, some national, some local, employing very different kinds of data and based on different analytic assumptions. Though the evidence raises important questions, it is impossible now to demonstrate that school integration, in itself, causes substantial white flight.

This chapter first discusses briefly the difficulties of sorting out the

---

* Brookings Institution.

various forces working toward accelerated suburbanization. Second, we describe the very severe long-term problem of flight *not* caused by desegregation plans but which tends to undermine the plans' viability. Third, we suggest that not only central cities but some inner suburbs as well are vulnerable to ghettoization in the absence of policies to alter the basic demographic trends in urban areas. Fourth, the analysis suggests that discussion of housing integration as an alternative to school integration is probably misleading. Finally, we discuss the policy implications of the imperfect information now available.

The Complexity of the Research Problem

At first glance the research problem appears to be relatively simple. The difference in white enrollment before and after desegregation is attributed to white resistance to the desegregation plan. These figures are commonly used by newspapers, local school officials, and desegregation opponents. Among other things, this method ignores the general trend toward declining enrollments, both in cities and in many suburbs. It also ignores the established patterns of white outmigration which developed long before the school issue was litigated. It neglects special local circumstances which occur simultaneously with desegregation.

Even when scholarly research attempts to make statistical provision for these trends, other complexities arise. Is school desegregation the sole cause of a decision to move, or does it merely trigger earlier departures by some families almost certain to move anyway? Are there other significant changes in the city or in the metropolitan area at the time that account for an observed change in enrollment and residence patterns? Is accelerated flight a continuing problem produced by desegregation, or is it a one-year spurt generated by the tumult of change? Does the statistical model exclude major influences on family choices? Inadequate treatment of any of these issues could produce seriously misleading policy conclusions.

Even simple definitions can have enormous implications for the meaning of research findings. Thus, in testing the proposition that whites are fleeing from school desegregation, the researcher must define "desegregation." Different definitions of this word can produce wide variance in the findings.

Most white flight research, including Coleman's, defines desegregation as any situation where there happen to be significant numbers of black and white children in the same school at a particular point in time. In the absence of a citywide desegregation plan, most such children in "desegregated" schools will actually be attending school on the periphery of an expanding ghetto. Usually, these are not integrated neighborhoods in any meaningful sense, but rather communities in rapid transition from all-white to all-black residential patterns. When one looks at enrollment patterns in such "desegregated" schools and observes the rapid shifts in the racial statistics, some conclude that the integration of the school "caused" its rapid resegregation. Actually, underlying these statistics is a very simple tautological principle—as ghettos expand, the neighborhoods they expand into become increasingly black.

The danger of reasoning from an inaccurate definition of desegregation in determining school policy can perhaps be illustrated by a comparative example from the housing field. Newark, New Jersey, in 1940 ranked as the most desegregated big city in the U.S., but during the 1960s it actually experienced an increase in segregation while most cities were moving in the opposite direction.[3] It is conceivable that an analyst could draw the conclusion from these data that residential integration is counterproductive and results in increasing segregation. If, on the other hand, one noted that the black and white housing markets in the city were highly segregated, except along ghetto boundaries, one could draw the more reasonable inference that rapid ghetto expansion produces an increasingly black city.[4] What appeared statistically to be integration was actually only rapid racial transition of neighborhoods. If one made the first kind of inference, the policy conclusion might be that nothing should be done to integrate housing. The second conclusion, on the other hand, would support a recommendation for a major effort to permit wider dispersion of the growing black population, thus producing a more stable pattern of integration.

Moving back to the school example, evidence that white flight increases after desegregation must be interpreted with considerable caution. If stabilizing the white population is a major long-term policy goal, it is very possible that desegregation over a much broader area, not no desegregation at all, is the best procedure. In fact, this conclusion is accepted by Coleman.[5] Given the fact that there is no way to prevent further expansion of the ghettos, spreading school and housing segregation are virtually inevitable in the absence of a powerful policy to alter the normal self-fulfilling prophecies of neighborhood transition.

This brief discussion of some of the complexities of white flight research does not mean that the question cannot be studied effectively. It does indicate, however, that results of tentative research should be read with great caution.

White Flight and Urban Change

Interpreting white flight research requires an implicit or explicit model of the process of racial change in a metropolitan area, particularly a set of assumptions about housing segregation, the nature of the causal relationships between school and housing decisions, and the future population prospects of central cities in the absence of school desegregation. White flight is related not only to school desegregation but also to the underlying demographics of the community, the consequences of division of a metropolitan area into many separate governments and school districts, the nature of the local housing market, and perhaps even to such elusive qualities as the area's racial climate and record of the local leadership in handling racial issues. To firmly establish any argument about white flight, one would need some kind of general theory of urban racial change to develop testable hypotheses about the factors causing white flight.

Convincing analysis requires treatment of the number of simultaneous changes influencing urban life and public attitudes during the past few years. The range and diversity of factors which might influence the rate of racial transition can be suggested by a simple, noninclusive list of common conditions in cities during the late 1960s and early 1970s.

1. Record levels of housing construction, overwhelmingly concentrated in the suburbs
2. Major urban riots
3. Rapid continued movement of urban jobs to suburban facilities
4. Trend toward racial polarization in city politics and the emergence of black political leaders
5. Increasing crime and public fears of violence
6. More rapid expansion of ghetto boundaries made possible by 1968 federal fair housing law
7. Increases in strikingly disproportionate central-city taxation in some areas
8. Decline in the actual level of central-city services in some cities
9. Housing subsidy programs of unprecedented magnitude which tended to accelerate racial transition in the city, create opportunities for lower-income whites in the suburbs, and sometimes end with the elimination of thousands of units from the central-city housing stock
10. Major financial incentives, in terms of downpayment and financing, for young families to purchase new outlying suburban housing

The basic analytic problem is that most of these major changes work in the same direction—toward increased suburbanization—and thus their effects can be easily confounded. Moreover, there are other, specifically educational, problems. Many city schools have deteriorating physical plants, and the local newspapers carry reports of steadily declining achievement test scores. Teacher strikes have eroded confidence and sometimes produced substantial enrollment declines. Financial crises have forced rising student-teacher ratios in some cities.

Separating out the influence of various elements is exceedingly difficult but vitally important if one is to draw any valid policy conclusions. It is difficult because the problems interact in shaping family decisions. Whites leaving Atlanta in 1973, for instance, decided not only in an atmosphere affected by a modest school integration plan but also in a climate of polarization over the drive of Maynard Jackson to become the South's first big-city black mayor.[6]

A family that leaves Detroit when a school integration plan is implemented will also be aware of the city's income tax, its 1967 riot, the extremely high level of violent crime, the cutbacks in the police force, the city's controversial black mayor, the massive housing abandonment in the city, the recent loss of more than a fifth of the city's job base, its severe current economic crisis, and so on.[7] While the school crisis might be the final factor that pushes the family to move *now*, the general condition of the city virtually guarantees that the family would move eventually and that it would not be replaced by a similar white family. Not only do the various forces work in the same direction, but several are simultaneously intensifying.

The indications that the school issue, in itself, is not a sufficient explanation for white flight can be found everywhere. If the changing racial composition of the public schools was the central problem, for example, one could expect a heavy increase in the enrollment of whites in relatively inexpensive Catholic schools, schools which are heavily concentrated in central cities. They are real alternatives for many of the Catholic ethnic concentrations directly threatened by racial change. These schools, however, have declined sharply in enrollment in recent years.[8]

Is It White Flight or Simply Flight?

The assumption that the rapid movement of white families from the central cities is a flight merely from racial contact has been substantially undermined by recent evidence that minority groups themselves are beginning to "flee" very rapidly to where they are allowed to buy suburban housing. Black public school enrollments are stabilizing or declining in a number of central cities, and black middle-class families are increasingly moving to their inner suburbs. Among middle-class black families who retain central-city residence, there are substantial numbers who have fled to private schools. The intensity of the black desire to escape central-city conditions is indicated by a survey of black Chicago residents, in which 54 percent said they would prefer to live in the suburbs.[9]

The situation in the Washington metropolitan area suggests possible future patterns. In the first four years of the 1970s the Washington black population fell by 5 percent. The city's suburbs, on the other hand, experienced an astonishing 61 percent increase in black population in this brief period. The decline in central-city black population during this period was more than twice as fast as the outmigration of the city's remaining whites. Almost three-fifths of the total suburban population growth during this period came from new black residents.[10]

More than a third of the black children in the Washington metropolitan area attended suburban schools by 1972, and the number is steadily rising.[11] District of Columbia public school statistics show that even among the blacks who remain in the city, about 10,000 are using private schools.[12] The city, in other words, is experiencing "massive black flight," and its public schools were becoming not simply black institutions, but black lower-class institutions. Elementary school enrollment declined 5.4 percent in the single year between fall 1973 and fall 1974.[13] Obviously these families are not fleeing contacts with blacks but are responding to both the problems of city life and the attractions of the suburbs.

The schools of California's largest cities indicate the complexity of the issue. All growth in black enrollment in the Los Angeles area is outside the central city. Although the Mexican-American enrollment has grown rapidly in the nation's second largest school system, the black enrollment is little changed since 1968 and recently entered a period of significant decline. The Chicano student population has expanded by 30 percent since 1968. During the last two school years, the black enrollment has actually dropped 5 percent.[14]

The results are even more confusing in San Francisco, the first big city outside the South to implement an extensive desegregation plan. The San Francisco schools have been experiencing not only white flight but also "black flight" and even "brown flight." From September 1972 to September 1974, San Francisco's black enrollment declined by a ninth, and its Latino enrollment fell by a twelfth.[15]

The California statistics could be interpreted as black resistance to contact with Mexican-Americans in Los Angeles and as black and brown hostility to San Francisco's growing numbers of Korean and Filipino students.[16] It is, of course, far more plausible to attribute the movement to many of the same long-term factors that shaped white suburbanization.

Policy Recommendations and Their Context

Failure to consider the accelerating decline of many of our largest central cities and their diminishing appeal for any family with any options can introduce a conservative bias into the interpretation of policy implications of research findings. If one focuses the research tightly on the short-term effect of school desegregation on white migration, and future research should actually demonstrate such an effect, the research could be read as evidence against doing anything. If one widens the focus to include the whole array of forces influencing locational decisions over a period of years, it is clear that the dominant trends point directly toward a particularly severe form of both racial and social class isolation in central-city school systems. If the latter diagnosis of the problem is correct, the policy implications are quite different. Assuming that the onset of school integration only highlights and perhaps temporarily accelerates already well-established social trends, one could recommend major efforts to change the structure of incentives and perceptions that have shaped these trends.

Public discussion of white flight research in recent months, usually based on newspaper interviews with Coleman, has focused on the assertion that school desegregation has greatly intensified outmigration. Several scholars, employing more sophisticated analytic techniques than Coleman's, have concluded that desegregation plans have no discernible effect, on the average, on the rate of white suburbanization.[17]

Yet, even if one were to concede the validity of Coleman's method of analysis and accept his results at their maximum force, his study suggests only that the initiation of desegregation in a city with half-black enrollment will produce an additional loss of 5.5 percent of the white students. This "flight" is significantly less than the same school system can expect to lose for other reasons in a normal year. In other words, the results show, at worst, that desegregation of a half-black big-city system might bring the schools to their final ghetto status about a year sooner than otherwise projected.[18]

Coleman finds that the effect is much weaker in the Northern cities and very small in cities below the top 22 districts. He has found no evidence of continued additional loss resulting from long-term impact of the desegregation plan after the first year.[19] In most cities where desegregation issues are still pending, in other words, the effect of school integration on population movements is uncertain, probably small or nonexistent, according to available data.

Research which focuses on the possible incremental effect of the initiation of desegregation is, of course, a valid intellectual undertaking. Policy recommendations, however, which are made without any reference to the broader causes of migration should not be taken seriously. If our central cities are moving very rapidly toward the condition prophesized by the 1968 Riot Commission report, then a policy proposal to slightly lower the rate of outmigration by ignoring unconstitutional school segregation can have only the most marginal importance.

Issues Needing Research

Serious recommendations about school desegregation policy should be based on analysis of alternatives that might lessen the incentives for the departure of the middle class and even provide some encouragement to the return of middle-class white and black families to the central city and its schools. Two policies suggest themselves, and both raise important research issues. First, one could try to determine why many cities experienced little or no loss after desegregation while some others had a massive drop in white enrollment. Closer study of the best and worst cases might well suggest either procedures and methods that can avoid this initial loss of enrollment or forms of federal assistance that would be particularly helpful. Similarly, there should be close analysis of Atlanta and Memphis, whose massive losses weighed heavily in the Coleman study.

More important, in the long run, there should be serious study of the value of metropolitan desegregation plans. Such plans are now in operation in a substantial number of the largest school districts in the South. Las Vegas also has one, and Louisville is implementing one. By eliminating segregation in predominantly white schools through entire metropolitan areas, these plans may diminish the incentives for suburbanization and eventually lower some of the barriers to return of middle-class families to the central cities and their schools.

The only research available on this issue, the study of Florida school districts reported by Giles and his colleagues, suggests that the metropolitan approach does indeed tend to avoid any significant transfer out of the public school system. This issue needs careful comparative research.

The White Flight Issue in Suburbia

Although the discussion of white flight has focused on central cities, the problem may actually become most serious in inner suburbs, when ghettos spill over city boundaries in a growing number of metropolitan areas. Because most suburban school districts are small, a relatively modest number of new black residents can often make a significant impact on a district's enrollment patterns. This can help create a self-fulfilling prophecy of transition to a ghetto school system.

This process is evident in two suburbs, Compton and Inglewood, adjoining the Watts ghetto in Los Angeles. Both communities went, in relatively short periods of time, from almost-all-white systems to almost completely black enrollments. One of the communities, Inglewood, had a desegregation plan. Compton did not. Yet both went through a brief biracial transition and then resegregated.[20] They behaved very much like a section of a big city undergoing racial transition. In fact, they are parts of a huge metropolitan city. The reason they went through the entire process so rapidly and completely, why they were so extremely vulnerable to white ghettoization, is that the entire system is really only a large neighborhood. The school district boundaries isolate the individual small suburb from the diversity of the metropolitan area. The small isolated nature of the school district, superimposed on a process of residential change based on monolithic ghetto expansion, meant that suburban districts once far ''whiter'' than the city became far more segregated than the city in a brief period of time.

Inglewood, a working-class suburb of almost 100,000 people, began receiving black residents in the 1960s, a number of whom left their homes in Compton after that suburb became part of the Los Angeles ghetto. By 1970, when a court ordered desegregation, there were about one-fourth black students in the schools and a substantially lower proportion of black residents. The next year, the percentage rose to 35. Within four school years the system had become overwhelmingly black. The court took the rare step of formally releasing the district from most parts of desegregation plan, since there were few whites left to integrate with.[21] An analysis of the dynamics of the Inglewood situation emphasized the futility and heavy social cost of attempting to deal with the issue one individual community at a time:

The freedom to leave encourages a high degree of rancor. People are able to take hard-line positions . . . because they are not ultimately dependent on a negotiated settlement. . . . The process is exacerbated by the fact that each individual decision to move out increases the pressures on the remaining residents to move.

When looked at in this way, the problem of school desegregation takes on metropolitan significance. People may relocate from community to community within the same metropolitan area without affecting their job and other important social relations. Relocation outside the metropolitan area is another matter. . . . In short, they have a stake in the metropolitan area that they do not have in a particular suburban community.[22]

Without a cross-district desegregation plan, the inner suburbs near city ghettos and the suburban communities most willing to practice genuine fair housing tend to become the focal points for black movement and for school resegregation. In the St. Louis metropolitan area, for example, the suburb of University City had been an early leader on housing integration. By 1972, its school enrollment was 55 percent black, with a larger black majority in the lower grades.[23]

The problem will become increasingly evident in the inner suburbs of New York and Newark. Even during the 1960s the inner ring of suburbs was losing 3,000 whites while gaining 9,000 blacks and 2,000 Puerto Ricans in an average year.[24] This problem became substantially more serious in the 1970s. Housing changes meant that the area was headed toward growing numbers of ghetto suburban school systems.

Where suburban school systems are small and black suburbanization

begins in earnest, the only alternative to continual repetitions of the Inglewood experience would be some kind of desegregation plan crossing
district lines, preferably with supporting housing policies. The most immediate and dramatic benefits of a metropolitan desegregation plan might
well accrue to inner suburbs.

School Desegregation and Housing Integration

The only way to truly avoid the problem of white flight and to accomplish
stable school integration, some researchers suggest, is to integrate housing.
Once civil rights laws strike down suburban housing discrimination, the
argument goes, the schools will be quietly integrated as a natural result of
changing residential patterns.

It may well be, however, that this argument can be turned on its head. It
is hard to imagine how stable housing integration, involving large numbers
of blacks, could be achieved in any reasonable period of time without a
framework of areawide integrated schools. Unless the normal process of
channeling black residents to limited areas breaks down completely, there
will be suburban ghettos with their own segregated schools. Once channeling is directed toward a particular area, that area tends to become steadily
more black unless new white families continue to move in to replace those
who depart in the normal process of rapid residential mobility.

Under the existing system there is virtually no incentive for a white
family desiring to avoid segregated ghetto schools to move into a
neighborhood with a substantial number of black neighbors. In all probability, based on past experience, the neighborhood school will become an
overwhelmingly black school in the near future.[25] Even those who would
accept integration will very seldom accept this. Therefore their logical
choice is to seek out one of the many segregated white areas in the
metropolitan community. Without a desegregation plan, in other words,
the white family often does not percieve a choice between an integrated and
an all-white school, but only between an all-white school and one that is
almost certain to become virtually all-black. The only way one can break
into this cycle of expectations is to assure families that the schools will be
integrated wherever they move and that they will not become overwhelmingly nonwhite anywhere. This assurance could powerfully support a serious campaign for housing integration, if federal, state, and local officials
ever decided to mount one.

Any stable large-scale residential integration, extending beyond communities with special institutions and particularly favorable attitudes,
probably requires solution of the problem of segregated schools. This
seems certainly true in considering residential integration in the inner-city

black neighborhoods. Americans have become so accustomed to thinking of ghetto expansion as an irreversible, inexorable process that there has been very little serious thought about the possibility of a significant movement back by young white families into central-city ghetto neighborhoods.

There are several reasons for thinking that such a reverse movement might be possible, at least in certain central cities which remain viable economic and cultural centers. The skyrocketing cost of housing, severe environmental restrictions on building in many suburbs, the increasing costs of supporting the two-car, high-energy consumption life-style, as well as the trend toward far smaller families and more working wives, are all compatible with a possible central-city revival. Such a reverse migration is now taking place in several parts of Washington, Philadelphia, and some other major cities.[26] The renovated communities have proved particularly attractive to young professionals, the very group that city leaders are most eager to attract and retain. Very few of the new residents, however, use the public schools. As a result, residence is largely limited to those without school-age children and those able to afford private schools. This means that the great bulk of middle-class families would have to pay a prohibitive penalty to live in the central city. If the central-city schools were integrated on a level that reflected the population distribution of the metropolitan area, this cost would be eliminated. The attractions of accessibility, diversity, energy economy, cultural opportunities, and the basically superior quality of older buildings might then permit a significant inmigration. Once such a migration reached a substantial scale, it would diminish the costs of maintaining school integration.

White Flight as a Triumph of National Housing Policy

The phenomenon described as "white flight" by students of school desegregation is often seen, in another light, from another angle, as a true triumph of the basic tools of U.S. housing policy during the post-World War II period. Facilitating white suburbanization has been a basic goal, explicitly at first and implicitly to this day. Federal policies have helped shape the environment in which every family makes its choice about where to live, and those policies have skewed the choice very heavily in favor of the suburbs. Even last year Congress enacted a major incentive for movement to the outermost suburbs. When these policies are superimposed on a dual housing market, where blacks are excluded from most new suburban housing, they are clearly policies fostering white flight.

The policies have taken many forms. Until 1950, the Federal Housing Administration openly favored segregated suburban developments in granting mortgage insurance, insurance commitments which aided both in the initial construction financing and in the sale of the housing. Until the late 1960s, HUD took no significant action against segregation in public housing.[27] The massive new housing subsidy programs created by the 1968 housing act were often used in ways that had the consequence of increasing segregation.[28] This year's large tax credit for the purchase of new homes unintentionally provides a powerful incentive for movement to the outer-most suburbs. The policies have drawn investment to the suburbs, created powerful financial incentives for young families to choose suburban homes, and often intensified and expanded central-city segregation.

One dramatic example of the relationship between federal housing policy and the departure of white families was provided in Detroit in the early 1970s. A program for low-income home ownership was implemented in a way that saddled poor minority families with overpriced deteriorated housing they could not affort to maintain. The process created a temporary artificially inflated market allowing lower-income white families to sell out and get enough money to leave for the suburbs. A former director of the Detroit FHA office, William Whitbeck, analyzed the results of a disaster which ultimately left the government holding 11,000 vacant, unusable houses:

What happened in Detroit is that the white flight from the city was facilitated by the FHA to the *n*th degree. Not only did the readily available FHA insured mortgages facilitate somebody selling and leaving the city, but of course we insured the other end of the transaction, when he bought a new house out in the suburbs. We greased the skids the whole way. It's no wonder that Detroit lost 190,000 people from 1960 through 1970. The system was like a greased runway.[29]

Federal housing policies have worked to facilitate exactly what is happening now. The results greatly reinforce segregation. The federal policies have been sustained, powerful, and effective. There has been no significant offsetting effort to retain or return young middle-class families to the central cities. If the problem is to be controlled, there surely must be one.

Policy Implications

Existing research on white flight and urban desegregation can support only limited policy recommendations. The current research findings suggest that the implementation of a desegregation plan, in itself, would have little or no impact on racial patterns in most communities where the issue is still open. The very limited experience with citywide desegregation plans in the North and West, however, means that this conclusion rests on a very modest empirical base. The data suggest that any possible effect of desegregation plans on migration patterns is largely limited to the nation's biggest cities, suggesting that desegregation of many smaller cities can be feasibly undertaken without accelerating white departures.

The available research suggests that the first year of desegregation is a critical period for decisions to leave the public schools or move to another school district. This problem might be moderated by expansion of the small federal program providing special assistance for the transition, as well as strong leadership supporting compliance with the law.

The research also contains some indications that the problems would be significantly diminished by metropolitan desegregation. While the evidence is limited, it strongly supports the argument that the process works better when it incorporates the racial and economic diversity of the metropolitan area and maintains the substantial white majorities in desegregated schools.

The basic forces generating both white and black suburbanization are many-faceted, and most are independent of school desegregation plans. There is no evidence that stopping school desegregation would stabilize central-city racial patterns. If the pattern of flight is to be significantly modified, positive, coordinated, and, often, metropolitanwide desegregation efforts dealing with both housing and schools will be required.

Notes

1. James Coleman and associates, *Equality of Educational Opportunity* (Washington: GPO, 1966).

2. Extraordinary public attention was focused on an article critical of busing written by David J. Armor ["The Evidence on Busing," *Public Interest*, No. 28 (Summer 1972), pp. 90-126]. The article did not reflect prevailing social science opinion [see: Thomas F. Pettigrew, Elizabeth L. Useem, Clarence Normand, and Marshall S. Smith, "Busing: A Review of 'The Evidence,'" *Public Interest* (Winter 1973), pp. 88-118].

3. John Tepper Marlin, "City Housing," *Municipal Performance Report* (November 1973), p. 17, citing data developed by Karl Taeuber and associates at the Institute for Research on Poverty at the University of Wisconsin.

4. Ibid., reporting data from Kurt Bayer, "A Social Indicator of the Cost of Being Black," unpublished Ph.D. dissertation, University of Maryland, 1971.

5. Statement at "Symposium on White Flight and School Desegregation," August 15, 1975.

6. *New York Times*, October 17, 1973.

198

7. Detroit Budget Department, City of Detroit, *Five Year Financial Forecast, 1975-1980*; Leonard Downie, Jr. *Mortgage on America* (New York: Praeger, 1974), p. 44.

8. Chris Ganley, ed., *Catholic Schools in America* (Denver: Curriculum Information Center, 1975), p. iv.

9. Metro Poll data reported in *Integrated Education*, January-February 1975, p. 9.

10. Data from Census Bureau and Washington Center for Metropolitan Studies, reported in *Washington Post*, May 18, 1975 and *Washington Star*, May 18, 1975.

11. HEW Data Management Center, "SMSA's Student/Teacher Data by Ethnicity," October 1973, p. 39.

12. District of Columbia Public Schools, Division of Research and Evaluation, *Data Resource Book*, 1974-75.

13. District of Columbia Public Schools, "Pupil Membership in Regular Day Schools on October 17, 1974, Compared with October 18, 1973," November 1975, p. 1.

14. HEW Office for Civil Rights, *Directory of Public Elementary and Secondary Schools in Selected Districts, Enrollment and Staff by Racial/Ethnic Group, Fall 1972*, p. 115; current district statistics from OCR files and earlier statistics from Los Angeles Board of Education Appeal Brief in *Crawford v. Board of Education of the City of Los Angeles*, p. 21.

15. OCR, *Directory of Public Elementary and Second Schools . . .*, p. 154 and 1974 statistics from school district reports.

16. *San Francisco Chronicle*, June 13, 1974, reports that the Korean population grew more than 100 percent and Filipino residents more than 50 percent from 1970 to 1973.

17. Paper by Reynolds Farley, in this symposium; Christine H. Rossell, "The Political and Social Impact of School Desegregation Policy: A Preliminary Report," paper delivered at the Annual Meeting of the American Political Science Association, September 1975; Charles T. Clotfelter, "School Desegregation, 'Tipping,' and Private School Enrollment," 1974, finds a very small effect in predominantly white school systems. Rossel's analysis, unlike Coleman's, actually measured the effects of desegregation plans. Her conclusion from an elaborate analysis of 86 northern school districts was as follows: ". . . school desegregation has little or no effect on white flight, as measured by change in percentage of whites enrolled in public schools. Even in the two high desegregating school districts that had significant white flight, it is minimal . . . and temporary. White flight stabilizes to a rate lower than the pre-desegregation period by the third year after desegregation in the only two districts that showed any significant

change. Desegregation under court order does not increase white flight, nor does massive desegregation in large school districts."

18. James S. Coleman, Sara D. Kelly, and John Moore, "Trends in School Segregation, 1968-73," unpublished Urban Institute Working Paper, July 1975, p. 53. Coleman suggests that extrapolation from his data indicates a far more dramatic initial loss in desegregation of a system like Detroit, with nearly three-fourths black pupils. Since no such citywide plans have been implemented, this conclusion is untested.

19. Ibid., p. 59

20. Leroy F. Aarons, "Compton, Calif., Looks Uneasily Over Its Shoulder at Watts," *Washington Post*, August 8, 1975.

21. Edna Bonacich and Robert F. Goodman, *Deadlock in School Desegregation* (New York: Praeger Special Studies, 1972), pp. 3-4, 26, 95-97.

22. Ibid., p. 86.

23. Office for Civil Rights, *Director of Public Elementary and Secondary Schools . . .*, p. 783.

24. Regional Plan Association, "The State of the Region: A Digest of Selected Trends through 1974," *Regional Plan News*, No. 97 (March 1975), pp. 26-27.

25. The impact of these expectations on housing prices is discussed in Charles T. Clotfelter, "The Effect of School Desegregation on Housing Prices," unpublished paper, 1974.

26. Conrad Weiler, *Philadelphia: Neighborhood, Authority, and the Urban Crisis* (New York: Praeger Special Studies, 1974).

27. Gary Orfield, "Federal Policy, Local Power, and Metropolitan Segregation," *Political Science Quarterly*, XCIX (Winter 1974-75), pp. 784-790.

28. U.S. Commission on Civil Rights, *Home Ownership for Lower Income Families: A Report on the Racial and Ethnic Impact of the Section 235 Program*, 1971.

29. Brian D. Boyer, *Cities Destroyed for Cash: The FHA Scandal at HUD* (Chicago: Follett, 1973), pp. 171-172.

About the Editors

Nelson F. Ashline has held public education administrative positions at suburban, urban, and state levels. He has lectured at the university level on educational policy and has served as a consultant to foundations and other private organizations. He currently serves as deputy superintendent of education for the State of Illinois. He received his training at Harvard University.

Thomas R. Pezzullo holds a doctor of philosophy degree from Boston College. He has served as a teacher of mathematics and science in the Newton public schools and is associate professor of education at the University of Rhode Island, where he has also served as assistant vice president for academic affairs and director of the Curriculum Research and Development Center. His principal research interest is in educational policy, particularly as it relates to education for the disadvantaged, compensatory programs, and the genetic/environment controversy.

Charles I. Norris is a research associate at the Curriculum Research and Development Center at the University of Rhode Island. He has a master's degree in teaching from Reed College and has been an executive officer aboard a Navy vessel, a stockbroker, and a teacher in public and private schools. He became interested in educational policy and inequality while a student of psychology.